Real Estate Practice & Law

Virginia

Eleventh Edition

Doris Barrell, GRI, DREI, Consulting Editor

Dearborn™
Real Estate Education

This publication is designed to provide accurate and authoritative information in regard to the subject matter covered. It is sold with the understanding that the publisher is not engaged in rendering legal, accounting, or other professional advice. If legal advice or other expert assistance is required, the services of a competent professional should be sought.

President: Dr. Andrew Temte
Executive Director, Real Estate Education: Melissa Kleeman-Moy
Development Editor: Adrienne Crezo

VIRGINIA REAL ESTATE PRACTICE & LAW ELEVENTH EDITION
©2017 Kaplan, Inc.
Published by DF Institute, Inc., d/b/a Dearborn Real Estate Education
332 Front St. S., Suite 501
La Crosse, WI 54601

Printed in the United States of America
First revision, March 2018
ISBN: 978-1-4754-5625-7

CONTENTS

INTRODUCTION

Although real estate activity in Virginia is subject to federal laws and regulations, it is controlled primarily by Virginia's laws, rules, and regulations and in some cases, by state or local common market practice. *Virginia Real Estate Practice & Law* offers real estate professionals a practical handbook of Virginia's real estate laws and rules. Every effort has been made to ensure that the information contained in this book is both relevant and current. There are numerous references to Virginia statutes in the Code of Virginia and the Virginia Administrative Code (VAC), and to the real estate regulations published by the Virginia Real Estate Board (REB). This enables readers to look up the law online or in most public and university libraries.

Virginia Real Estate Practice & Law is a component of Dearborn™ Real Estate Education's Complete Learning System. It may be used effectively with other Dearborn products:

- *Modern Real Estate Practice*
- *Real Estate Fundamentals*
- *Mastering Real Estate Principles*
- *Virginia Real Estate Principles online course*

The conversion chart on the inside front cover indicates which unit or units in some of the national products correspond with your Virginia-specific text. We hope the conversion chart will be helpful as you study for your real estate exam.

Each unit in this book is followed by a quiz. As you finish each unit, and before going on to the next, be sure that you can answer each question and that you understand all the material covered. When you have completed the course, take the 75-question practice examination. An answer key for all questions is included before the Appendix.

ABOUT THE CONSULTING EDITOR

Doris Barrell, GRI, DREI, has been in the real estate business for over 36 years, working first for a builder-developer, then as a general brokerage agent, and for nine years as managing broker for a 60-agent office in Alexandria, Virginia. She has brought this wealth of real-life experience into the classroom and in her writing on the subjects of real estate finance, agency, fair housing, ethics, diversity, and legal and legislative issues.

Doris is author of *Real Estate Finance Today, Know the Code: Real Estate Ethics, Everyday Ethics in Real Estate, and Essentials of Real Estate Finance, 15th Edition*, all published by Dearborn Real Estate Education. She is also a teaching consultant for the International Real Property Foundation, bringing real estate education to countries in Eastern Europe and Southeast Asia. Additionally, Doris has served as a senior instructor for NeighborWorks® America training institutes held in cities throughout the United States and as a Master Trainer for the National Association of REALTORS®.

ACKNOWLEDGMENTS

This new edition owes much to its reviewer, Roger Smith, associate broker, Long & Foster Real Estate, Inc.

Earlier editions of *Virginia Real Estate Practice & Law* were made possible with the assistance of JoAnn Kokindo, associate broker, Long & Foster Real Estate, Inc.; F.A. Dan Daniels, ABR, principal broker of Governmental Employees Realty Associates, Alexandria, Virginia; and Florence L. Daniels, GRI, Associate Broker of Governmental Employees Realty Associates, Alexandria, Virginia.

UNIT
1

Virginia Real Estate Law

LEARNING OBJECTIVES

When you have completed this unit, you will be able to

> **state** the purpose and responsibilities of the Real Estate Board (REB) and the Common Interest Community (CIC) Board;
> **describe** important provisions of Chapter 21 of Title 54.1 including the Virginia Real Estate Transaction Recovery Fund;
> **explain** the application of the Virginia Residential Property Disclosure Act in a real estate transaction;
> **identify** other state and federal legislation affecting real estate practice; and
> **define** the following key terms:

broker	Loan Estimate (LE)	sole proprietor
claimant	principal broker	stigmatized property
Closing Disclosure (CD)	salesperson	subrogate
firm		

OVERVIEW

The practice of real estate in the Commonwealth of Virginia is governed under the Code of Virginia in Title 54.1 – Professions and Occupations, and Title 55 – Property and Conveyances. The Virginia General Assembly is solely responsible for creating and amending the Code of Virginia. The general assembly meets in January or February of each year with any resulting changes to the code usually taking effect on July 1 of the current year (although some exceptions may be made). For example, changes to agency law usually require a longer time before enactment to allow time for the Virginia Real Estate Board (REB) to prepare new rules, regulations, and required forms.

TITLE 54.1—PROFESSIONS AND OCCUPATIONS

Chapter 3

Chapter 3 of Title 54.1 covers the Department of Professional and Occupational Regulation (DPOR). The mission of the DPOR is to serve and protect the public through

- licensure of qualified individuals and businesses in professions that, if not regulated, may harm the public's health, safety, and welfare; and

- enforcement of laws pertaining to professional conduct.

The Board for Professional and Occupational Regulation consists of nine members appointed by the governor for staggered four-year terms. The board meets at least four times a year. Each of the regulatory boards within the DPOR is a separate board with all administrative functions under the direction and supervision of the director of the DPOR.

Real Estate Board (REB)

As part of the DPOR, the REB is charged with issuing regulations that further describe what will be expected of both **salespersons** and **brokers**. The board is authorized to license real estate brokers, to prescribe standards for licensure and professional conduct, and to regulate schools offering real estate courses. The board is also authorized to develop criteria for evaluating and approving continuing education course credits. The board administers the Virginia Real Estate Transaction Recovery Fund and is authorized to administer and enforce the provisions of the Virginia Fair Housing Law. The board is periodically charged to develop a residential property disclosure statement form in accordance with Chapter 27 of Title 55. All regulations must be consistent with the Code of Virginia. The agency rules and regulations of the REB can be found in the VAC, Title 18—Professional and Occupational Licensing. The REB is Agency 135. A detailed discussion of Virginia real estate license law is covered in Unit 8—Virginia Real Estate License Law.

Common Interest Community (CIC) Board

The CIC Board is a separate agency within the DPOR (Agency 48). The board was established to regulate CIC managers by means of a licensure program. Also included under the CIC Board are four acts that were formerly regulated by the REB. Further discussion regarding these four acts will be in Unit 3—Interests and Forms of Ownership.

- Condominium Act
- Real Estate Time-Share Act
- Real Estate Cooperative Act
- Property Owners' Association Act

The licensure program for CIC Managers requires licensing for **firms** providing management services. Permanent regulations for CIC Managers became effective April 1, 2010. Each CIC Manager must have at least one qualifying supervisory employee with five years of experience in providing management services, and each must complete a comprehensive 80-hour CIC Manager Training Program, approved by the CIC Board. In addition, 50% of persons who have principal responsibility for management services will have to meet specific experience requirements, hold a specified designation, or complete an introductory 16-hour CIC Manager Training Program approved by the CIC Board.

The board is responsible for creating regulations regarding the establishment of procedures by each association for the resolution of written complaints from its members.

The Office of the Common Interest Community Ombudsman was established to assist members in understanding their rights and the processes available to them, to provide information and answer inquiries from members and other citizens, to receive notices of final adverse decisions, to provide information to the director for an annual report, to monitor changes in federal and state laws relating to common interest communities, and to ensure that members have access to the services provided by the CIC office.

Agency Rules and Regulations for the CIC Board are found in the VAC in Title 18, Agency 48. Reference is also made to the CIC Board in Unit 3—Interests and Forms of Ownership.

Rules and Regulations

The most recent issue of the rules and regulations for both the REB and the CIC Board are available from the DPOR. All licensees, real estate brokers, and real estate salespersons are responsible for staying informed about licensing laws, regulations, and current changes. The current real estate regulations went into effect November 1, 2015.

The REB can be contacted with questions about the laws or regulations governing the practice of real estate in Virginia via email (reboard@dpor.virginia.gov) or phone (1-804-367-8526).

Information is also available on the internet. Search *Code of Virginia* or *VAC* on the Virginia General Assembly Legislative Information System (LIS) at http://leg1.state.va.us/lis.htm. This website also provides information on historical and current actions taken by the general assembly.

References may be made throughout this text to the Code of Virginia, Title 54.1, Chapter 2— Professions and Occupations (§ 54.1 et seq.) and Title 55—Property and Conveyances or to the VAC, Title 18 (18 VAC 135-10 et seq.) or (18 VAC 48-10 et seq.).

CHAPTER 21

Chapter 21 of Title 54.1 covers real estate brokers and salespersons in Article 54.1-2100 (Definitions) through Article 54.1-2146 that allows licensees to maintain required documents electronically in accordance with the Uniform Electronic Transaction Act.

Brokerage Definitions

In Virginia, a real estate broker is defined by statute as

> any person or business entity, including, but not limited to, a partnership, association, corporation, or limited liability corporation, who, for compensation or valuable consideration (i) sells or offers for sale, buys or offers to buy, or negotiates the purchase or sale or exchange of real estate, including units or interest in condominiums, cooperative interest... or time-shares in a time-share program... or (ii) leases or offers to lease, or rents or offers for rent, any real estate or the improvements thereon for others. (§ 54.1-2100)

In common practice, the word *broker* may refer to a firm, a **sole proprietor** who transacts real estate business, a managing broker for a branch office of a larger firm, or a person who holds a broker's license but practices under the supervision of a **principal broker** (i.e., an associate broker). It is important to note that the brokerage relationship is established between the broker (principal broker or sole proprietor) as the agent and the client as the principal. All supervising brokers, managing brokers, associate brokers, and salespersons are general agents of the principal broker. There can only be one principal broker of a brokerage.

The statutory definition of a real estate salesperson is

> any person, or business entity of not more than two persons unless related by blood or marriage, who for compensation or valuable consideration is employed either directly or indirectly by, or affiliated as an independent contractor with, a real estate broker, to sell or offer to sell, or to buy or offer to buy, or to negotiate the purchase, sale, or exchange of real estate, or to lease, rent or offer for rent any real estate, or to negotiate leases thereof, or of the improvements thereon. (§ 54.1-2101)

Although a salesperson may generally perform the same functions as a broker, the salesperson must be employed by or affiliated with a licensed real estate broker. Brokers are expected to supervise all activities of the salespersons affiliated with their company and are responsible for the actions of every salesperson.

Brokers and salespersons can be further defined according to their specific roles within a brokerage firm. Any licensed broker or salesperson may prepare written contracts for the sale, purchase, option, exchange, or rental of real estate provided the preparation of such contracts is incidental to a real estate transaction in which the licensee is involved and does not charge a separate fee for preparing the contract (§ 54.1-2101.1). A *firm* is defined as any sole proprietorship (broker-owned or non-broker-owned) partnership, association, LLC, or corporation, other than a sole proprietorship (principal-broker-owned) that is required by regulation to obtain a separate brokerage firm license.

[handwritten margin note: Real Estate agents are not attorneys]

A *sole proprietor* is an individual, not a corporation, who is doing business under his own name or under a legally registered fictitious name. A licensed broker who is a sole proprietor has the same responsibilities as a principal broker. A sole proprietor who is not licensed must designate a licensed broker to perform the duties of a principal broker.

The principal broker is designated by each firm to ensure compliance with Chapter 21 of Title 54.1 of the Code of Virginia and to receive all communications and notices from the REB that may affect the firm or its licensees. The principal broker has responsibility for the activities of the firm and all of its licensees.

Additional definitions relating specifically to licensees will be covered in Unit 8. Two other general definitions included in the statute are the following:

■ *Common source information company*—Any person or entity that compiles or provides information regarding real estate for sale or lease and other data and includes, but is not limited to, a multiple listing service (MLS)—no broker or salesperson license required

■ *Distance learning*—Instruction delivered by an approved provider through a medium other than a classroom setting

Licensing Requirements

Any person or business entity that performs or advertises brokerage services must be licensed by the REB as established in Chapter 21, Section 54.1-2104. The general powers of the REB and all specific licensing requirements are described in Unit 8 of this course. The license may be granted in a fictitious name, that is, a name other than that of the principal broker.

IN PRACTICE

A principal broker who wishes to operate and be called ABC Realty must obtain a broker's license as a principal broker, and ABC Realty must obtain a separate firm license.

A salesperson whose name is difficult to say and wishes to be known by a pseudonym must obtain a license in her real name with a "DBA" (doing business as) for the pseudonym endorsement.

A salesperson who heads a team of licensees within a brokerage firm and wishes to advertise under the team name must obtain a business entity license for the team in addition to the required individual licenses. All advertising must still provide the brokerage firm name.

Additional regulations for a firm license include the following:

 Every member or officer who actively participates in brokerage business must hold a license as a broker.

 Every employee or independent contractor who acts as a salesperson must hold a license as either salesperson or broker.

 A salesperson and a broker may not be principals in a firm together. By law, all salespersons come under the supervision of a principal broker.

Public Notice Requirements

Every principal broker must have the following readily available to the public: the business entity or firm license, the managing broker's license, and a roster of every salesperson and broker assigned to the office. If a firm has more than one physical location (e.g., branch offices), then all actual licenses are to be held at the firm's main office, with the exception of the entity's branch office license, which must be available at the branch office. Every resident real estate broker must maintain a place of business in Virginia.

A separate branch office license must be issued for each branch office of a brokerage firm, including the name of the supervising broker. The branch office license and a roster of every salesperson and broker assigned to the branch office must be available to the public in each branch office. As of January 1, 2017, supervising brokers must provide the name and license number for each supervising broker of a branch office. After that date, upon renewal or transfer of a licensee's license to a branch office, the supervising broker must inform the Virginia REB of each licensee's name and license number.

Any person or firm engaging in unlicensed real estate activity will be subject to action by the REB and a civil penalty not to exceed $1,000 for any real estate transaction or the compensation received. (§ 54-1.2105.2)

The requirements for licensure stated here pertain only to the practice of real estate in the Commonwealth of Virginia as governed by Title 54.1, Chapter 21 of the Code of Virginia and Title 18 of the VAC. Further licensing or authority to conduct a brokerage business at a specific physical location is usually required by local jurisdictions.

Exemptions

Not everyone who performs an act of real estate brokerage or related real estate activities is required to hold a Virginia real estate license. The following are a few examples of persons exempt from the state licensing requirement:

- Individual persons or firms or their employees who are selling or renting their own property
- Any person acting without compensation as attorney-in-fact under a power of attorney issued by a property owner
- Attorneys involved in real estate transactions in their normal role as attorneys
- Any person acting as a receiver, trustee, administrator, or executor
- Licensed auctioneers selling real estate at public auction

A complete list of exemptions will be reviewed in Unit 8.

Virginia Real Estate Transaction Recovery Fund

The Virginia Real Estate Transaction Recovery Fund (§ 54.1-2112 et seq.) was established for the purpose of reimbursing parties who suffer monetary loss due to a licensee's improper or dishonest conduct.

✻ Must have exhausted all other avenues

Maintenance of the Fund

The establishment and maintenance of the fund is the duty of the director of the DPOR. The cost of administering the fund is paid out of interest earned on deposits. The REB may, at its discretion, use part of the interest earned by the fund for research and education for the benefit of licensees.

Each new licensee, whether a salesperson a or broker, must pay $20 into the fund. The fund's minimum balance is $400,000. If the balance of the fund falls below $400,000, the REB may assess each active and inactive licensee a proportionate amount to bring the balance to the statutory minimum. No licensee may be assessed more than $20 during any two-year period ending on June 30 of even-numbered years. Licensees who fail to pay the assessment within 45 days of receiving the first notice are given a second notice. Failure to pay the assessment within 30 days of the second notice results in automatic suspension of the licensee's license. The licensee will be suspended until such time as the director receives the amount due. The REB has the power to assess all licensees at one time or on individual licensees' renewals.

✻ At the close of each fiscal year, if the balance of the fund is more than $2 million, the excess amount over $2 million is transferred to the Virginia Housing Trust Fund (see Virginia Housing Development Authority [VHDA] in Unit 6—Real Estate Financing).

Claims Procedure

Legislation passed in 2016 clarified the position of a **claimant** as follows:

The claimant shall not himself be (i) a regulant, (ii) the personal representative of a regulant, (iii) the spouse or child of the regulant against whom the judgment was awarded, or (iv) a lending or financial institution or any person whose business involves the construction or development of real property. (§ 54.1-2114A)

- A person who files a claim for payment from the fund must first obtain a judgment against the licensee from a Virginia court of competent authority. Originally, the law required judges to make a specific judgment of "improper or dishonest conduct" in order to find in favor of a claimant. A new law in 2015 eliminated the need for the prescriptive judgment and clarified the eligibility requirements for consumers to make a claim under the Transaction Recovery Fund. Following a judgment against the licensee, the claimant must conduct or make a reasonable attempt to conduct debtor's interrogatories to determine whether the licensee has assets, including any listings and commissions due.

- The person must take all legally available actions for the sale or application of any assets disclosed in the debtor's interrogatories.

- The person must file a claim with the bankruptcy court, if the licensee has filed bankruptcy.

If any portion of the claim remains unsatisfied, the individual may file a claim with the REB requesting payment from the fund for the unsatisfied portion of the claim within 12 months from the date of the final judgment. (§54.1-2114)

A claimant must have pursued all legal means for possible recovery before a claim can be filed with the REB. On receipt of a claim, the REB will promptly consider the request and notify the claimant, in writing, of its findings.

Limitation on Recovery

The amount of the claim is limited to actual monetary damages suffered in the transaction, court costs, and attorney's fees. The claim cannot include interest, punitive, or exemplary damages, even though these amounts may have been included in the judgment awarded by the court.

If at any time the amount of claims to be paid from the fund would deplete the fund to an amount below the statutory minimum of $400,000, the processing of all claims will be suspended. The REB will assess licensees as previously outlined. As funds become available to satisfy the pending claims, the claims will be paid in the order in which they were originally received.

In all cases, the REB may withhold payment of any claim for 12 months if it has reason to believe that additional claims may be filed. In the event that there are multiple claims against a licensee that exceed the maximum allowable payment from the fund, each claimant will receive a proportionate share of the total payment.

Single transaction: In a single transaction, the maximum payment from the fund to all injured parties is $50,000. The maximum amount any single claimant may recover from the fund based on a single transaction is $20,000, regardless of the number of claimants.

Multiple transactions: If the same licensee is involved in multiple fraudulent transactions during any two-year period ending June 30 of even-numbered years, the maximum payment to all claimants combined is $100,000.

If a payment is made from the fund, the claimant must **subrogate** the rights to the REB. Subrogation permits the REB to take action against the licensee to recover the amount of claims paid due to the licensee's misconduct.

Penalty

Payment from the fund causes the licensee's license to be immediately revoked. The respondent may also be subject to other disciplinary action by the REB. The licensee may not apply for a new license until the fund has been repaid in full, plus interest at the judgment rate of interest from the date of payment from the fund.

Repayment to the fund does not guarantee that the license will be reissued. The REB may take disciplinary action against a licensee for a disciplinable violation whether or not the licensee has reimbursed the fund.

Law of Agency

The Virginia law of agency is covered in articles Section 54.1-2130 through Section 54.1-2144 and will be discussed in detail in Unit 2—Brokerage Relationships and Agency.

TITLE 55—PROPERTY AND CONVEYANCES

The chapters from Title 55—Property and Conveyances that have significant impact on the practice of real estate in Virginia are the following:

- Chapter 1—Creation and Limitation of Estates
- Chapter 4.2—Condominium Act
- Chapter 21—Virginia Real Estate Time-Share Act
- Chapter 24—Virginia Real Estate Cooperative Act
- Chapter 26—Property Owners' Association Act

The five chapters listed previously will be covered in Unit 3—Interests and Forms of Ownership.

- Chapter 13—Landlord and Tenant is covered in Unit 9—Leasing Real Estate in Virginia.
- Chapter 27—The Virginia Residential Property Disclosure Act is covered in Unit 1— Virginia Real Estate Law.
- Chapter 27.3—Real Estate Settlement Agents (formerly CRESPA) is covered in Unit 7—Transfer of Title.
- Chapter 36—Fair Housing is covered in Unit 10—Virginia Fair Housing Law.

Virginia Residential Property Disclosure Act

The Virginia Residential Property Disclosure Act has undergone significant changes since first being enacted in 1992. The act has always applied to transfers by sale, exchange, installment land sales contract, or lease with option to buy for residential property of one-to four-dwelling units. The act applies whether or not the transaction is with the assistance of a licensed real estate broker or salesperson (§ 55-517). Most property owners attempting to sell a property on their own are not aware that they are also subject to this act.

[handwritten margin note: Continuous/ Latent defect w/ home]

Exemptions

There are exemptions to the provisions of the act, which include the following:

- Transfers pursuant to court order

- Transfers pursuant to a foreclosure sale

- Transfers made in the course of administration of an estate guardianship, conservatorship, or trust

- Transfers from one or more co-owners solely to one or more other co-owners

- Transfers made between spouses resulting from divorce or property settlement

- Transfers made by virtue of the owner's failure to pay federal, state, or local taxes

- Transfers to or from any governmental entity

- Transfers involving the first sale of a dwelling—the builder still being responsible to disclose all known material defects which would constitute a violation of applicable building code

Duties of Licensees

A licensee representing an owner has a duty to inform the owner of the owner's rights and obligations under the Virginia Residential Property Disclosure Act. The seller is directed to the REB website for the proper disclosure form, which is to be given to the purchaser before making an offer to purchase. The timely provision of the disclosure form is essential. If the purchaser does not receive the form before ratification of the contract, the contract can be terminated.

A licensee representing a purchaser has a duty to inform the purchaser of the rights and obligations under the act. The purchaser is also directed to the REB website to see the list of seller representations. The licensee has no further duties to the parties (§ 55-523). The REB website is www.dpor.virginia.gov/News/Residential_Property_Disclosures/.

Any purchaser who is a party to a real estate purchase contract subject to this section may provide in such contract that the disclosures provided on the REB website be printed off and provided to such purchaser. (§ 55-519C)

Disclosure Forms

In 2007, the general assembly implemented a new law eliminating the old disclosure and disclaimer forms. This form was subject to frequent changes over the years and created a concern that a wrong form could be used, putting the contract in jeopardy. The new form contained only disclosures mandated by the general assembly. The REB was first charged with developing a residential property disclosure form by January 1, 2008. In 2014, the REB was again charged with developing a new disclosure statement form to meet the requirements of Chapter 27 of Title 55 including the inclusion of required notice on the REB website.

As of July 1, 2011, the Residential Property Disclosure Statement Notice to Seller and Purchaser directs the purchaser to a website maintained by the REB for a list of seller's representations (see Figure 1.1 and Figure 1.2). Although the responsibility for receiving disclosure information has been shifted to the purchaser, a licensee can print out the site's contents and provide it to the purchaser at the seller's discretion or if required by contract.

See www.dpor.virginia.gov/News/Residential_Property_Disclosures/.

In 2015, the law added language to the disclosure statement advising the purchaser to exercise due diligence in investigating whether there is a storm water retention maintenance agreement on the property. Some localities are adding storm water facilities on individual properties and requiring homeowners to maintain them or risk penalties. The law also advises purchasers to exercise due diligence by obtaining a flood certification or mortgage lender determination of whether the property is located in a special flood hazard area which would require flood insurance.

Three sections of the Virginia Residential Property Disclosure Act were updated in 2016:

- The statement dealing with the condition of the real property and improvements was updated to add that the seller makes no representations with regard to any covenants and restrictions that may be recorded in the land records. That section was also amended to remove the word *certified* before home inspection in anticipation of the requirement that all home inspectors be licensed as of July 1, 2017.

- The statement that the seller makes no representations with respect to adjacent parcels has been amended to include that seller is not making representations about any zoning classification or permitted uses of adjacent parcels.

- The statement dealing with wastewater systems now says the purchaser should exercise due diligence with regard to costs associated with maintaining, repairing, or inspecting any wastewater system, including costs related to pump-out of septic tanks.

The last page of the disclosure statement contains additional written disclosure requirements that cover:

- **First Sale of a Dwelling:** The builder must disclose in writing all known material defects that would constitute a violation of any building code.

- **Planning District 15:** The builder or owner of property in this district must disclose any previous or present mining operations.

- **Section 55-519.1:** Requires disclosure of any military air installation (noise and crash potential)

- **Section 55-519-4:** Requires disclosure if property used to manufacture methamphetamine

- **Section 32-1-164.1:** Requires disclosure regarding validity of septic system operating permits

Reference is also made to the Virginia Condominium Act, the Virginia Real Estate Cooperative Act, and the Virginia Property Owners' Association Act disclosure requirements.

FIGURE 1.1:   Residential Property Disclosure Statement

RESIDENTIAL PROPERTY DISCLOSURE STATEMENT
NOTICE TO SELLER AND PURCHASER

> The Virginia Residential Property Disclosure Act (§ 55-517 et seq. of the Code of Virginia) requires the owner of certain residential real property, whenever the property is to be sold or leased with an option to buy, to furnish this form to the purchaser and to refer the purchaser to a Virginia Real Estate Board website for additional information.
>
> Certain transfers of residential property are excluded from this requirement (see § 55-518).

Property Address/
Legal Description: _____

The owner makes no representations with respect to the matters set forth and described at the RESIDENTIAL PROPERTY DISCLOSURES web page. The purchaser is advised to consult the website (http://www.dpor.virginia.gov/dporweb/reb_consumer.cfm) for important information about the real property.

The undersigned owner(s) represents that there are no pending enforcement actions pursuant to the Uniform Statewide Building Code (§ 36-97 et seq.) that affect the safe, decent, and sanitary living conditions of the real property described above of which the owner has been notified in writing by the locality, nor any pending violation of the local zoning ordinance which the violator has not abated or remedied under the zoning ordinance, within a time period set out in the written notice of violation from the locality or established by a court of competent jurisdiction, except as disclosed on this statement.

_____
_____
_____
_____
_____
_____

The owner(s) acknowledge having carefully examined this statement and further acknowledge that they have been informed of rights and obligations under the Virginia Residential Property Disclosure Act.

_____ _____   _____ _____
         Owner   Date   Owner   Date

The purchaser(s) acknowledge receipt of a copy of this disclosure statement and further acknowledge that they have been informed of their rights and obligations under the Virginia Residential Property Disclosure Act.

_____ _____   _____ _____
       Purchaser   Date   Purchaser   Date

DPOR 7/11

FIGURE 1.2:   Residential Property Disclosures

RESIDENTIAL PROPERTY DISCLOSURE STATEMENT
NOTICE TO SELLER AND PURCHASER

The Virginia Residential Property Disclosure Act (§ 55-517 et seq. of the *Code of Virginia*) requires the owner of certain residential real property, whenever the property is to be sold or leased with an option to buy, to furnish this form to the purchaser and to refer the purchaser to a Virginia Real Estate Board website for additional information.

Certain transfers of residential property are excluded from this requirement (see § 55-518).

Property Address/
Legal Description: _____

The owner makes no representations with respect to the matters set forth and described at the RESIDENTIAL PROPERTY DISCLOSURES web page. The purchaser is advised to consult the website (http://www.dpor.virginia.gov/News/Residential_Property_Disclosures/) for important information about the real property.

The undersigned owner(s) represents that there are no pending enforcement actions pursuant to the Uniform Statewide Building Code (§ 36-97 et seq.) that affect the safe, decent, and sanitary living conditions of the real property described above of which the owner has been notified in writing by the locality, nor any pending violation of the local zoning ordinance which the violator has not abated or remedied under the zoning ordinance, within a time period set out in the written notice of violation from the locality or established by a court of competent jurisdiction, except as disclosed on this statement.

_____
_____
_____
_____
_____
_____

The owner(s) acknowledge having carefully examined this statement and further acknowledge that they have been informed of rights and obligations under the Virginia Residential Property Disclosure Act.

_____   _____
Owner   Date   Owner   Date

The purchaser(s) acknowledge receipt of a copy of this disclosure statement and further acknowledge that they have been informed of their rights and obligations under the Virginia Residential Property Disclosure Act.

_____   _____
Purchaser   Date   Purchaser   Date

DPOR 7/11

Legislation enacted in 2011 requires the disclosure on both sales and leasing transactions of known defective drywall on the appropriate REB disclosure form (§ 55-519.2). As of July 1, 2014, disclosure must be made if the seller has actual knowledge that a home was once used to create methamphetamine, unless the property has been thoroughly cleaned according to Virginia Department of Health guidelines.

At or before settlement, the owner is only required to disclose any material change from the original disclosures. The recertification form was eliminated in 2014.

Time for Disclosure and Purchaser's Options

The disclosure is required before contract ratification by the seller and buyer. If the disclosure is received after contract ratification, the sole remedy for the purchaser is to terminate the contract by giving written notice to the seller. Once the disclosure is received by the buyer, notice to terminate must be given to the seller

- within three days if the notice is hand-carried;
- within five days of postmark if the notice is mailed;
- before settlement;
- before occupancy if occupancy occurs before settlement; or
- before loan application where the loan application discloses that the right of contract terminations ends when the loan application is taken.

The purchaser may allow the contract to remain valid if she provides a notice of waiver of rights to terminate the contract or remains silent and does nothing.

If the purchaser elects to terminate the contract in accordance with the disclosure law, it may be done without penalty. Any monies already paid by the purchaser, such as earnest money deposits, must be returned.

Buyer's Recourse

If the buyer learns of defects that were either not disclosed or were misrepresented in the disclosure statement, the buyer is entitled to seek recourse. Any action brought under this act must be commenced within one year from the date the disclosure was delivered. If no disclosure was delivered, action must be commenced within one year of settlement, or within one year of occupancy in the event of lease with option to buy.

The owner is not liable for any error, inaccuracy, or omission of information in the disclosure form if the information was provided to the owner by a reliable third party, such as a surveyor, engineer, appraiser, home inspector, or public authority. The owner is also not liable if she reasonably believed the information to be correct and there was no gross negligence involved.

Liability for Licensee

A real estate licensee cannot be liable for misrepresentation if he relied on information provided by a client, public record, or reliance on representations of another regulated professional (this was clarified as of July 1, 2014). However, a licensee must disclose material adverse facts pertaining to the physical condition of the property that are actually known by the licensee (§ 54.1-2131B, 18 VAC 135-20-300(2)).

IN PRACTICE

A real estate salesperson, is hosting an open house during a rainstorm. While no one is being shown the property, he notices that there is a leak in the attic and water seepage in the basement. He must disclose that information to any prospective buyers as an adverse material defect in the property, regardless of the owner's wishes. If he fails to inform a prospective buyer about the leaking and seepage, he may be found guilty of misrepresentation.

Stigmatized Property

Stigmatized property refers to any property that is made undesirable by some event or circumstance that had no actual effect on its physical structure, environment, or improvements. For example, a house in which a homicide, felony, or suicide occurred may be tainted by that event and be difficult to sell. Buyers may hesitate to make an offer on a property that is reputed to be haunted or one in which the current or former occupant suffered from a communicable disease.

Disclosure of this type of information, which in Virginia has been determined to be immaterial, is not required. In fact, a licensee who represents a seller and discloses stigmatizing information to a buyer could be construed as having breached responsibilities to the client if the buyer cancels the contract due to the disclosure. The failure to disclose this information does not subject either the owner or a licensee to disciplinary action by the courts or the REB. There is also no disciplinary action of a licensee who does disclose such information as long as the seller has approved of such disclosure. The only topic of disclosure that is specifically prohibited is any discussion of HIV or AIDS. If information is disclosed regarding persons infected with HIV, a licensee could be in violation of fair housing laws and the federal privacy act.

OTHER LEGISLATION AFFECTING REAL ESTATE PRACTICE

State and Local Law

Mandatory Licensing for Home Inspectors

The 2016 general assembly approved legislation to transition the voluntary certification program for home inspectors to a mandatory licensing requirement effective July 1, 2017. A license to practice as a home inspector will be issued to

- an individual holding an unexpired certificate as a home inspector issued before June 30, 2017; or
- an applicant who has successfully
  - completed the educational requirements required by the board;
  - completed the experience requirements required by the board; and
  - passed the examination approved by the board.

The board will issue a license with the new residential structure endorsement to any applicant who completes a training module developed by the board in conjunction with the Department of Housing and Community Development based on the International Residential Code component of the Virginia Uniform Statewide Building Code.

The general assembly in 2014 created the First-Time Homebuyers' Savings Accounts to be used for real estate transaction costs listed on the settlement statement (Closing Disclosure). The accounts are to be held at a participating financial institution and may contain cash or other marketable securities. Account holders may contribute up to $50,000 (post-tax) and withdraw the principal and any interest earned up to a total of $150,000 without paying state taxes (federal taxes would still be imposed.). Funds withdrawn for other purposes are subject to recapture taxes and penalties.

First-Time Homebuyers Savings Accounts

The general assembly in 2014 created the First-Time Homebuyers' Savings Accounts to be used for real estate transaction costs listed on the settlement statement (Closing Disclosure). The accounts are to be held at a participating financial institution and may contain cash or other marketable securities. Account holders may contribute up to $50,000 (post-tax) and withdraw the principal and any interest earned up to a total of $150,000 without paying state taxes (federal taxes would still be imposed.). Funds withdrawn for other purposes are subject to recapture taxes and penalties.

Vested Property Rights

Legislation passed in 2014 clarifies the vested rights of owners of properties that were built before current zoning regulations were in effect or where permits can no longer be located. This bill states that so long as the homeowner has been paying taxes on the property for the past 15 years, the structure is deemed legal but nonconforming. When repairing or replacing a vested structure, the homeowner may be asked to bring the structure up to current code, but cannot be forced to remove it.

Virginia Underground Utility Damage Prevention Act

An additional statute that can have impact on residential property is the Virginia Underground Utility Damage Prevention Act, which requires that anyone planning construction on any site must contact "Miss Utility" so that flags can be placed to protect existing utility lines. The latest information says to "dial 811 before you dig" or call 1-800-552-7001.

The act states that, "no person... shall make or begin any excavation or demolition without first notifying the notification center for that area." (§ 56-265.17 A)

This also pertains to real estate signs placed on utility easements in the front of properties to increase visibility for potential customers. The notification center must be called before excavating to install a sign. Hand digging is exempt from the act (see website http://va811 .com for a presentation on hand digging).

For additional information regarding the act, contact the State Corporation Commission's Division of Utility and Railroad Safety at 1-800-552-7945 or visit www.scc.virginia.gov /urs/index.aspx.

Chesapeake Bay Preservation Act

This act was originated in 1988 but has had several revisions over the years, the most recent being in 2013 when certain boundaries were changed. The residential property disclosure statement makes reference to the act in the section on resource protection areas. Areas subject to the act must follow certain regulations regarding building or other activities that could affect waters running into the Chesapeake Bay.

Federal Law

In addition to fair housing law, there are other federal laws that directly affect the practice of real estate. Although this information is not part of the state examination for licensure, it is important background knowledge for those intending to practice real estate in the Commonwealth of Virginia.

National Do Not Call Registry

The federal government created the National Do Not Call Registry to help consumers avoid unwanted telemarketing calls. Anyone can register online at www.donotcall.gov or by calling 1-888-382-1222. As of June 2003, cell phone numbers can also be placed on the register. Violators are subject to civil penalties of up to $16,000 per violation. As of 2016, computer-generated robocalls are also prohibited.

Exemptions

Individuals who use cold calling as a prospecting tool must comply with the provisions of the National Do Not Call Registry. Exemptions to the rule are as follows:

- Consumers with whom the caller has an existing relationship (this applies to existing clients and customers and extends for up to 18 months after the end of a transaction)
- In response to a consumer inquiry or application (calls can be made for up to three months after the inquiry)
- Persons who have granted express written permission to call

In addition, the rules do not apply to

- charities,
- political organizations,
- telephone surveyors, or
- certain nonprofit organizations.

On January 1, 2005, the FTC and FCC rules made it mandatory to check a phone number against a version of the registry that is no more than 31 days old before placing a telemarketing call. An annual fee is charged for accessing individual area codes (the fee per area code in 2016 was $59 or $16.28 for all area codes). Five area codes are available at no cost. A salesperson should always check with the broker before making random calls.

Visit https://telemarketing.donotcall.gov to register and obtain current fees.

CAN-SPAM Act

The CAN-SPAM Act of 2003 (Controlling the Assault of Non-Solicited Pornography and Marketing) became effective January 1, 2004. It was designed to create a national standard to control the growing problem of deceptive or fraudulent commercial email and outlines a series of practices that email senders must follow. It does not just apply to bulk email; it covers all electronic mail messages with the primary purpose of advertising or promoting a product or service (for example, an email notice for a new listing in the neighborhood).

Each separate email in violation of the CAN-SPAM Act is subject to a penalty up to $16,000. The main CAN-SPAM requirements are listed following:

- Don't use false or misleading header information.
- Don't use deceptive subject lines.
- Identify the message as an advertisement.
- Tell recipients where you are located (a physical postal address).
- Tell recipients how to opt out of receiving future emails from you.
- Honor opt-out requests promptly (within 10 days).
- Monitor what others are doing on your behalf (for example, even if you hire a marketing company, you are still responsible).

unsubscribe option

CAN-SPAM information can be found at www.ftc.gov/tips-advice/business-center /guidance/can-spam-act-compliance-guide-business.

The Fair and Accurate Credit Transaction Act (FACTA) was enacted in 2003 and is primarily concerned with credit report issues. There is part of the act, however, that deals with protecting the consumer from identity theft that does involve office procedures for a real estate firm.

The FACTA Disposal Rule requires office policies to

FACTA information can be found at www.ftc.gov with a search entry of "FACTA".

FACTA

The Fair and Accurate Credit Transaction Act (FACTA) was enacted in 2003 and is primarily concerned with credit report issues. There is part of the act, however, that deals with protecting the consumer from identity theft that does involve office procedures for a real estate firm.

The FACTA Disposal Rule requires office policies to

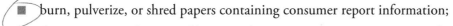

- burn, pulverize, or shred papers containing consumer report information;
- destroy or erase electronic files or media containing consumer report information; and
- conduct due diligence and hire a document destruction contractor to dispose of material identified as consumer report information.

FACTA information can be found at www.ftc.gov with a search entry of "FACTA".

MAP Rule

An FTC ruling on Mortgage Acts and Practices—Advertising Rule (MAP Rule), which took effect on August 19, 2011, impacts real estate professionals who provide specific information about mortgage loan products to consumers. The rule does not apply to purely informational communications not designed to cause the purchase of a particular good or service. Providing a buyer general information about market rates for different types of mortgage products would not be subject to the MAP Rule because these are not related to a specific product. Completing a prequalification process with the buyer to determine the price range of properties that the consumer may be eligible to purchase also does not require compliance with the MAP Rule.

American Taxpayer Relief Acts

Anyone who has purchased a home understands that there is usually a significant tax deduction for interest paid on a mortgage loan. A real estate licensee may wish to point this out, but should never be in a position of giving tax advice to a client. There are certain aspects of recent tax bills that are directly related to real estate transactions and are included here for general information.

Tax Deductions

The American Taxpayer Relief Act of 2012 was signed into law on January 2, 2013. The bill extended mortgage cancellation tax relief for homeowners or sellers who had some of their mortgage debt forgiven by a lender, typically in a short sale or foreclosure sale for sellers and in a modification for owners. Without the extension, any debt forgiven would have been taxable. Legislation each year has continued to extend the Mortgage Forgiveness Debt Act—currently through 2017.

The deduction for mortgage insurance premiums for tax filers making less than $100,000 remains a deduction until the Adjusted Gross Income (AGI) exceeds $109,000. The tax credit for energy-efficient home improvements is now limited to solar, wind, geothermal, and fuel-cell technology. State and local property taxes remain deductible.

In 2014, legislation simplified the home office deduction. Instead of providing detailed expense records, taxpayers can now simply deduct $5 for every square foot of home office space, up to a maximum of 300 square feet, or $1,500. The simplified expense is reported on Schedule C along with other business expenses. A home office deduction is allowed even though the licensee may have an assigned space in the brokerage firm's office.

National Flood Insurance

The ability to obtain flood insurance at a reasonable cost is important to more than 5.6 million businesses and homeowners throughout the country. In July 2012, Congress passed the Flood Insurance Reform Act, ensuring that the program would remain in effect for another five years. In March 2014, Congress passed the Homeowner Flood Insurance Affordability Act, which provides new or renewed National Flood Insurance Policies (NFIP), which includes a surcharge depending on the use and type of policy in place.

The availability of affordable flood insurance can impact real estate transactions in over 21,000 communities nationwide in areas where the Federal Emergency Management Agency (FEMA) flood maps indicate that flood insurance is required in order to obtain approval for a mortgage loan. To identify a community's flood risk, FEMA conducts a Flood Insurance Study. The study includes statistical data for river flow, storm tides, hydrologic/hydraulic analyses, and rainfall and topographic surveys. FEMA uses this data to create the flood hazard maps that outline your community's different flood risk areas. These Flood Insurance Rate Maps (FIRMS) can be seen by providing an address and zip code on the FEMA website www.newfloodmap.com. Mortgage lenders may not require flood insurance coverage exceeding the replacement value of the property's improvements.

Consumer Financial Protection Bureau (CFPB)

The Dodd-Frank Wall Street Reform and Consumer Protection Act of 2010 established the Consumer Financial Protection Bureau (CFPB). Its central mission is stated as making consumer financial products and services work better for Americans whether applying for a mortgage, selecting a credit card, or using any type of consumer financial products.

The CFPB released new rules on how mortgage servicers must treat borrowers, which took effect on January 10, 2014 and apply to all mortgage servicers with 5,000 or more loans. The goal of the new regulations is to ensure that servicers do not take advantage of borrowers who fall behind on their payments. The new CFPB rules are discussed further in Unit 6.

TILA-RESPA Integrated Disclosures (TRID)

Rulemaking authority for the Truth in Lending Act (TILA)—Regulation Z and the Real Estate Settlement Procedures Act (RESPA)—Regulation X was transferred to the CFPB in July 2011. After four years of study, research, and revisions TILA-RESPA Integrated Disclosures (TRID) was made mandatory on October 3, 2015. Under TRID, the **Loan Estimate (LE)** that replaced the initial Truth in Lending statement and Good Faith Estimate (GFE) must be delivered to a borrower within three days of application. Upon receipt of the LE, the borrower has 10 days to proceed with the transaction or walk away.

The other new form created by the CFPB is the **Closing Disclosure (CD)** which replaced the final TILA statement and the HUD-1 Settlement Statement. The CD must be delivered to the borrower at least three days before settlement. The CD has very little tolerance for any changes from the original LE. Any significant change from the original LE may require new documentation to be prepared causing a delay in settlement. Prior to the new TRID rules, the settlement agent prepared a HUD-1 Settlement Statement. The new CD form is now prepared by the lender and combines the old HUD-1 statement and the final Truth in Lending statement.

TRID is triggered by an application for a "federally related mortgage loan." Construction-only loans, vacant land, and properties with 25 acres or more did not fall under RESPA, but are now subject to TRID. Business, commercial, and agricultural loans are still exempt.

Regulations for Drones

New federal regulations allow for the operation of drones beyond 15 miles of Washington, D.C. Virginia REALTORS® interested in using drones for marketing will be subject to FAA requirements for commercial drone operators. The procedure involves registering the aircraft with the FAA, obtaining an FAA-issued pilot's license, and obtaining a Section 333 exemption, which allows for operation of the drone in public airspace. The licensing and approval process is complicated and interested REALTORS® might want to consider using a third-party operator already approved by the FAA. See the FAA website for further information.

SUMMARY

The practice of real estate in the Commonwealth of Virginia is governed under the Code of Virginia in Title 54.1—Professions and Occupations, and Title 55—Property and Conveyances. Chapter 3 of Title 54.1 covers the DPOR, which administers both the REB and the CIC Board. Rules and regulations for both are covered in the VAC as Agency 135 for the REB and Agency 48 for the CIC.

Chapter 21 of Title 54.1 covers real estate brokers and salespersons and includes brokerage definitions, licensing and public notice requirements, and exemptions. The Virginia Real Estate Transaction Recovery Fund was established to reimburse parties who suffer monetary loss due to a licensee's improper or dishonest conduct and is maintained by the DPOR. Each new licensee pays $20 into this fund and if at any time the balance falls below $400,000, all licenses will be assessed. The 2016 general assembly passed legislation to clarify the position of claimants from this fund. There are also set limitations on the amount that may be recovered.

Many of the chapters from Title 55 are covered in detail in other units of this course: Creation and Limitation of Estates, Condominium Act, Virginia Real Estate Time-Share Act, Virginia Real Estate Cooperative Act, and Property Owners' Association Act in Unit 3; Landlord and Tenant in Unit 9; Settlement Agents in Unit 7; and Fair Housing in Unit 10. The Virginia Residential Property Disclosure Act is covered in this unit with a discussion of exemptions, duties of licensees, and disclosure forms. The time for disclosure and purchaser's options, buyer's remorse, and liability for licensees are covered along with a brief explanation of stigmatized properties.

Other legislation affecting real estate practice on both the state and federal level make up the final section of the unit. The most significant on the state level are the new requirement for home inspectors to be licensed as of July 1, 2017, the creation of the First-Time Homebuyers' Savings Accounts, and the Virginia Underground Utility Damage Prevention Act. A review of relevant federal laws is included here for reference although they will not be included on the state portion of the licensing exam.

UNIT I QUIZ

1. The Real Estate Board (REB) rules and regulations are found in *consistent with*
   A. the Code of Virginia. ✓
   B. the Virginia Constitution.
   C. the Virginia Administrative Code (VAC).
   D. the general assembly minutes.

2. The REB is authorized to do all of the following *EXCEPT*
   A. license brokers and salespersons.
   B. develop criteria for evaluating and approving continuing education courses.
   C. regulate the Property Owners' Association Act. *under CIC*
   D. enforce provisions of the Virginia Fair Housing Law.

3. The Virginia Real Estate Transaction Recovery Fund is administered by
   A. the Board for Professional and Occupational Regulation.
   B. the REB.
   C. the CIC Board.
   D. the VAC.

4. The current real estate regulations went into effect
   A. January 1, 2015.
   B. July 1, 2015.
   C. October 3, 2015.
   D. November 1, 2015.

5. The Common Interest Community (CIC) Board regulates all of the following *EXCEPT*
   A. the Condominium Act.
   B. the Real Estate Time-Share Act.
   C. the Real Estate Cooperative Act.
   D. the Residential Property Disclosure Act. *REB*

6. The CIC was established to regulate CIC managers by means of
   A. an established fee structure.
   B. licensure.
   C. annual testing.
   D. written procedures.

7. The Office of the Common Interest Community Ombudsman was established to do all of the following *EXCEPT*
   A. assist members to understand their rights.
   B. provide information and answer inquiries from members.
   C. officiate in making adverse decisions.
   D. provide information to the director for an annual report.

8. The term *broker* may refer to all of the following *EXCEPT*
   A. a brokerage firm.
   B. a sole proprietor transacting real estate business.
   C. a managing broker for a branch office.
   D. a principal in a brokerage relationship. *clients*

9. By Virginia statutory definition, a salesperson may perform all of the following functions *EXCEPT*
   A. offer a residence for sale.
   B. negotiate an exchange.
   C. serve as managing broker.
   D. lease rental apartments.

10. When a licensee acts as an independent contractor and *NOT* as a standard agent, the relationship is governed by
    A. the common law of agency.
    B. a standard Virginia REB contractor agreement.
    C. a written agreement between licensee and client.
    D. a buyer agency agreement.

11. An individual wants to sell her own house. Which of the following statements is *TRUE*?
    A. She does not need a real estate license to sell her own property.
    B. In Virginia, anyone who sells real property must have a real estate license.
    C. An individual may obtain a temporary real estate license in order to legally sell her own house.
    D. She may only sell her own house without a real estate license if she is an attorney.

12. All of the following are exempt from the state licensing requirements *EXCEPT*
    A. a person acting without compensation as attorney-in-fact.
    B. an attorney involved in a real estate transaction in his normal role as attorney.
    C. an officer of a firm who actively participates in brokerage business.
    D. a licensed auctioneer selling real estate at a public auction.

13. The Virginia Real Estate Transaction Recovery Fund was created to
    A. protect consumers from unscrupulous settlement attorneys.
    B. provide funding for the Virginia Housing Development Authority (VHDA).
    C. reimburse consumers who suffer monetary loss due to a licensee's misconduct.
    D. establish a fund for research and education of licensees.

14. The REB may assess each active and inactive licensee a proportionate amount whenever the Transaction Recovery Fund falls below a minimum balance of
    A. $20 per licensee.
    B. $400,000.
    C. $1 million.
    D. $2 million.

15. Exemptions to the Virginia Residential Property Disclosure Act provisions include all of the following *EXCEPT*
    A. transfers pursuant to a foreclosure sale.
    B. transfers made without the assistance of a licensed real estate broker.
    C. transfers made between spouses resulting from a divorce.
    D. transfers involving the first sale of a dwelling.

16. As of July 1, 2011, a full list of seller representations was made available to a purchaser by
    A. the listing agent.
    B. the seller.
    C. the REB website.
    D. the buyer agent.

17. If a purchaser does *NOT* receive the proper property disclosure before contract ratification, the contract may be terminated
    A. within three days of occupancy.
    B. within five days of settlement.
    C. any time before settlement.
    D. before loan application with no right of contract termination.

18. Which federal organization is responsible for identifying flood areas?
    A. Federal Emergency Management Agency (FEMA)
    B. Department of Housing and Urban Development (HUD)
    C. Environmental Protection Agency (EPA)
    D. U.S. Fish and Wildlife Service

19. Exemptions to the provisions of the National Do Not Call Registry include all of the following *EXCEPT*
    A. clients and customers for a period of 18 months from last transaction.
    B. within 18 months of a consumer inquiry.
    C. charitable organizations.
    D. political organizations.

20. Legislation that directly affects the policies and procedures of a brokerage firm includes all of the following *EXCEPT*
    A. cold calling for prospects (National Do Not Call Registry).
    B. emailed newsletters (CAN-SPAM).
    C. maintenance of client records (FACTA).
    D. purchase of flood insurance (NFIP).

UNIT 2

Brokerage Relationships and Agency

LEARNING OBJECTIVES

When you have completed this unit, you will be able to

> **define** agency and brokerage relationships and how to originate and terminate the relationship;
> **explain** the disclosure requirements for brokerage relationships and agency representation;
> **list** the statutory duties for clients and customers;
> **describe** typical components of listing and buyer agency agreements; and
> **define** the following key terms:

agency	designated agent	net listing
agent	dual agent or representative	property management
brokerage relationship	independent contractor	agreement
client	limited service agent	standard agent
customer	Megan's Law	standard or statutory agency
defective drywall	ministerial acts	

OVERVIEW

The concept of common law of agency as it relates to real estate brokerage no longer exists in Virginia. In 1995, the Virginia General Assembly expressly abrogated the common law of agency in real estate transactions (§ 54.1-2144). In its place, the legislature enacted an agency statute that codifies the agency relationships between brokers, buyers, sellers, landlords, tenants, and property managers (§ § 54.1-2130–54.1-2146). This is called **standard or statutory agency**.

One aspect of the Virginia agency law that differs from the common law of agency is that there is no longer imputed liability on the part of either the client or the broker. The client is not liable for misrepresentations made by a licensee, nor is a broker liable for misrepresentation on the part of another broker engaged to assist in a real estate transaction. In both cases, liability for another's actions would occur only if the client or broker knew, or should have known, of the misrepresentation or failed to take steps to correct it.

Knowledge or information between clients or brokers is not imputed. Each is responsible only for actual knowledge or information, although liability may still occur in a case of unlawful housing discriminatory practices.

AGENCY AND BROKERAGE RELATIONSHIPS

Commercial Transactions

Changes in **agency** law found in Title 54.1, Sections 2130 through 2142.5 that were amended and reenacted in 2016 are underlined. Minor changes occur throughout the act to differentiate between residential and commercial transactions. **Brokerage relationship** and agency disclosure forms were also modified to reflect the change.

Residential real estate means real property containing one to four residential dwelling units and the sale of lots containing one to four residential dwelling units.

Commercial real estate generally refers to property of more than one to four residential units but does not include single-family residential units such as condominiums, townhouses, apartments, or homes in a subdivision even though these units may be part of a larger building or parcel of real estate containing more than four residential units.

The 2016 general assembly enacted legislation eliminating the previous classifications of licensees for commercial transactions. Commercial agents will now act as **agents** or **independent contractors**. They will no longer be known as **standard agents** and will not be allowed to practice as **limited service agents**. The new ruling eliminates the need for a disclosure of brokerage relationship form and written brokerage agreement in commercial transactions. However, a disclosure form for dual agency or representation is still required for commercial transactions.

The law now clarifies that the disclosure requirements pertaining to **defective drywall** and the provisions of the fair housing statutes do not apply to commercial transactions.

Definitions

Virginia's statute Section 54.1-2130 provides the following definitions, rearranged here into similar categories.

Agency is defined as any relationship in which a real estate licensee acts for or represents a person as an agent by such person's express authority in a commercial or residential real estate transaction. Agency includes representation of a **client** as a standard agent or a limited service agent. *Agent* means a real estate licensee who is acting as (i) a standard agent in a residential real estate transaction, (ii) a limited service agent in a residential real estate transaction, or (iii) an agent in a commercial real estate transaction.

A *standard agent* is defined as a licensee who acts for or represents a client in an agency relationship in a residential real estate transaction. A standard agent has the obligations provided by statute and any additional obligations agreed to by the parties to the brokerage agreement.

A *limited service agent* is a licensee who represents a client in a residential transaction pursuant to a brokerage agreement that ensures that the agent will not provide one or more duties as proscribed under agency law in the category of promoting the best interest of the client, such as marketing activities, drafting and negotiating contracts, receiving and presenting offers and counteroffers, and assisting the client to fulfill contract obligations. All other statutory duties with regard to confidentiality, ordinary care, accounting, and compliance with all statutes and regulations are still required. The limited service agent must provide the client with copies of any disclosures required by federal or state law, the rights and obligations under the Virginia Residential Property Disclosure Act and any rights or obligations for the sale of a condominium or property subject to the Property Owners' Association Act. Specific disclosure is required for a limited service agent.

A **designated agent** or representative is a licensee assigned by the broker to represent a client when a different client is also represented by the broker in the same transaction. In this way, two licensees from the same brokerage firm can take part in the same transaction while retaining standard agent duties to their clients. This differs from a **dual agent or representative** where a licensee has a brokerage relationship with both seller and buyer, or landlord and tenant, in the same transaction.

A licensee can also act as an independent contractor. An independent contractor is not an agent, has the obligations agreed to in the brokerage agreement, and is still subject to certain provisions of agency law with regard to confidentiality, ordinary care, accounting, and disclosures.

A *brokerage agreement* is the written agreement creating a brokerage relationship between a client and a licensee, stating whether the licensee represents the client as an agent or as an independent contractor. A *brokerage relationship* is a contractual relationship between a client and a licensee who has been engaged by the client to procure a seller, buyer, option, tenant, or landlord who is ready, willing, and able to sell, buy, option, exchange, or rent real estate on behalf of the client. Although it is often the salesperson who initiates the brokerage relationship with the client, it is in fact the broker who has the brokerage relationship with the client. In this context, the word *broker* refers to the brokerage firm.

E X A M P L E

XYZ Realty, as a non-broker-owned sole proprietor, may have hired Mary Smith to act as principal broker of the firm. The broker-client relationship is with XYZ Realty (the broker), not with Mary Smith.

The brokerage relationship is limited to a broker and a client. A *client* is a person who has entered into a brokerage relationship with a broker licensee. Any other party to the transaction with whom the licensee does not have a brokerage relationship, but for whom the licensee performs **ministerial acts**, is a **customer**.

Ministerial acts are defined as routine acts that a licensee can perform for a person that do not involve discretion or the exercise of the licensee's own judgment.

A **property management agreement** is the written agreement between a property manager and the owner of real estate for the management of the real estate.

Significant changes with regard to both designated and dual agency disclosure went into effect on July 1, 2012. Due to the complexity of the changes, every applicant for relicensure as either a broker or a salesperson before July 1, 2014 was required to take a minimum three-hour continuing education course on the changes to residential standard agency.

Establishing a Brokerage Relationship

In addition to establishing new rules and standards for agency relationships in real estate transactions, the statute provides that neither compensation nor use of a common source information company, such as an MLS, creates a brokerage relationship. (§ 54.1-2141)

Before entering into a brokerage relationship, the licensee must advise the prospective client of

- the type of brokerage relationship proposed by the broker;
- the broker's compensation; and
- whether the broker will share the compensation with a broker who may have a brokerage relationship with another party to the transaction.

As of July 1, 2012, all brokerage agreements must

- be in writing;
- have a definite termination date (if no date specified, brokerage relationship terminates after 90 days);
- state the amount of the brokerage fees and how and when such fees are to be paid;
- state the services to be rendered by the licensee;
- include such other terms of the brokerage relationship as have been agreed to by the client and the licensee; and
- in the case of brokerage agreements entered into in conjunction with the client's consent to dual representation, include the additional disclosures set out in Section 54.1-2139.

Commencement and Termination of Brokerage Relationship

The brokerage relationship begins at the time the client engages a broker. Ideally, the relationship terminates when the brokerage agreement's terms have been completely performed. However, the relationship may also be terminated by

- the expiration of the agreement;
- a mutual agreement to terminate;
- a default by any party; or
- the licensee's withdrawal when a client refuses to consent to disclosed dual agency.

All brokerage relationships must have a definite termination date. If no date is specified, the statute establishes a mandatory termination date of 90 days after the commencement of the brokerage relationship (§ 54.1-2137B).

Once a brokerage relationship has terminated or expired, the licensee owes no further duties to the client. However, the licensee is nonetheless required to account for all monies and property relating to the brokerage relationship and keeping confidential all personal and financial information received from the client.

DISCLOSURE REQUIREMENTS

Brokerage Relationships

Virginia agency law requires full disclosure of any existing brokerage relationships. It is essential that the party to the transaction who is not the client of the licensee and who is not represented by another licensee clearly understand that the licensee represents only the licensee's client. Although the licensee must treat a customer honestly and to disclose any material adverse facts about the physical condition of the property, the agent's primary responsibility is to protect and promote the best interest of the client.

At the time of the first substantive discussion about a specific property in a residential real estate transaction with an actual or prospective buyer, seller, landlord, or tenant who is not a client of the licensee and who is not represented by another licensee, a licensee must disclose any broker relationship he has with any other party to the transaction. The disclosure must be made in writing at the earliest practical time but no later than the time when specific real estate assistance is provided for sales transactions or at the time of a lease application or in the lease, whichever occurs first. Disclosure is not required for lease terms of less than two months. All written disclosure forms must be signed by all parties.

As of July 1, 2016, a disclosure of brokerage relationship form must be used, as illustrated in Figure 2.1.

FIGURE 2.1:   Disclosure of Brokerage Relationship

DISCLOSURE OF BROKERAGE RELATIONSHIP IN A RESIDENTIAL REAL ESTATE TRANSACTION

The undersigned do hereby acknowledge disclosure that the licensee

_____ (name of broker or salesperson) associated with

_____ (Name of Brokerage Firm) represents the following party in a

real estate transaction:

☐   Seller(s)   or   ☐   Buyer(s)

☐   Landlord(s) - 13m   or   ☐   Tenant(s)

_____   _____

Date   Name

_____   _____

Date   Name

Note that this form is required for the person who is not the client of the agent and is not represented by another licensee. Signature of this disclosure by a client is not required because a brokerage relationship has been previously established by an exclusive right to represent, a buyer agency agreement, or an exclusive right to sell.

If the required disclosure is given in combination with other disclosures or information, the disclosure must be conspicuous, printed in bold lettering, all capitals, underlined, or within a separate box (§ 54.1-2138A). If the licensee's relationship with any party to the transaction changes, all clients and customers involved in the transaction must be informed (in writing) of the change. Copies of all disclosures that are a part of an executed lease or a consummated transaction must be kept for three years.

Limited Service Agent Disclosure

A licensee may act as a limited service agent in a residential real estate transaction only pursuant to a written and signed brokerage agreement in which the agent discloses (i) that the licensee is acting as a limited service agent, (ii) provides a list of the specific services that will be provided, and (iii) a list of the specific duties of a standard agent that will not be provided to the client. The disclosure must be conspicuous and printed either in bold lettering or all capitals, and must be underlined or in a separate box. Language that complies substantially with the following must be included in the agreement:

> By entering into this brokerage agreement, the undersigned do hereby acknowledge their informed consent to the limited service agent in a residential real estate transaction by the licensee and do further acknowledge that neither the other party to the transaction nor any real estate licensee representing the other party is under any legal obligation to assist the undersigned with the performance of any duties and responsibilities of the undersigned not performed by the limited service agent. (§ 54.1-2138.1)

Disclosed Dual Representation

In Virginia, a licensee may represent both parties in the same real estate transaction—seller and buyer or landlord and tenant—only with the written consent of all clients in the transaction. The client's signature on the written disclosure form is presumptive evidence of the brokerage relationship. Under the July 1, 2012, revisions to agency law, a licensee may act in an agency relationship with a client as either a standard or a limited service agent. A licensee acting as an independent contractor is now called a *representative* (not an agent).

In response to concerns that clients agreeing to dual agency were not being adequately represented, Section 54.1-2139 was revised, effective July 1, 2012. The new disclosure form points out that the client may be disadvantaged by dual representation. It specifies that the dual agent or representative may not give advice as to terms, offers, or counteroffers or the suitability, condition, or needed repairs of the property and that the licensee will be acting without real knowledge of the client's needs and experience.

The much stronger disclosure form was required as of July 1, 2012. Section 54.1-2139 specifically states that a licensee may not act as either a dual agent or representative without the written consent of all parties to the transaction. The new disclosure form provides for disclosure of the client being represented (seller, buyer, landlord, or tenant) and the type of representation (standard agent, limited service agent, independent contractor). See the sample residential disclosure form in Figure 2.2 and commercial disclosure form in Figure 2.3. A separate form is available for disclosure of dual agency or dual representation in a commercial real estate transaction. (§ 54.1-2139.01)

FIGURE 2.2: Disclosure of Dual Agency or Dual Representation in a Residential Real Estate Transaction

DISCLOSURE OF DUAL AGENCY OR DUAL REPRESENTATION IN A
RESIDENTIAL REAL ESTATE TRANSACTION

The undersigned do hereby acknowledge disclosure that the licensee

_____ (name of broker or salesperson) associated with

_____ (Brokerage Firm) represents more than one party in this residential

real estate transaction as follows:

A. Brokerage Firm represents the following party (select one):
  ☐ Seller(s)   ☐ Buyer(s)   ☐ Landlord(s)   ☐ Tenant(s)

As a (select one):
  ☐ standard agent   ☐ limited service agent   ☐ independent contractor

Brokerage Firm represents another party (select one):
  ☐ Seller(s)   ☐ Buyer(s)   ☐ Landlord(s)   ☐ Tenant(s)

As a (select one):
  ☐ standard agent   ☐ limited service agent   ☐ independent contractor

B. Brokerage Firm disclosure and client acknowledgement of the following (select one):
☐ Brokerage Firm represents two existing clients in the transaction and the undersigned acknowledge the following:
  The undersigned understand that the foregoing dual agent or dual representative may not disclose to either client any information that has been given to the dual agent or representative by the other client within the confidence and trust of the brokerage relationship except for that information which is otherwise required or permitted by Article 3 (§ 54.1-2130 et seq.) of Chapter 21 of Title 54.1 of the Code of Virginia to be disclosed.

☐ Brokerage Firm represents one existing client and one new client in the transaction and the undersigned acknowledge the following:
  The undersigned understand:
  1. That following the commencement of dual agency or representation, the licensee cannot advise either party as to the terms to offer or accept in any offer or counteroffer; however, the licensee may have advised one party as to such terms prior to the commencement of dual agency or representation;
  2. That the licensee cannot advise the buyer client as to the suitability of the property, its condition (other than to make any disclosures as required by law of any licensee representing a seller), and cannot advise either party as to what repairs of the property to make or request;
  3. That the licensee cannot advise either party in any dispute that arises relating to the transaction;
  4. That the licensee may be acting without knowledge of the client's needs, client's knowledge of the market, or client's capabilities in dealing with the intricacies of real estate transactions; and
  5. That either party may engage another licensee at additional cost to represent their respective interests.

FIGURE 2.2: Disclosure of Dual Agency or Dual Representation in a Residential Real Estate Transaction (continued)

The undersigned by signing this notice do hereby acknowledge their informed consent to the disclosed dual representation by the licensee.

_____   _____
Date   Name (One Party)

_____   _____
Date   Name (One Party)

_____   _____
Date   Name (Other Party)

_____   _____
Date   Name (Other Party)

FIGURE 2.3:   Disclosure of Dual Agency or Dual Representation in a Commercial Real Estate Transaction

DISCLOSURE OF DUAL AGENCY OR DUAL REPRESENTATION
IN A COMMERCIAL REAL ESTATE TRANSACTION

The undersigned do hereby acknowledge disclosure that the licensee

_____ (name of broker or salesperson) associated with

_____ (Brokerage Firm) represents more than one party in this

commercial real estate transaction as follows:

A. Brokerage Firm represents the following party (select one):
   ☐ Seller(s)   ☐ Buyer(s)   ☐ Landlord(s)   ☐ Tenant(s)

As a (select one):
   ☐ standard agent   ☐ limited service agent   ☐ independent contractor

Brokerage Firm represents another party (select one):
   ☐ Seller(s)   ☐ Buyer(s)   ☐ Landlord(s)   ☐ Tenant(s)

As a (select one):
   ☐ standard agent   ☐ limited service agent   ☐ independent contractor

The undersigned understand that the foregoing dual agent or dual representative may not disclose to either client any information that has been given to the dual agent or representative by the other client within the confidence and trust of the brokerage relationship except for that information which is otherwise required or permitted by Article 3 (§ 54.1-2130 et seq.) of Chapter 21 of Title 54.1 of the Code of Virginia to be disclosed.

The undersigned by signing this notice do hereby acknowledge their informed consent to the disclosed dual representation by the licensee.

_____   _____

Date   Name (One Party)

_____   _____

Date   Name (One Party)

_____   _____

Date   Name (Other Party)

_____   _____

Date   Name (Other Party)

A dual agent or representative does not terminate any brokerage relationship by making the required disclosures of dual representation. (§ 54.1-2139E) As mentioned previously, a licensee may withdraw from representing a client who refuses to consent to disclosed dual agency. The licensee may withdraw under such circumstances without liability and may continue to represent the other client. Furthermore, the licensee may continue to represent the client who refused dual representation in other transactions. (§ 54.1-2139F)

Disclosed Designated Agency

The new legislation effective July 1, 2012, also affected designated agents. Section 54.1-2139.1 reestablished the broker's authority to designate agents or representatives to work with different clients in the same transaction. The required disclosure form is a disclosure of designated agency or representatives as illustrated in Figure 2.4.

FIGURE 2.4: Disclosure of Designated Agency or Representatives

DISCLOSURE OF DESIGNATED AGENTS OR REPRESENTATIVES

The undersigned do hereby acknowledge disclosure that the licensee

_____ (name of Broker and Firm) represents more than one party in this

real estate transaction as indicated below:

☐ Seller(s) and Buyer(s)   ☐ Landlord(s) and Tenant(s)

The undersigned understand that the foregoing dual agent or representative may not disclose to either client or such client's designated agent or representative any information that has been given to the dual agent or representative by the other client within the confidence and trust of the brokerage relationship except for that information which is otherwise required or permitted by Article 3 (§ 54.1-2130 et seq.) of Chapter 21 of Title 54.1 of the Code of Virginia to be disclosed.

The principal or supervising broker has assigned

_____ (broker or salesperson) to act as Designated Agent or Representative for the one party as indicated below:

☐ Seller(s)   ☐ Buyer(s)   ☐ Landlord(s)   ☐ Tenant(s)

As a (select one):

☐ standard agent   ☐ limited service agent   ☐ independent contractor

_____ (broker or salesperson) to act as Designated Agent or Representative for the other party as indicated below:

☐ Seller(s)   ☐ Buyer(s)   ☐ Landlord(s)   ☐ Tenant(s)

As a (select one):

☐ standard agent   ☐ limited service agent   ☐ independent contractor

The undersigned by signing this notice do hereby acknowledge their consent to the disclosed dual representation by the licensee.

_____   _____
Date   Name (One Party)

_____   _____
Date   Name (One Party)

_____   _____
Date   Name (Other Party)

_____   _____
Date   Name (Other Party)

IN PRACTICE

The principal broker of a brokerage firm, through the actions of agent M, has established a brokerage relationship with a prospective buyer by having her sign an exclusive right-to-represent agreement. The buyer decides to make an offer on a property that is listed with the same firm with agent B as the listing agent. The broker may now designate agent M to be the designated agent for the buyer and agent B to be the designated agent for the seller. Both designated agents will be able to meet all of the statutory obligations of duties to their clients. The principal broker will remain in a dual agency position with equal responsibility to both clients.

If the buyer wished to purchase a property listed with the same firm with agent M as listing agent, agent M could then enter into a disclosed dual agent role where she would have statutory responsibilities to both clients. The brokerage firm would have brokerage relationships with both the buyer, through the signing of an exclusive right-to-represent agreement, and the seller, through the signing of a listing agreement.

Another alternative is for agent M to withdraw from the buyer representation brokerage agreement with the buyer and continue to represent only the seller. The buyer would then be a customer instead of a client. The statutory obligation is to treat the buyer honestly and disclose any adverse material defects in the property. Agent M would also be able to perform ministerial acts for the buyer, but her primary responsibility is to the seller.

In all cases where dual agency or designated agency is practiced, the need for written consent of all parties to the transaction is a requirement of the statute. The disclosure may be combined with other disclosures but must be conspicuous, printed in bold lettering, all capitals, underlined, or within a separate box.

STATUTORY DUTIES

The Virginia agency statute (§ § 54.1-213–54.1-2135) establishes specific duties for a licensee who is in an agency relationship as a standard agent with a seller, buyer, landlord, or tenant or to manage real estate.

Duties to a Client

The seven specific duties outlined in the statute are basically the same for all clients. The only variation is in the duty to promote the best interests of the client. These variations will be noted separately. Licensees engaged to manage real estate do not have a duty to promote the best interests of the client.

The statutory duties for a client require that licensees

- perform according to the terms of the brokerage relationship;
- promote the best interests of the client by
  - (seller and landlord only) conducting marketing activities seeking a sale or lease at the price and terms established in the brokerage relationship or at a price and terms acceptable to the client (once the property is under contract, the licensee is not obligated to seek additional offers unless required to do so under the brokerage agreement or sales contract);

- (buyers and tenants) seeking a property at a price and terms acceptable to the client (licensee is not obligated to seek other properties while the client is party to a purchase contract or lease);

- (sellers and buyers) assisting in the drafting and negotiating of offers and counteroffers, amendments, and addenda and in establishing strategies for accomplishing the client's objectives;

- (landlords and tenants) assisting in the drafting and negotiating of leases or letters of intent;

- receiving and presenting in a timely manner written offers and counteroffers even when the property is subject to a contract of sale or lease; and

- providing reasonable assistance to satisfy the client's contract obligations and to facilitate settlement of the purchase contract or finalize a lease;

■ maintain confidentiality of all personal and financial information received from the client during the brokerage relationship and any other information characterized as confidential by the client, unless the client consents in writing to its release or its release is required by law;

■ exercise ordinary care;

■ account in a timely manner for all money and property received in which the client has or may have an interest;

■ disclose to the client all material facts related to the property or concerning the transaction of which the licensee has actual knowledge; and

■ comply with all requirements of this article, all applicable fair housing statutes and regulations, and all other statutes and regulations that are not in conflict with this article.

In the case of a residential transaction, a licensee must also disclose to the seller the buyer's intent to occupy the property as a principal residence (§ 54.1-2132B). This disclosure is often stated in the body of a purchase agreement.

Duties to a Customer

The traditional fiduciary responsibilities that were a part of the common law of agency are basically included in the new statutory duties but with far less implied liability.

Customers, the parties with whom the licensee does *not* have a brokerage relationship, must be treated honestly and may not knowingly be given false information. In addition, they must be informed of any material adverse facts regarding the property's physical condition of which the licensee has actual knowledge. As of July 1, 2011, the law specifically requires disclosure of defective drywall. As of 2014, disclosure is required if the property was used for the manufacture of methamphetamine. The term *physical condition of the property* refers to the land and any improvements. It does not refer to

■ matters outside the boundaries of the land,

■ adjacent or other properties in proximity,

■ matters relating to governmental land use regulations, or

■ matters relating to highways or public streets.

Any such disclosure must be made in writing. No legal action may be brought against a licensee for making such required disclosures. This was further clarified as of July 1, 2011:

> A licensee shall not be liable for providing false information if the information was (i) provided to the licensee by the licensee's client; (ii) obtained from a governmental entity; (iii) obtained from a nongovernmental person or entity that obtained the information from a governmental entity; or (iv) obtained from a person licensed, certified, or registered to provide professional services in the Commonwealth, upon which the licensee relies, and the licensee did not (a) have actual knowledge that the information was false or (b) act in reckless disregard of the truth. (§ 54.1-2142.1)

A licensee having a brokerage relationship with a client is permitted to assist customers (the party with whom the licensee does not have a brokerage relationship) by performing ministerial acts. The performance of ministerial acts does not violate the licensee's brokerage relationship with the client. Similarly, the brokerage relationship is not violated if the licensee shows alternative properties to prospective buyers (or tenants) or represents other sellers (or landlords).

Property Management

Licensees who are engaged to manage real estate are required by Virginia law to perform according to the management agreement, exercise ordinary care, disclose all material facts concerning the property of which the licensee has actual knowledge (specifically the existence of defective drywall), maintain confidentiality of information, account for all money and property received, and comply with all relevant real estate and fair housing laws and regulations. The licensee is expected to perform services in accordance with the property management agreement. Licensees are permitted to represent other owners in the management of real property and to represent the owner as seller or landlord under a brokerage agreement. (§ 54.1-2135)

As of July 1, 2012, Section 54.1-2135 has been expanded to require that property management agreements must be in writing and must have a definite termination date or duration (if not, the agreement will terminate in 90 days). The agreement must state the amount of the management fees and how they are to be paid, state the services to be rendered by the licensee, and include any other terms agreed upon by the owner and the property manager.

AGENCY AGREEMENTS

When licensees assist buyers, sellers, tenants, landlords, and property owners, some type of written agreement must formalize an agency relationship. The listing agreement is probably the most widely used instrument for representing a seller in the sale of a property. The buyer agency or buyer representation agreement is technically a listing agreement for buyers.

Listing Forms

Although there are no standard listing or buyer representation forms used throughout the entire Commonwealth, the Virginia Association of REALTORS® (VAR) creates standard forms that are available in print and software versions, which are used in many parts of the state. Additionally, several large associations, such as the Northern Virginia Association of REALTORS® (NVAR), have standard forms available for use in large regional, multijurisdictional areas. These are available in print, software, and online subscription.

It should be noted that while an oral listing or buyer representation agreement may be legal in Virginia, such an agreement would not be enforceable, based on the statute of frauds.

IN PRACTICE

In a listing form, the blanks are rarely optional. All blanks should be filled in. If an item does not apply in a particular transaction, the notation N/A (not applicable) should be used. Finding accurate information for each item may require additional research.

Some items on the listing forms may have to be entered as approximations, such as the mortgage balance—until a payoff statement is available from the lender—or the exact age of the dwelling. Accurate figures should be used wherever possible. Any changes involving financial responsibility, such as a price change, dates, or other major seller commitments, must be authorized in writing by the seller.

SELLER REPRESENTATION—SELLER AGENCY AGREEMENT

Seller Representation

Types of Listing Agreements

The standard types of listings—open, exclusive agency, and exclusive right-to-sell—are all legal in Virginia. Many brokers will not accept open listings, however, because there is no guarantee of payment for time and money spent on the listings. Also, open listings may not be allowed by many MLS systems. All listing agreements must include a definite termination date. The owner must be furnished a copy of the listing at the time it is signed.

Virginia REB regulations specifically prohibit **net listings** (18 VAC 135-20-280(5)). A net listing is an agreement in which an owner specifies a particular dollar amount that she must net from the sale or rental of a property; the broker may keep any amount over the seller's net that is generated by the transaction. Under a net listing, it is difficult to balance the broker's responsibility to the principal with the broker's own interest in making a profit. Because this practice is not permitted in Virginia, brokers must inform prospective clients that their fee will be a percentage of the selling price, a commission, or a flat fee for services.

EXAMPLE

A homeowner called a Richmond real estate broker and told her that he wanted to sell his house. "I don't have time to be bothered with percentages and bargaining and offers and counteroffers," he explained. "I just need to walk out of this deal with $150,000 in my pocket. If you sell this place for more than that, you can keep the rest." The broker knew that comparable homes were selling for well over $200,000. Also, the broker knew that net listings are illegal in Virginia. What should the broker do?

The broker should explain that net listings are illegal in Virginia and advise him of the current range of values for properties like his. The broker can then negotiate a commission or fee for the services she will provide, sign a listing agreement with the owner, and proceed to market the property.

Typical Listing Information

A listing agreement (Exclusive Right to Represent Seller) usually contains information such as the following:

- Assurances that the seller has not entered into a listing agreement with another broker

- Complete list of what items (chattels) convey with the property, including items of personal property

- The sales price

- Specific terms of the agreement

- Disclosure of any retainer or administration fees required by the agent or the agent's firm and whether these fees will be refunded to the seller at the conclusion of the transaction

- Statement of the broker's duties; because the document will establish a brokerage relationship, a recital of the statutory duties of a broker is appropriate (see § 54.1-2131, Licensees Engaged by Sellers)

- Statement of any duties owed by the client

- Description of the purpose of the agreement

- Complete disclosure of how the broker will be paid

- Recital of disclosed dual or designated agent representation—statement of applicability of federal, state, and local disclosures include, but are not limited to, the following:

  - Lead-based paint

  - Mold

  - **Megan's Law** (information about registered sex offenders must be made available to the public)

  - Defective drywall

  - Disclosure statements

  - POA or condominium inclusion

- Local disclaimer information; some local MLS systems have regional disclosure information or information that sellers should know before entering into a sales agreement

- Fair housing statement

- Recital of any other provisions pertaining to the brokerage relationship

- Statement describing how the listing agreement may be terminated by either party

A property owner is now allowed to opt out of having the property displayed on the internet. The owner can also either authorize or not authorize specific elements on the broker's website, such as showing third-party comments or reviews, or an automated estimate of the market value of the property. Electronic signatures are now allowed as long as all parties agree to use them as shown on the form.

Buyer Representation

Buyer Agency Agreement

A buyer's agent establishes a brokerage relationship with a client through a buyer representation agreement.

An exclusive right-to-represent buyer agreement typically contains information such as the following:

- Assurances that the buyer has not entered into a buyer representation agreement with another broker

- Information about other properties that the buyer may have been shown by other agents

- Specific terms of the agreement

- Disclosure of any retainer or administration fees required by the agent or the agent's firm and whether these fees will be refunded to the buyer at the conclusion of the transaction

- Statement of the broker's duties; because the document will establish a brokerage relationship, a recital of the statutory duties of a broker is appropriate (see § 54.1-2132, Licensees Engaged by Buyers)

- Statement of any duties owed by the client

- Description of the purpose of the agreement

- Complete disclosure of how the broker will be paid

- Recital of disclosed dual or designated agent representation local disclaimer information; some local MLS systems have regional disclosure information on information that buyers should know before entering into a purchase agreement

- Fair housing statement

- Recital of any other provisions pertaining to the brokerage relationship

- Statement describing how the listing agreement may be terminated by either party

All of the statutory requirements for brokerage relationships and agency can be found in the Code of Virginia under Title 54.1, Chapter 21, Section 54.1-2130 through 54.1-2146.

Search the Code of Virginia on the Virginia General Assembly Legislative Information System (LIS) website at http://leg1.state.va.us/lis.htm.

SUMMARY

The common law of agency was abrogated by the Virginia General Assembly in 1995 in favor of legislation that codified the agency relationship between brokers and clients. Minor changes were made to the agency statutes found in Title 54.1 in 2016 to better differentiate between residential and commercial transactions.

A licensee may act as either a standard agent, or a limited service agent. Most of duties to be performed for a client are the same with the exception of the duty to promote the best interests of the client. The limited service agent can choose to not perform certain aspects of that duty. A designated agent is named by the broker in order for two agents from the same firm to work in the same transaction. A non-agency relationship of independent contractor is also part of the law. The independent contractor performs according to the brokerage agreement but is still obligated to most of the agency duties.

All agents work subject to a written brokerage agreement that establishes the brokerage relationship. Before entering into a brokerage relationship, the licensee must advise the prospective client of the type of brokerage relationship proposed, the broker's compensation, and how that may be shared. As of 2012, all brokerage agreements must be in writing, have a definite termination date, state the amount of fees, the services to be rendered, include any other terms as agreed upon and any additional disclosures needed. Agency law requires full disclosure of brokerage relationships to any party to the transaction that is not a client of the licensee or is not represented by another license. Limited service agent and disclosed dual or designated representation requires additional disclosure.

The law specifies these statutory duties for clients: to perform according to the terms of the brokerage relationship, promote the best interests of the client (this section is slightly different depending on the type of client), maintain confidentiality of all personal and financial information, account for all money and property received, disclose all material facts related to the property and comply with all statutes and regulations. Customers must be treated honestly and must be informed of any material adverse facts regarding the property's physical condition, not to include matters outside the boundaries, adjacent or other properties, matters relating to government land use regulations, or matters relating to highways or public streets. Ministerial acts are routine actions that require no judgment on the part of the agent and may be performed for persons other than a client. Licensees engaged to manage real estate have most of the same duties and must have a written agreement with a definite termination date, the amount of management fees and how to be paid, services to be rendered, and any other agreed upon terms.

The agency agreement with a seller is the listing form: either open, exclusive agency, or exclusive right-to-sell. Net listings are prohibited. The agency agreement with a buyer is the buyer agency agreement.

UNIT 2 QUIZ

1. Changes made to agency law in 2016 regarding licensees engaged in commercial real estate include
   A. commercial agents are no longer defined as standard or limited service agents.
   B. the disclosure of brokerage relationship form is no longer required in commercial transactions.
   C. the disclosure form for dual agency or representation is still required in a commercial transaction.
   D. all of these.

2. *Agent* is now clearly defined as a real estate licensee who is acting as any of the following *EXCEPT*
   A. a standard agent.
   B. a limited service agent.
   C. an independent contractor.
   D. an agent in a commercial real estate transaction.

3. Routine services that do *NOT* involve a licensee's experience or discretion are called
   A. transactional acts.
   B. routine brokerage.
   C. ministerial acts.
   D. customer service.

4. A brokerage relationship can be terminated by any of the following *EXCEPT*
   A. one party unilaterally firing the other.
   B. expiration of the agreement.
   C. a default by either party.
   D. a licensee's withdrawal when the client refuses to consent to dual agency.

5. Broker A is representing a buyer in the purchase of a town house listed with broker B. Broker A has a signed exclusive right-to-represent contract with the buyer. He will need to have a disclosure of brokerage relationship form signed by
   A. the buyer.
   B. the sellers of the town house.
   C. both the buyer and the sellers of the town house.
   D. no one because the sellers have their own agent.

6. Acting as a limited service agent is allowed as long as the written brokerage agreement includes all of the following *EXCEPT*
   A. licensee is acting as a limited service agent.
   B. licensee may also serve as an independent contractor.
   C. a list of specific services to be provided.
   D. a list of specific duties of a standard agent that will not be provided.

7. Salespersons M and T are licensees who are both affiliated with the same realty firm. M has listed a house, and T has a likely buyer. What is the *BEST* option for the supervising broker?
   A. The broker should do nothing because neither salesperson wishes to act as disclosed dual agents.
   B. The broker should insist that one of the salespersons sign a disclosed dual agency agreement with the buyers and sellers.
   C. The broker may assign the salespersons as designated agents, providing a disclosure form to the sellers only.
   D. The broker may assign the two salespersons as designated agents and provide a disclosure form to be signed by both the sellers and the prospective buyers.

8. A prospective buyer calls the listing agent about a home she is interested in. She tells him that she has a signed buyer agency agreement with another licensee, but he is out of town and she would like the listing agent to show her the home. When should the listing agent have her sign an agency disclosure form?
   A. Immediately, over the phone
   B. When he shows her the listing
   C. After she signs a new buyer agency agreement with him
   D. Never, none will be needed

9. A prospective buyer calls a licensee and spends 20 minutes talking about her real estate needs. They agree to meet and go for a drive to look at neighborhoods but never discuss or visit any specific property. The licensee should have her sign a disclosure of brokerage relationship form
   A. when she gets in the car.
   B. when she arrives at the office.
   C. before she leaves the car.
   D. never, no written disclosure is required yet because no specific assistance was given.

10. All of the following are specific statutory duties owed to a seller or buyer client *EXCEPT*
   A. to perform the terms of the brokerage agreement.
   B. to always be obedient to the client's demands.
   C. to maintain confidentiality forever.
   D. to promote the best interests of the client.

11. The specific duty that falls under the duty to promote the best interests of the client that only applies to sellers and landlords is the duty to
   A. conduct marketing activities.
   B. seek a price and terms acceptable to the client.
   C. assist in the drafting and negotiating of offers and counteroffers.
   D. provide assistance to satisfy the client's contract obligations.

12. The phrase *physical condition of the property* only would refer to
   A. a gas station on the corner.
   B. the empty field behind the house.
   C. defective drywall in the house.
   D. plans for widening the street.

13. As of July 1, 2012, property management agreements must include all of the following *EXCEPT*
   A. be in writing.
   B. have a suggested termination date of one year.
   C. state the amount of management fees.
   D. state the services to be rendered.

14. A seller offers a broker a listing agreement that contains the following clause: "Seller must receive the amount of $60,000 from the sale of this property. Seller agrees that the selling agent will receive, as her total compensation, any proceeds that remain beyond that amount after satisfaction of seller's mortgage loan and any closing costs incurred by seller." Based on these facts, the broker
   A. must decline this listing agreement because the clause violates REB regulations.
   B. must decline this listing agreement because it is not the standard form used in Virginia.
   C. may accept this listing agreement because the clause is standard in an open listing.
   D. may accept this listing agreement because it specifically limits the amount of the compensation.

15. A typical right-to-represent buyer agreement should contain all of the following *EXCEPT*
   A. statement of the duties to be performed.
   B. disclosure of how the broker will be paid.
   C. marketing plan.
   D. assurance that buyer has not entered into any other buyer representation agreement.

- Will meet next week.

UNIT 3

Interests and Forms of Ownership

LEARNING OBJECTIVES

When you have completed this unit, you will be able to

> **explain** a transfer of interest through eminent domain, descent and distribution, or easement;
> **define** the different types of tenancy used in Virginia;
> **describe** forms of co-ownership, including cooperative, condominium, and time-share;
> **explain** the elements of the Virginia Property Owners' Association Act; and
> **define** the following key terms:

augmented estate	estate	resale certificate
automatic survivorship	homestead exemption	tacking
condemnation	intestate	tenancy by the entirety
condominium	joint tenancy	tenancy in common
cooperative	just compensation	tenancy in partnership
easement by necessity	land trust	testate
easement by prescription	law of descent and distribution	time-share ownership
elective share	public offering statement (POS)	unsecured debts
eminent domain		

OVERVIEW

An estate in land is the character and extent of ownership interest that a person has in real property. Virginia recognizes all the major estates in land, such as inheritable fee simple absolute, defeasible, and determinable estates and noninheritable life estates, including conventional, ordinary with rights of, remainder, reversion, or pur autre vie. Specific areas of ownership interest will be covered in this unit.

Land trusts are permitted in Virginia. A land trust is a trust in which the assets consist of real estate. While the deed to a trustee may appear to confer full powers to deal with the real property and complete legal and equitable title to the trust property, the trustee's powers are in fact restricted by a trust agreement mentioned in the deed. The agreement typically gives the beneficiary full powers of management and control. However, even the beneficiary cannot deal with the property as if no trust existed. Land trusts generally continue for a definite term.

EXAMPLE

The deed of trust used as collateral in the financing of a property gives the power of sale to the trustee acting on behalf of the beneficiary (the lender).

TRANSFER OF OWNERSHIP

The most common method of transfer of ownership is through the purchase and sale of a property. There are, however, other legal ways to accomplish a transfer of property that are provided for in the Virginia Constitution and statutes. The material presented in this section is provided for general background information only. Any question about legal issues should be brought to the attention of appropriate legal counsel. Real estate licensees are definitely not authorized to provide legal opinions for their clients.

Eminent Domain

In Virginia, the power of **eminent domain** is provided by both state constitution and statutes. (§ 25.1) Virginia law provides that easements, ingress and egress rights, flowage rights, and all similar rights and uses constitute property. As a result, **just compensation** must be paid if they are taken or damaged by the Commonwealth through the power of eminent domain, sometimes called a *taking*. This process is called **condemnation**.

In November 2012, an amendment to the constitution was passed that limits the state's power of eminent domain to only taking private property for public use and not giving it to a private landowner even if it would result in job creation.

Just compensation means the fair market value of the property at the time of the taking. Payment of just compensation is a prerequisite to passing of title to the property. In addition, the Commonwealth must have made a genuine but ineffectual effort to purchase the property directly before beginning condemnation proceedings.

If the parties do not agree on what constitutes just compensation for the land, commissioners are appointed to hold a hearing and determine the amount. Virginia's Condemnation Act provides for a two-stage proceeding. First, the court determines the fair market value of the land taken and the damage, if any, to the remaining land. Second, if payment occurs, the court determines the rights and claims of all persons entitled to compensation.

Required Disclosure

Real estate licensees must disclose to all interested parties that a condemnation is planned for a parcel or an entire area. If a seller is aware that a governmental authority has made an offer to acquire the property and that condemnation proceedings are contemplated, prospective buyers should be made aware of this information. Because condemnation can affect the value of both the condemned property and neighboring properties, it is an important consideration for buyers and sellers alike.

E X A M P L E

A portion of a homeowner's property was condemned for street construction. This had an adverse impact on the value of the homeowner's remaining property. However, the value of adjacent parcels increased as a result of the improved access provided by the street.

Descent and Distribution in Marital Estates

In 1991, the Virginia legislature abolished the concepts of dower and curtesy. The Augmented Estate and Elective Share Act defines to whom a deceased person's property is distributed if the individual dies **intestate**, that is, without having executed a valid will. The **law of descent and distribution** is similar to the old dower and curtesy statutes because it establishes the rights of ownership to property by a surviving spouse and others.

The statute defines property or **estate** as including

- insurance policies,
- retirement benefits (exclusive of Social Security),
- annuities,
- pension plans,
- deferred compensation arrangements, and
- employee benefit plans.

Intestate Distributions

This discussion of descent and distribution is a simplified overview of a very complex law (see the Code of Virginia, Title 64.2 Wills, Trusts, and Fiduciaries, Subtitle II. Wills and Decedents' Estates, for more detailed information).

The act defines the rights of natural children, adopted children, children by previous marriages, illegitimate children, children of surrogates, and children born by in vitro fertilization.

IN PRACTICE

Real estate licensees are cautioned that their involvement in real estate transactions involving part of an estate can open the door to complications that may arise from claims by the heirs. Legal counsel is strongly advised.

If a person dies **testate**, that is, having executed a valid will, but fails to specifically devise or bequeath all property, the undistributed property is treated as if the person died intestate.

When a person dies intestate, distribution is made first to the surviving spouse. If there are children or their descendants, two-thirds of the estate passes to the children with the remaining third to the surviving spouse. If there is no surviving spouse or children, the estate is distributed in accordance with the Virginia Code rules of descent and distribution. (§ 64.2-200)

E X A M P L E

A man died without having made a valid will. His estate, valued at $785,950, was distributed among his surviving spouse and three children as follows:

The surviving spouse: $261,983.33 = ⅓ of $785,950

Each of the children: $174,655.55 each = ⅔ divided by 3

If he had left a valid will disposing of $500,000 of the estate, the remaining $285,950 would be distributed to his spouse and children as follows:

Surviving spouse: $95,316.67 = ⅓ of $285,950

Each of the children: $63,544.44 each = ⅔ of $285,950 divided by 3

Although a surviving spouse could be named in a will to receive certain property and to be further entitled to receive a share of the surplus, it is possible for the spouse to renounce the will and claim an **elective share** of the **augmented estate** with the same distribution as if the deceased died intestate. (See § 64.2-302, Chapter 3 Rights of Married Persons, Article 1, Elective Share of Surviving Spouse.)

Augmented Estate

An augmented estate consists of the property, both real and personal, owned by the deceased at the time of death. The value of the augmented estate is the value that remains after the payment of funeral expenses, the cost of the estate administrator, and personal debts of the decedent.

Items that can be excluded from the augmented estate include

- property owned by the surviving spouse;
- property owned by the decedent and another, with right of survivorship;
- property conveyed during the marriage with the consent of the surviving spouse;
- property acquired by the decedent as a gift, by will or intestate succession from someone other than the surviving spouse; and
- property transferred before January 1, 1991, if such transfer was irrevocable as of that date.

If a claim for an elective share is made, the surviving spouse receives one-third of the estate if there are children. If there are no children or descendants of children, the surviving spouse is entitled to one-half of the estate. (§ 64.2-305)

Other Considerations

A surviving spouse has the right to possess and occupy the principal family residence during the time that the estate matters are being settled although the residence may be a part of the augmented estate of the deceased.

If a spouse willfully deserts or abandons the other spouse until the death of the deserted spouse, the deserting spouse is barred from all interest of the other by intestate succession, elective share, exempt property, family allowance, and homestead allowance.

A surviving spouse may be entitled to the Virginia Homestead allowance of $15,000. If there is no surviving spouse, the $15,000 is divided equally among any minor children. The homestead allowance is in lieu of any share passing to the spouse or children by will or intestate distribution.

EASEMENT

Simply put, an easement is a right to use someone else's land. The most common easement is a utility company's right to access and use a landowner's land (property) for the purposes of delivering the utility either to the landowner or other landowners.

Creating an Easement

An easement may be acquired by express grant or may be created by covenant or agreement. In Virginia, the owner of a dominant tenement may convey the land without the easement. When the easement is not an **easement by necessity**, that is, not necessary for access to the property, and the appurtenance is expressly excluded by the grant, it will not convey. When a grantor conveys land by a deed that describes the property as bounded by a road or street that the grantor owns, the grantor is implying that a right-of-way exists. The grantee acquires the benefit of the easement automatically.

If the width of a right-of-way is not specified in the grant, it is limited to the width as it existed at the time of the grant. An **easement by prescription** is somewhat similar to the acquisition of property by adverse possession and the two terms are often confused. An easement by prescription differs from adverse possession in significant ways, as shown in Figure 3.1.

FIGURE 3.1:   Easement by Prescription vs. Adverse Possession

Criteria	Easement by Prescription	Adverse Possession (See Chapter 8)
Use of the property	Use of the property occurs with the knowledge and acquiescence of the landowner	Use of the property is hostile and without the true owner's permission
Prescriptive period	20 years	15 years
Tacking allowed?	Tacking is permitted	Tacking is not permitted

In an action to establish an easement by prescription in Virginia, the court must find that use of the property was

- adverse,
- under a claim of right,
- exclusive,
- continuous,
- uninterrupted, and
- with the knowledge and acquiescence of the landowner.

In Virginia, the prescriptive period is 20 years. **Tacking**—combining successive periods of continuous uninterrupted use by different parties—is permitted in Virginia.

When an easement is terminated, no document needs to be recorded in the clerk's office of the county where the land is located.

VIRGINIA HOMESTEAD EXEMPTION

Under Virginia's **homestead exemption**, a householder is entitled to hold a certain amount of real or personal property exempt from **unsecured debts**. The total value of the property may not exceed $5,000, plus $500 for each dependent. If the householder is 65 or older or a veteran with 40% or more disability, the allowance is $10,000.

Only a householder or head of a family may have the benefit of the homestead exemption. A married couple living together may both be deemed householders if each contributes to maintaining the household.

The exemption does not apply against

- claims for the purchase price of the homestead property,
- mechanics' liens, and
- claims for taxes.

The claim to homestead must be made by deed in the case of real property or by an inventory under oath for personal property. The owner of the homestead may sell or encumber the homestead property.

The key words in the homestead exemption are unsecured debts. For example, a credit card balance is an unsecured debt. On the other hand, because a mortgage or a deed of trust is secured by real property, it has priority over the homestead exemption. The property may be sold at foreclosure to satisfy a secured debt.

In addition to the homestead estate, the householder is entitled to hold certain other items of real and personal property exempt from sale for the satisfaction of a debt, such as a family bible, wedding and engagement rings, family portraits and heirlooms not to exceed $5,000 in value, a burial plot and preneed funeral contract not to exceed $5,000, $1,000 worth of clothing, $5,000 worth of household furnishings, firearms not to exceed $3,000 in value, all animals owned as pets, medically prescribed health aids, items needed for an occupation or trade up to $10,000 in value, motor vehicles not to exceed $6,000 in value, tax refund or governmental payment attributed to Child Tax Credit, and unpaid spousal or child support.

IN PRACTICE

A real estate agent may be unaware that a homestead deed has been filed. The exemption is usually revealed in a title search conducted by an attorney or title examiner. The agent should be aware that the filing could indicate financial difficulties or even pending bankruptcy, or that judgments may be recorded.

A full discussion of the Virginia Homestead Exemption can be found in the Code of Virginia, Title 34.

FORMS OF HOMEOWNERSHIP

There are many forms of homeownership available in Virginia, including several types of ownership by two or more parties. The first part of this section deals with co-ownership of a single property; the second half is dedicated to co-ownership within a greater complex of other homeowners.

Co-Ownership

An individual is said to own property in severalty. When two or more people purchase a property, the term is "tenancy". The significant part of which type of tenancy is selected is concerned with rights of inheritance.

JOINT TENANCY

Virginia's **joint tenancy** is similar to that of most other states, insofar as the four unities of time, title, interest, and possession must be present. However, Virginia's interpretation of *unity of interest* is that one joint tenant cannot be a tenant for life and another for years. Similarly, one tenant cannot be a tenant in fee and another a tenant for life. Joint tenancy is always created by an act of the parties, never by descent or operation of law.

P.I.T.T.

The doctrine of **automatic survivorship** has been abolished in Virginia. The legislature was intended to place joint tenants in the same situation as tenants in common as far as augmented estates were concerned. If the deed expressly creates a joint tenancy with right of survivorship (as in common law), then on the death of a joint tenant, the entire estate continues in the surviving tenant or tenants. The surviving spouse of the deceased joint tenant has no liability, and the deceased's creditors have no claim against the enlarged interests of the surviving tenants. Property owners who wish to have a property pass at their death to particular persons frequently create a joint tenancy as a substitute for a will.

Deed must state right of survivorship

A tenant in common or a joint tenant who commits waste may be liable to the other cotenant(s) for damages. By statute, a joint tenant or a tenant in common may demand an accounting from a cotenant who receives more than a fair share of rents and profits from the property. Similarly, joint tenants or tenants in common who improve a common property at their own expense are entitled to file a partition suit to divide and sell the property to obtain compensation for the improvements. However, if one tenant makes improvements without the consent of the other, the amount of compensation is limited to the amount by which the value of the common property has been enhanced.

Tenancy in Common

In Virginia, **tenancy in common** may be created by

- an express limitation to two or more persons to hold land as tenants in common;
- a grant of part interest in one's land to another;
- a devise or grant of land to two or more persons to be divided between them;
- a breakup of estates in joint tenancy; and
- the dissolving of a **tenancy by the entirety** as a result of the divorce or mutual agreement of the parties.

↳ marriage - you are one!

A tenant in common may convey undivided interest; however, a contract by one tenant in common relating to the whole estate is voidable by any cotenant that did not join in the contract.

A deceased cotenant's interest, in passing through his will or to his heirs, is subject to the statute of Wills and Decedents Estates, which protects the rights of the surviving spouse (see Augmented Estate earlier in this unit). Tenancy in common carries no right of survivorship, and the interest of the deceased does not automatically pass to a surviving cotenant.

Tenancy by the Entirety

Tenancy by the entirety is a special type of joint tenancy honored in Virginia that is created between spouses. There is no right to partition or to convey a half interest. The tenancy is indestructible except by mutual agreement or divorce, in which case the tenancy by the entirety is converted into a tenancy in common.

Property held by spouses as tenants by the entirety is legally an asset of both parties. If one spouse contracts to convey the property, that spouse cannot do so alone. The conveying spouse would be answerable to the would-be purchaser for the inability to perform.

IN PRACTICE

If a married woman has retained her maiden name, the deed should grant to "John Doe and Mary Jones, husband and wife, as tenants by the entirety," not to "Mary Doe, also called Mary Jones."

Neither spouse alone may encumber the property. Any debts that could become liens on the property must be entered into jointly by both parties.

Community Property

There are no community property laws in Virginia.

Tenancy in Partnership

A partnership may own real property, but each individual partner's interest is considered personal property. A partner is co-owner with the other partners of real property as a tenant in partnership.

Tenancy in partnership has the following features:

- A partner (subject to the partnership agreement) has an equal right with the other partners to possess the property for partnership purposes but may not possess it for any other purpose without the other partners' consent.

- A partner's right in a property is not assignable unless all the partners assign their rights in the same property.

- A partner's right in the property is not subject to creditors, except for a claim against the partnership itself. When partnership property is attached for a partnership debt, no rights can be claimed under homestead exemption laws by any partner or by the representative of a deceased partner.

- On the death of a partner, that partner's interest in partnership property passes to the surviving partners. If the decedent was the last surviving partner, that right in the property vests in the decedent's legal representative. The surviving partner, or legal representative, has no right to possess the property for anything other than a partnership purpose.

- A partner can transfer property on behalf of all the partners if acting within the scope of the firm's business and purposes. Partners may transfer partnership property among themselves, provided all partners consent.

IN PRACTICE

Whenever a real estate licensee represents a buyer who is purchasing partnership-owned property, the licensee should have an attorney review the partnership agreement to ensure that a general partner with power to bind all other general partners executes conveyance. It is desirable to have a written resolution of the partnership authorizing the sale.

CORPORATIONS

A corporation may acquire and convey real property in its corporate name. A contract entered into by a corporation under an assumed name may be enforced by either party. If an instrument bears both a corporate seal and the signatures of the responsible corporate officers, it is presumed to be a corporate instrument, even if it lacks the required number of signatures or the corporate name.

IN PRACTICE

Anyone who purchases real estate from a corporation should require a written corporate resolution that duly authorizes the sale of property by the corporation.

CO-OWNERSHIP WITHIN A COMMUNITY

Some forms of ownership involve the use of a **public offering statement** (POS). The sale of a **cooperative**, a **condominium,** or a time-share requires the POS to fully and accurately disclose the characteristics of the project. Additionally, the Virginia Property Owners Association Act may require the use of the POS.

Common Interest Community (CIC) Board

Condominiums, cooperatives, time-shares, and the property owner associations fall under the authority of the CIC Board. A CIC Manager is defined as a person or entity that provides management services to an association for a fee or other compensation. Management services may include the following:

- Acting for the association in its business, legal, financial, or other transactions
- Executing the resolutions and decisions of an association or enforcing the rights secured by law
- Collecting, disbursing, or otherwise controlling money or other property
- Preparing budgets, financial statements, or other financial reports
- Arranging, conducting, or coordinating meetings of the association or its governing body
- Negotiating contracts or arranging for services on behalf of the association
- Offering or soliciting to perform any services on behalf of an association

The CIC Manager must be licensed by the CIC. The CIC Board has disciplinary authority to issue fines, suspend or revoke CIC licenses, issue cease and desist letters or injunctions, or to revoke an association's registration. (If the community manager is a real estate licensee, disciplinary authority belongs to the REB.)

Unit 3

The CIC Ombudsman office provides assistance and information to association members regarding the rights and processes available to them through their associations. The Ombudsman is not an advocate for homeowners or community associations, but remains neutral and cannot provide legal advice. The Ombudsman office also receives complaints and notices of final adverse decisions from individuals who believe an association violated CIC laws or regulations. The complaint procedure does not begin until complainants have proceeded through the established complaint procedure of the POA or condominium association. Enforcement remains with the CIC Board.

Legislation enacted in 2011 states that no association or CIC Manager can require payment at the time requests are made for packets, certificates, or updates. The fees are to be collected at settlement. If settlement does not occur within 90 days, the fees may be assessed against the lot or unit owner. (For non-CIC managed associations the law is unclear as to time of payment.)

The law does not require a signed receipt for the hand delivery but does when delivered by electronic means.

IN PRACTICE

A licensee should make sure that a purchaser signs a receipt for delivery of a resale packet or certificate that states that the packet received should contain all the required disclosures, not that the packet is complete. This allows time for the purchaser to review the packet within the three-day right-of-recession period.

Cooperative Ownership

Cooperative ownership is governed by the Virginia Real Estate Cooperative Act. (§§ 55-424–55-506) The CIC is charged with administrative responsibility for the Virginia Cooperative Act. A cooperative is, "real estate owned by an association, each of the members of which is entitled, by virtue of his or her ownership interest in the association, to exclusive possession of a unit."

A cooperative is created by a Declaration of Cooperative, filed in the clerk's office of the circuit court in the district in which the real estate is located. A cooperative has both common elements and limited common elements. When an individual purchases a cooperative unit, she is purchasing shares in the corporation (considered personal property) and signing a proprietary lease that allows for use of that particular unit.

The cooperative association may adopt and amend bylaws, rules, and regulations; adopt and amend budgets; hire and discharge management agents; regulate the use, maintenance, and repair of common elements; impose charges; and exercise other powers conferred by the declaration and bylaws.

Unless otherwise provided by the cooperative declaration, the association is responsible for the common elements and the proprietary lessee is responsible for the individual unit. The association has a lien on the cooperative interest for unpaid assessments. Nonpayment of assessment may be cause for eviction and resale of the cooperative interest.

Sale of a Cooperative Interest

In the case of an initial sale of the cooperative, the purchaser must be given a POS. The POS must be provided before conveyance and not later than the date of the contract. If this does not occur, the seller has a financial liability. (§ 55-483)

Before the contract for the resale of a cooperative interest is executed or before conveyance, the purchaser must be given, among other things, a proprietary lease, a copy of the declaration, bylaws, rules and regulations of the association, and a certificate containing the following statements:

- Disclosure of the effect of any right of first refusal or other restraint on transferability
- The amount of the monthly common expense assessment, as well as any unpaid expense currently due or payable from the sale and from the lessee
- Any other fees payable by proprietary lessees
- Any capital expenditures anticipated by the association for the current and next two succeeding fiscal years
- The amount of reserves for capital expenditures designated for specific projects
- The most recent regularly prepared balance sheet and income/expense statement
- The current operating budget of the association
- Unsatisfied judgments and pending suits
- Insurance coverage
- Health or building code violations against the unit or common elements
- Remaining term of any leasehold estate and provisions for extensions or renewal, if any
- Disclosure that the POS is available for inspection
- Deductibility of any real estate taxes and interest
- Restrictions in the declaration that may affect the amount received by the proprietary lease holder on sale, condemnation, or loss to the unit or cooperative upon termination of the cooperative
- Certification that the association has filed the required reports to the CIC

Alternately, the documents can be provided after the ratification of a contract when the contract is made contingent on the receipt of such documents and when it provides for the statutory rescission period to the purchaser.

IN PRACTICE

In the sale of a cooperative interest, it is the seller's obligation to provide a buyer with the required information. The real estate licensee, however, may facilitate the transfer of information from the seller to the buyer as a service to the client.

Buyer's Right to Rescind

In Virginia, purchasers of a cooperative interest have certain rights to rescind the contract. In an initial sale, (the first time the cooperative interest is sold after the cooperative is established), the buyer has the right to rescind within 10 days following ratification of the contract or after receiving the POS, whichever is later. When a cooperative unit is resold, that is, by an owner to a buyer, the purchase contract is voidable by the purchaser until the certificate has been provided and for five days thereafter or until conveyance, whichever occurs first. (§ 55-484)

Condominium Ownership

The CIC is charged with the administrative responsibility for the Virginia Condominium Act. (§ § 55-79.39–55-79.103)

A condominium can be a multiunit structure, an attached single-family dwelling, such as a town home, or a detached single-family dwelling. Commercial properties may also be condominiums. It is important to recognize that a condominium is a form of ownership and not a type of property or structure. The owner of property may convert the property to condominium status. The owner is called the declarant because she must declare her intent to have the property considered a condominium.

The declarant must provide declaration instruments to the CIC that includes the following:

- Name of the condominium (the name must include the word *condominium)*
- Name of city and county where the condominium is located
- Legal description by metes and bounds
- Description or delineation of the horizontal and vertical boundaries of each unit
- Description or delineation of all common elements and any limited common elements
- The allocation to each unit of the undivided ownership interest in the common elements
- A statement of the declarant's obligation to complete improvements not yet completed (specific to type and quality, size or capacity, and time for completion)

There may be additional requirements if the condominium contains any convertible land or is an expandable, contractible, or leasehold condominium.

In addition, the declarant must submit a copy of the bylaws under which the condominium will operate. The bylaws must be specific regarding such issues as

- the form of self-governance for the unit owners;
- whether there are to be trustees, a board of directors, or other officers;
- their exact duties and the means by which they are to be appointed or elected;
- the extent to which the governing or executive body may delegate responsibilities to a management agent;
- the accounting and management records that will be maintained;
- a schedule of meetings of all owners and of the executive body;
- statutory requirements for meeting notices (21 days); and
- the rules and regulations that will apply to all owners.

Condominium Public Offering Statement

The declarant must also provide a POS. The POS discloses all characteristics of the condominium and makes known all unusual and material circumstances or features. The POS must include

- the name and principal address of the declarant;
- a narrative description of the condominium, including the number of units and future plans for the addition of more units;

- copies of the declaration and bylaws, a projected budget, and provisions for reserves;

- copies of any management contract or lease of recreational areas, including a statement of the relationship between the declarant and the managing agent;

- a description of the status of construction, zoning, permits, or other compliance with state or local statute or regulation;

- the terms of any encumbrances, liens, or easements that affect the title;

- the terms and conditions of any financing offered to purchasers;

- provisions of warranties;

- a statement that purchaser may cancel the contract within 10 days of delivery of the POS, or within 10 days of the contract date, whichever is later;

- a statement of the declarant's obligation to complete planned improvements;

- a statement identifying the common and limited common elements along with any user fees;

- a statement of any limitation on the number of persons who may occupy a unit; and

- a statement setting forth any restrictions or limitation on the right to display the flag of the United States, including size, place, and manner of display. (§ 55.79-90)

Initial Sale of a Condominium Unit

At the initial sale of a condominium unit, the purchaser receives a copy of the POS along with the sales contract. The first purchaser of a condominium unit has the right to rescind a ratified contract, without penalty, within five days (reduced from 10 days in 2014), for any reason. The five-day period begins with the date of contract ratification or on receipt of the POS, whichever is later. The right to rescind cannot be waived. The right to cancel must be listed on the first page of the purchase contract in bold, 12-point type.

At closing, the purchaser acquires a fee simple interest in the individual unit and an undivided percentage interest in the common elements as a tenant in common with the other unit owners. At this time, the purchaser assumes responsibility for the individual unit purchased.

The declarant remains responsible for all unsold units and for the overall management and maintenance of the condominium development until 75% of the units are sold. At that point, responsibility for maintenance and management of the property shifts to the owners' association. The declarant becomes a member of the association as owner of the remaining units.

Voting Rights

Each unit owner has an assigned ownership interest and voting rights in the governance of the condominium. This interest is usually in proportion to the size of each individual unit and the amenities of the unit. The exact percentage of ownership interest is established in the declaration.

Bylaw Changes

The Condominium Act states that two-thirds of the total voting interest is required to change the bylaws.

Termination

Once a property has been declared a condominium, its status can be changed by abandoning or dissolving it; 80% of the voting interest must approve the termination of a condominium's status.

Statutory Lien Rights

The unit owners' association has a statutory lien on every unit for unpaid assessments levied against the unit. This lien is secondary to real estate tax liens and other liens recorded before the filing of the original condominium declaration.

Resale of a Condominium Unit

All unit owners have the right to resell their individual units. In the event of an intended resale, the seller must obtain certain documents from the unit owners' association. These documents are collectively called the **resale certificate**.

The unit owners' association must furnish the resale certificate upon the written notice request of any unit owner within 14 days of the receipt of such request. Payment of actual costs of preparing the resale certificate may be required of the unit owner requesting it as a prerequisite to its issuance, but the total fee may not exceed a total of $163.97 for two hard copies or $136.64 for an electronic version. An additional expedited fee (certificate must be delivered within five days) may be charged up to $54.66. An additional hard copy may be ordered for $27.33. The declarant may also charge a $109.31 fee for inspection of the unit as a requirement for preparing the resale certificate. Up to $54.66 may be charged for updates to the certificate to be collected at settlement. Fees were adjusted for inflation in 2013 based on the U.S. Average Consumer Price Index (CPI). The fees will automatically adjust again in 2018. (§ 55.79.97:1)

In response to complaints from agents that condos and POAs were overcharging, HB 1674 was passed by the general assembly, effective July 1, 2011, that explicitly prohibits unauthorized resale packet fees. The bill also amends the Condominium Act to include a right of cancellation if a resale packet is unavailable.

The resale certificate must be current as of the date specified on the resale certificate but not more than 12 months old. This means that the seller may obtain the certificate in advance of any purchase contract and have it immediately available for the purchaser. The buyer's rights to receive the certificate and to cancel the contract are waived if the right is not exercised before settlement.

Right to Rescind

The certificate must be provided to the purchaser. The purchaser may cancel the contract under the following conditions:

■ Within three days after the date of the contract if the certificate was provided to the purchaser on or before the date that the purchaser signs the contract

- Within three days after receiving the certificate if hand-delivered or by electronic means
- Within six days of the postmark date if the certificate is mailed (§ 55.79.97)

Legislation passed in 2011 allows buyers to electronically deliver notice of cancellation under the POA and Condominium Acts.

Condominium Disclosure Packet

The documents required in the resale certificate include the following:

- A statement of any expenditure of funds requiring an assessment in addition to the regular assessment
- A statement of all assessments and other fees or charges currently imposed
- A statement whether there is any other entity or facility to which the unit owner may be liable for fees or charges
- A statement of the status and amount of any reserve or replacement fund
- A copy of the current budget and statement of current financial position
- A statement of any pending suits or judgments
- A statement setting forth what insurance coverage is provided for all unit owners
- A statement that any improvements or alterations made to the unit are not in violation of the condominium instruments
- A copy of the current bylaws, rules and regulations, and architectural guidelines
- A statement of whether the condominium is subject to the Property Owners' Association Act
- A copy of notice given to the unit owner of any current or pending rule or architectural violation
- A copy of approved minutes of unit owners' association meetings for previous six months
- Certification that the association has filed the annual report to the CIC
- A statement of any limitation on number of persons who may occupy a unit
- A statement setting forth any restrictions on right of unit owner to display the flag of the United States
- A statement setting forth any restriction, limitation, or prohibition on the right of a unit owner to install or use solar energy collection devices
- A statement indicating any known project approvals currently in effect issued by secondary mortgage market agencies (§ 55.79.97)

Contract Disclosure Requirement

Whenever a condominium unit is sold, the contract must include disclosure that (i) the unit is located within a development which is subject to the Condominium Act, (ii) the act requires the seller to obtain from the unit owners' association a resale certificate and provide it to the purchaser, (iii) the purchaser may cancel the contract within three days after receiving the resale certificate or being notified that the resale certificate will not be available, (iv) if the purchaser has received the resale certificate, the purchaser has a right to request a resale certificate update or financial update in accordance with Section 55-79.97:1, as appropriate, and (v) the right to receive the resale certificate and the right to cancel the contract are waived conclusively if not exercised before settlement. The disclosure may be included in the printed contract or as a separate addendum.

If the unit is governed by more than one association, the purchaser's right of cancellation may be exercised within the required time frames following delivery of the last resale certificate or disclosure packet.

Time-Share Ownership

Following are two types of **time-share ownership** recognized by the Virginia Time-Share Act (§ 55-360 et seq.):

- *Time-share estate* means a right to occupy a unit, or any of several units, during five or more separate time periods over a period of at least five years. The time-share estate includes renewal options, coupled with either a freehold interest or an estate for years, that is, a lease, in all or part of a time-share project.

- *Time-share use* means a right to occupy a time-share unit or any of several time-share units, during five or more separate time periods over a period of at least five years, including renewal options, not coupled with a freehold estate or an estate for years in a time-share project. Time-share use does not mean a right subject to a first-come, first-served, space-available basis that exists in a country club, motel, or health spa.

The CIC Board is charged with the administrative responsibility for the Time-Share Act.

Creation of a Time-Share

The developer of a time-share project must file and record with the CIC a time-share instrument that defines the project being created. This process establishes a time-share association in accordance with the Virginia Nonstock Corporations Act. (§ 13.1-801)

A time-share association must be set up before any time-share estates may be sold. The project must be named, and the name must include the words *time-share, time-share interest, interval ownership, vacation ownership,* or other terms recognized in the industry.

Some of the items that are to be included in the time-share instrument include

- the name of the time-share project;
- the complete address and legal description of the project; and
- a description of the property. (§ 55.367)

Time-Share Public Offering Statement

The POS filed for a time-share project is similar to the POS filed for a condominium. The developer may not convey any interest or advertise the property until the POS has been approved. If the time-share is being converted from another type of ownership, additional information is required regarding repairs made during the preceding three years and the physical condition of the structure. The purpose and value of reserve funds must be disclosed.

If the property to be converted is currently leased, tenants must be given 90 days' notice of the intent to convert the property to a time-share project. The tenants then have 60 days in which to contract with the developer to purchase the unit currently occupied if that unit is to be part of the overall project. Tenants on month-to-month leases must be given 120 days' notice to vacate.

Right to Rescind

The purchaser of a time-share interest at the project's initial sale has seven calendar days from execution of contract in which to cancel the contract without penalty. The developer must deliver the POS to the purchaser before the execution of the contract. The cancellation period commences on the date of contract ratification. If the seventh day falls on a Sunday or legal holiday, the right to cancel will expire on the day following the Sunday or legal holiday. The purchaser's right of cancellation cannot be waived, which must be identified in the contract.

Furthermore, if there are material changes to the POS before settlement and after the initial time of contracting to purchase, the developer must provide the purchaser with the amended statement. The purchaser's right of cancellation is reinstated.

Deposits

Money received by the developer as earnest money deposits or down payments must be placed in an escrow account established by the developer and held there through the rescission period. The developer also must post a surety bond with the REB in the amount of $25,000 or the amount of the deposits received, whichever is greater. If any purchaser exercises the statutory right of rescission, the developer has 45 days in which to refund all monies paid by the purchaser.

Advertisements

Advertisements used for the marketing of time-share interests that offer gifts or prizes must clearly disclose the retail value of the gift or prize offered. The ad must also disclose the terms and conditions under which the gift is offered, the odds of actually winning a prize, and the number of gifts or prizes to be awarded. The ad must include the offer's expiration date and a statement that the offer is made for the purpose of soliciting the purchase of a time-share estate.

Transfer of Control

The developer remains in control of the project until 90% of the time-share estate has been sold or when all amenities and facilities have been completed, whichever is later. This is called the *developer control period*. The developer control period may not exceed 10 years after the sale of the first time-share interest. At the conclusion of the developer control period, the time-share owners' association assumes control and responsibility for the management and maintenance of the project. The developer must transfer control of the project to the owners' association without charging any fee. The owners' association may appoint or elect a managing agent for the project.

The owners' association has a statutory lien on every time-share estate in the project for unpaid regular and special assessments. The bylaws of the association may be changed by a vote of the owners. Should the owners decide to terminate the time-share project, approval by 51% of the voting interest of the association is required.

Resale of Time-Share

A resale of a time-share interest by any person other than the developer is subject to rules similar to those governing the resale of a condominium. The seller must obtain a resale certificate from the owners' association. The certificate contains a copy of the time-share instruments; current financial statements; current bylaws; current rules and regulations of the association; fees and assessments; a disclosure of any liens that may be pending on the time-share for nonpayment of fees; and a statement of pending litigation against the developer, owners' association, or managing entity relative to the time-share project. The association may charge up to $50 for the certificate of resale.

The buyer in a time-share resale has the right to rescind the contract within five days following receipt of the certificate of resale or actual transfer, whichever occurs first. This right is without penalty and may be for any reason. Once the contract has closed, however, all rights of rescission are waived.

Statute of Limitations

Any action for misrepresentation of information in the project instruments, the POS, or any contract must be initiated within two years of the date of the contract.

VIRGINIA PROPERTY OWNERS' ASSOCIATION ACT

The Virginia Property Owners' Association (POA) Act sets forth requirements for the formation and operation of the property owners' association. Each association subject to the act is governed by covenants, deed restrictions, POSs, bylaws, and other restrictions designed to manage, regulate, and control the specific development, community, subdivision, or neighborhood and their common areas, if any. The specifics of the various governing documents vary among associations (Code of Virginia, Title 55, Chapter 26, §§ 55-508–55-516.2).

The CIC Board is charged with the administrative responsibility for the Virginia POA Act.

An association may be either self-managed or an independent management company may be employed to manage the affairs of the association. The act allows for a board of directors that may consist of property owners, developer representatives, and even representation from the independent management company, if used. Actions of the board, meetings, records, budgets, reports, and other association functions are governed by the act and the specific association documents. The board has the power to establish, adopt, and enforce rules with respect to the use of common areas and other areas of responsibility as established in the original declaration. A majority of votes from a quorum of the property members is usually required to repeal or amend rules and regulations. Violations of rules and regulations by the member property owner may result in the member being suspended from use of the common area facilities.

Property owners may be assessed routine fees, as allowed by the association documents, for the maintenance and upkeep of the association and common areas. Special assessments may be levied by the association. These special assessments usually require a majority vote of the property owners in accordance with the association's bylaws. Failure of a property owner to pay the authorized assessments entitles the association to place a lien on the property. (§ 55-516)

Exemptions

Condominiums, cooperatives, time-shares, and campgrounds are exempt from the POA Act. However, if one of these types of ownership is located within an area that has been declared to be under the POA Act, the property is subject to both sets of regulations.

IN PRACTICE

Reston, Virginia, is a very large planned unit development (PUD) and properties there are subject to POA fees. There are also several condominium projects within the PUD that are subject to both condo and POA fees.

Additional exceptions to disclosure packet requirements include disposition of a lot

- by gift,
- pursuant to court order,
- by foreclosure or deed in lieu of foreclosure,
- by sale at auction, or
- to a person not acquiring the lot for a personal residence. The person acquiring the lot must nevertheless be obligated to abide by the declaration, bylaws, rules and regulations, and architectural guidelines of the association. (§ 55-509.10)

Disclosure Requirements

Because each association may impose certain restrictions and fees on the member property owners, potential purchasers must receive sufficient information before settlement about the association in order to make an informed decision to continue with the purchase. Therefore, any party who sells property subject to the act must include a statement in the sales contract to the effect that the

- property is located in a development that is subject to the POA Act;
- act requires that the seller obtain a disclosure packet from the POA and provide that packet to the buyer;
- buyer may cancel the contract within three days after receiving the packet or being advised that the packet will not be provided;
- buyer has the right to request an update of the packet; and
- rights to cancel the contract are waived if those rights are not exercised before closing.

If the contract does not contain these disclosures, the sole remedy for the buyer is to rescind the contract before closing. (§ 55-511)

POA Disclosure Packet

The information in the POA disclosure packet must be current as of the date of the packet. This allows the property owner to have a packet available for the buyer at the time of contract.

The association must make the packet available within 14 days after an owner/member, or an owner/member's authorized agent, files a written request. The association may charge a fee reflecting the actual cost for preparation of the packet but must not exceed $163.97 for two hard copies or $136.64 for an electronic version. An additional hard copy can be purchased for $27.33. The association's failure to deliver the packet in a timely manner waives any claim for delinquent assessments or fines. (§ 55-509.5) All condominium resale certificates and disclosure packets for professionally managed POAs received an adjustment in fees in 2013 based on the U.S. CPI. Another adjustment will be made in 2018. The amount of $109.31 can be charged for an inspection required before issuing the disclosure packet.

An association that is not professionally managed may charge $0.10 per page or a total of $100 for actual costs in preparing the packet. The cost for a disclosure packet update cannot exceed $50.

Contents of the POA Disclosure Packet

Each disclosure packet must include the name of the association plus the name and address of the registered agent, if incorporated. The packet must also include

- a statement of any expenditure that would require an additional assessment during the current or succeeding fiscal year;
- a statement of all assessments and other fees currently imposed;
- a statement whether there is any other entity or facility to which the lot owner may be liable for fees or charges;
- the current reserve report and a statement of the status and amount of any reserve or replacement fund;
- a copy of the current budget plus statement of income and expenses, including a statement of the balance on any loans;
- a statement of any pending suit or unpaid judgment;
- a statement of what insurance coverage is provided for lot owners and what is expected of each individual lot owner;
- plans for any improvement or alteration of lot or uses of common areas;
- any restrictions on the placement of For Sale signs or flags;
- a statement setting forth any restriction, limitation, or prohibition on the right of a lot owner to display any flag, including restrictions as to size, place, and manner of placement; and
- certification that the association has filed with the CIC Board the required annual report.

The Association Disclosure Packet must include the following attachments, if any:

- A copy of the current declaration, articles of incorporation and bylaws, and all rules and regulations or architectural guidelines adopted by the association
- A copy of notice given to the lot owner of any current or pending violation of rules
- Copies of last six months' minutes of the association meetings

An informational form prepared by the CIC Board must accompany all POA disclosure packets. The purpose of this form is to describe the special circumstances and the relationship between lot owners and the association in order to educate the prospective purchasers and foster a better understanding between the property owners and the association. A copy of this form is available on the Virginia Association of REALTORS® website.

Purchaser's Right to Request Update

The purchaser may submit a copy of the contract to the association with a request for updating of the disclosure packet. The association must respond within 10 days and has the right to charge the purchaser a fee for preparation of the new packet that reflects the actual cost but not to exceed $54.66. The purpose of this request for update of the packet is to both assure the buyer that there have been no changes and to identify the specifics of any material changes. If there have been any material changes, the buyer has no recourse for cancellation of the contract unless that right had previously been agreed on in the purchase contract.

IN PRACTICE

When purchasing a property bound by a POA, it is wise to include terms in the contract allowing the purchaser to request an update and to be able to void the contract if an update to a previously provided POA packet is not forthcoming within a specified period.

Purchaser's Right to Rescind

The purchaser has the right to cancel the contract

- within three days after the date of the contract, if the packet or notice that the packet is unavailable was provided before signing of the contract;

- within three days after receiving the packet or notice that the packet is not available (if hand-delivered or by electronic means); or

- within six days after the postmark date of either the packet or the notice that the packet is not available was sent by U.S. mail.

The purchaser may also cancel the contract any time before settlement if not notified that the disclosure packet will not be available nor the packet delivered.

If the purchaser elects to rescind, the notice of rescission must be hand-delivered or sent by U.S. mail, return receipt requested, to the owner. Rescission is without penalty, and the purchaser is entitled to a full refund of any earnest money given. Any rights to rescind the contract must be exercised before closing.

Legislation now provides for the delivery of association disclosure documents electronically as long as the association maintains a website link for 90 days and does not charge any additional fees, beyond a $54.66 update fee for a 12-month period. Buyers are also allowed to electronically deliver notice of cancellation under the POA and Condominium Acts.

A complete discussion of interests and forms of ownership of real estate in Virginia may be found in the Code of Virginia, Title 55—Property and Conveyances; see the table of contents, Title 55, at http://leg1.state.va.us/lis.htm.

Recent Changes to Condominium and POA Acts

Changes Made by the 2014 General Assembly

Several miscellaneous items regarding condominiums or POAs were passed by the 2014 general assembly, including the following:

- The process for members of a condo or POA to inspect association records was clarified. Residents are permitted to inspect records during normal business hours with five business days' written notice to a professionally managed association or 10 business days' written notice to a self-managed association.

- Associations may not assess a late fee of more than 5% for nonpayment of assessments unless otherwise stated in the association documents.

- Associations may not charge separate inspection fees for unimproved lots or charge sellers for website access to request the resale disclosure packet. The choice of electronic delivery is at the option of the seller. Five electronic copies are to be provided for the same fee to the seller, seller's agent, purchaser, purchaser's agent, and one additional person. If the resale packet is delivered using a commercial mail delivery service, the right of cancellation is set at three days following delivery.

- An association may take action against a unit owner in general district or circuit court for violations of the condo or POA instruments. The owner must be given written notice and time to correct the violation. The prevailing party may recover court costs and reasonable attorneys' fees.

- No association may ban the installation of solar collection devices unless the ban is specifically outlined in the recorded declarations.

Changes Made by the 2016 General Assembly

Numerous changes were made to both the Virginia POA and Condominium Acts in 2016, especially regarding the rental of units. Changes effective July 1, 2016 include the following:

- Prohibits unit owners' associations from conditioning or prohibiting the rental of a unit, making an assessment, or imposing a rental fee or any other fee except as expressly provided by law

- Prohibits associations from evicting tenants or requiring the association to be given a power of attorney to evict tenants; and prohibits associations from requiring a power of attorney from landlords who are represented by an agent with a property management agreement

- Prohibits associations from requiring use of their particular lease or addendum

- Provides that unit owners may designate a licensed broker to act as the owner's authorized representative with respect to the lease

- Prohibits associations from demanding a copy of the lease for a rented unit—can require that the name of the tenants, authorized occupants, authorized agents and vehicle information be provided

- Defines, for purposes of delivering the disclosure packet, who the purchasers' and sellers' designated agents are, and that delivery of the packet is effected by using one of the methods outlined in the Code of Virginia

- Stipulates that if a unit is governed by more than one association, the three-day right of rescission does not begin until the date that the last packet or resale certificate has been delivered

- Adds right of cancellation under the Condominium Act if the purchaser is notified that the resale certificate is unavailable when requested (mirrors provisions already in the POA Act)

- Confirms that sellers will continue to be able to obtain condo/HOA documents and delay payments for such documents until settlement so long as settlement occurs within 60 days

- Prohibits a locality from requiring the consent of a condo association, homeowners' association, or real estate cooperative before the issuance of a permit, certificate or license, including a building permit or a business license

SUMMARY

Virginia recognizes all the major estates in land, including land trusts. The most common method of transfer of ownership is through the purchase and sale of a property but there is also eminent domain, descent and distribution in marital estates, and easement. The Commonwealth can take private property through the process of condemnation, but it must be for public use and just compensation must be paid.

The old rights of dower and curtesy have been abolished. The Augmented Estate and Elective Share Act defines how the property is distributed if an individual dies intestate (without a valid will). Generally, the distribution is to the surviving spouse, or one-third to the spouse and the two-thirds divided among any children. A surviving spouse can renounce the will and claim an elective share of the augmented estate. The law is complicated and appropriate legal counsel should always be sought.

An easement may be acquired by express grant or may be created by covenant or agreement. An easement by necessity grants access to a property. An easement by prescription requires that use of the property was adverse, exclusive, continuous, and with the knowledge of the landowner. Not to be confused with adverse possession (15 years), the prescriptive period is 20 years and tacking is permitted.

Under Virginia's homestead exemption, a householder is entitled to hold a certain amount of real or personal property exempt from unsecured debts. The total value of the property may not exceed $5,000, plus $500 for each dependent. If the householder is 65 or older or a veteran with 40% or more disability, the allowance is $10,000. Certain items may be held in addition to the homestead estate.

There are many forms of homeownership in Virginia. An individual owns property in severalty. Two or more people have a tenancy, which can be joint tenancy, tenancy in common, tenancy by the entirety, or tenancy in partnership. There can also be co-ownership within a community such as a cooperative, condominium, or time-share. Specific disclosures are required for the purchase of any of these properties or for property that is within a development that falls under the Virginia POA Act.

Condominiums, cooperatives, time-shares, and POAs now fall under the authority of the CIC Board. The CIC Manager must be licensed and is subject to disciplinary authority by the CIC Board. The CIC Ombudsman office provides assistance and information to association members regarding the rights and processes available.

Unit 3

A cooperative ownership differs from a condominium in that the buyer purchases shares in the corporation that owns the property and receives a proprietary lease for use of the property. In an initial sale, the purchaser has the right to rescind the contract within 10 days. For a resale, the contract is voidable for five days after receipt of the resale certificate. A condominium is a fee simple form of ownership. The first purchaser of a condominium unit has the right to rescind within five days. For later resales, the contract may be canceled within three days after receipt of the resale packet. Time-share ownership can be either a time-share estate or time-share use. The initial sale can be rescinded within seven days; a resale may be rescinded within five days after receipt of the certificate of resale. Specific disclosure is required in the contract to purchase a cooperative, condominium, or time-share unit.

Most residential developments today fall under the Virginia POA. Routine fees may be assessed for maintenance and upkeep, which are generally much less than those for a condominium. Failure to pay the assessment gives the association the right to place a lien on the property. The purchaser has the right to cancel the contract within three days after receipt of the POA Disclosure Packet and has the right to request an update.

UNIT 3 QUIZ

1. Which of the following does *NOT* constitute the exercise of eminent domain by the process of condemnation?
   A. A county taking a farmer's cropland for a highway
   B. The state taking private woodland for the construction of a roadside visitor center
   C. A county zoning ordinance change
   D. Port Authority of Hampton Roads taking riparian rights for a pier

2. All of the following items could be excluded from an augmented estate *EXCEPT*
   A. a condominium owned by the deceased spouse.
   B. a small farm willed to the deceased by his grandmother.
   C. a beach property sold with the spouse's consent.
   D. a 52-foot sailboat purchased during the marriage.

3. Which of the following statements concerning the homestead exemption is *TRUE*?
   A. Exemption is automatic; every homeowner has one.
   B. The homeowner's filing for homestead exemption indicates financial difficulties.
   C. The homestead exemption is protection against claims for taxes, mechanics' liens, and deeds of trust against the property.
   D. The family bible, wedding rings, and burial plots are in addition to the $5,000 exemption.

4. All of the following are true of an easement by necessity *EXCEPT*
   A. it must be an appurtenant easement.
   B. both the dominant and the servient estates must have at some time in the past been owned by the same person.
   C. inconvenience is a basis for the easement.
   D. the only reasonable means of access is over the servient estate.

5. A married couple owns real property as tenants by the entirety. One spouse dies owing money to creditors. In this situation, the surviving spouse owns the entire property
   A. in severalty and is liable to the creditors.
   B. and is not liable to the creditors.
   C. except for a share owned by the creditors.
   D. and the creditors cannot make any claim to the property.

6. Which of the following is *TRUE* regarding Virginia's community property laws?
   A. Since 2001, the Virginia statute is patterned after California's statute.
   B. Virginia only recognizes some community property provisions.
   C. Augmented estates are the same as community property provisions.
   D. Virginia is not a community property state.

7. Two partners in a successful accounting practice are in the process of purchasing a small office condominium for their practice. They would *NOT* be able to take title as
   A. tenants by the entirety.
   B. tenants in common.
   C. joint tenants.
   D. tenants in partnership.

8. Contracts for the initial purchase of a cooperative interest may be rescinded without penalty how many days after either contract ratification or receipt of the POS?
   A. 5 days
   B. 10 days
   C. 14 days
   D. 21 days

9. If a condominium unit owner fails to pay the homeowners association's assessment against his unit, the association may
   A. place a lien against the unit.
   B. garnish the owner's wages.
   C. do nothing; as a stockholder, the unit owner has priority.
   D. revoke the unit owner's privileges and rights.

10. A recently retired woman has a ratified contract to purchase a two-bedroom condominium unit. She is now suffering from buyer's remorse and wishes to back out of the contract. She has not yet received the condominium documents. After hand delivery of the documents, she will have how many days to cancel the contract?
    A. 3 days
    B. 5 days
    C. 7 days
    D. 10 days

11. When the owner's interest in a time-share includes either a freehold interest or an estate for years, it is what type?
    A. Time-share use
    B. Time-share estate
    C. Time-share fee
    D. Time-share demise

12. A man recently visited a brand-new time-share project on the Eastern Shore. If he decides to make an offer on the property, how long will he have to cancel the contract without penalty?
    A. None; he is bound to the contract
    B. 3 calendar days after ratification of contract
    C. 7 calendar days after ratification of contract
    D. 10 calendar days after ratification of contract

13. A military couple has decided they no longer wish to purchase the town house that they currently have under contract. The town house is covered by the POA Act. The couple can cancel their contract
    A. whenever they wish.
    B. within 10 days after ratification of contract.
    C. within 3 days after receiving the POA disclosure packet.
    D. within 14 days after receiving the property disclosure packet.

14. Both the Condominium Act and the POA Act have a set limit on the amount that may be charged for preparation of the required document packet of
    A. $163.97 for two hard copies.
    B. up to $325.
    C. actual cost of copying.
    D. any amount they choose.

15. In 2016, both the Condominium Act and the POA Act were amended with regard to the rental of units. Changes effective July 1, 2016 include all of the following *EXCEPT*
    A. prohibits association from prohibiting the rental of a unit.
    B. prohibits associations from evicting tenants.
    C. prohibits associations from requiring the names of tenants.
    D. prohibits associations from demanding a copy of the lease.

UNIT 4

Real Estate Taxes and Other Liens

LEARNING OBJECTIVES

When you have completed this unit, you will be able to

> **describe** taxation liens, including exemptions, transportation issues, and special assessments;
> **explain** a mechanic's lien and how it may be implemented;
> **define** judgments and other types of liens; and
> **define** the following key terms:

broker's lien	money judgment lien	vendor's lien
landlord's lien	principle of uniformity	vested rights
lis pendens	"run with the land" seller affidavit	writ of execution
mechanic's lien	special assessment	writ of possession

OVERVIEW

Real estate taxes in Virginia are levied according to the provisions of Article X of the Virginia Constitution. The article specifies that all property must be levied at fair market value and must be uniform upon the same class of subjects within the territorial limits of the authority levying the tax (i.e., residential, commercial). This **principle of uniformity** does not prevent differences in taxation or the classification for taxation purposes of properties according to use in a business, trade, or occupation. The general assembly is given the authority to legislate laws for the levying and collecting of real estate taxes and to provide for a difference in the rate of taxation in certain circumstances. Virginia real and personal property tax records are managed by the County Assessor Office in each Virginia county. Many counties provide an online searchable database where searches can be made by address, owner name, or map number.

TITLE 58.1—TAXATION

Title 58.1 of the Code of Virginia contains the general laws regarding taxation. (§ 58.1-3200 et seq.) Based on Article X, Section 4 of the Virginia Constitution, all taxable real estate is to be assessed for local taxation. Taxable real estate includes a leasehold interest in a case where the land or improvements are exempt from taxation by the owner.

Exemptions

Section 6 of Article X of the constitution provides for the following exemptions from taxation:

- Property owned by the Commonwealth
- Real estate and personal property owned and used by churches or religious bodies for worship or residence of ministers
- Private or public nonprofit burying grounds or cemeteries
- Property owned by nonprofit public libraries or institutions of learning
- Intangible personal property
- Property used for religious, charitable, patriotic, historical, benevolent, cultural, or public park and playground purposes
- Property subject to a perpetual easement permitting inundation by water
- Property of any veteran determined to have a 100% service-connected disability who occupies the property as a personal residence (An amendment was passed on November 5, 2014 that allows an exemption for the surviving spouse of a soldier killed in action as long as the assessed value of the property does not exceed the average value for the locality; the exemption applies to both dwelling and land, not to exceed one acre.)

Further clarification in 2016 includes manufactured homes, whether or not on wheels, and whether or not the veteran or spouse owns the land the manufactured home sits on. The home will be tax exempt, the land will not.

The governing body of any county, city, or town may provide for the exemption or deferral of taxation for real estate owned and occupied by anyone at least 65 years old or permanently and totally disabled. (§ 58.1-3217) As of March 24, 2011, the law authorizes local governments to establish annual income or financial worth limitations as a condition of eligibility. Partial exemptions may also be granted for property in a redevelopment or conservation area, for certain rehabilitated, renovated, or replacement residential structures, and energy-efficient buildings.

Buildings that are listed on the Virginia Landmarks Register, not including the real estate or land on which they are located, are declared as a separate class of property and may be levied at a different rate as long as the building is maintained so as to retain the characteristics for which it was originally listed.

The controlling factor in determining whether private property is exempt from taxation is the use of the property. Public property, however, may be exempt from taxation without regard to its use. All nonexempt tangible personal property is subject to taxation by the local authority. Examples include aircraft, mobile homes, campers, and watercraft assessed at market value.

Zoning Effects on Taxes

Legislation in 2014 clarified the **vested rights** of owners of properties that were built before current zoning regulations were in effect or where permits can no longer be located. This bill states that so long as the homeowner has been paying taxes on the property for the past 15 years, the structure is deemed legal but non-conforming. When repairing or replacing a vested structure, the homeowner may be asked to bring the structure up to current code, but cannot be forced to remove it.

Taxes vary according to the type of zoning where a property is located. A new law in 2015 reformed the Board of Zoning Appeals (BZA) process which changed the burden of proof requirements to obtain a variance from a local zoning ordinance. The original requirement that a variance was needed due to "unnecessary or unreasonable hardship to the property owner" was changed to "unreasonably restricts the utilization of the property." The new law requires that property owners and local government be given equal time to present their cases at the BZA hearing. The property owner has the burden of proof by a preponderance of the evidence in a request for a variance. The law also establishes a statewide standard for private property owner variance request hearings allows for and regulates communications between all parties involved and amends the appeal process.

Legislation passed in 2016 extends protection for business owners if a locality issues a notice of zoning violation for use on a specific property after the business owner has paid taxes and operated for more than 15 years. The law provides that in such a case, the business owner has a right to file for rezoning or use a permit without payment of filing or related fees.

Transportation Issues

As part of Virginia's transportation plan, regional localities are now allowed to address their own specific transportation issues by raising funds independently. For example, earlier legislation had allowed counties and cities within the Northern Virginia Transportation Authority and the Hampton Roads metropolitan planning areas to permit real property zoned for commercial or industrial uses to be declared a separate class of real property for local taxation. All regional localities will now have this option.

Virginia Governor McDonnell's plan for solving the short and long-term transportation funding needs of the Commonwealth of Virginia became a reality at the conclusion of the 2013 general assembly. Titled the 2013 Transportation Funding and Reform Package, the plan is expected to generate over $3.1 billion to be invested in the Commonwealth's transportation network over the course of the next five years.

The 2013 transportation legislation

- eliminated the $0.175 per gallon tax on motor fuel, replaced by 3.5% tax on gasoline and 6% tax on diesel fuel;

- imposed a $64 annual registration fee on hybrid, alternative fuel, and electric motor vehicles; (This was repealed in 2014 with refunds issued.)

- raised the sales and use tax across the Commonwealth to 5.3%;

- increased the sales tax on motor vehicles to a total of 4.15% over four years;

- reclassified texting while driving as a primary offense with fines of $125 for first violation and $250 for any subsequent violation;

- generated additional revenue in Northern Virginia by raising the sales tax to 6%, hotel occupancy tax by 2%, and the real estate grantor's tax to $0.25 per $100; and

- directed $160 million in funding for mass transit capital improvements, operating costs, and special projects beginning in 2014.

The legislation provided for regional self-help provisions allowing localities to address their own specific transportation issues by raising funds independently.

EXAMPLE

The Fairfax County Board of Supervisors voted to create a Tysons Transportation Tax District to generate funds for transportation improvements to help develop the Tysons area into a walkable urban area. The board has the ability to levy a tax on all taxable real property within the service district, expected to be between $0.06 and $0.08 per $100 of assessed value. The combination of demographics, traffic congestion, and energy costs are shifting demand throughout the country to urban, walkable neighborhoods, especially for young professionals and retirees.

Assessments

Taxes "**run with the land**," meaning that the owner is responsible for paying real estate taxes for the current tax year from the date of purchase until the end of the year. In Virginia, the buyer is said to own the property on the date of closing or settlement. Taxes should be prorated between the seller (vendor) and the buyer (vendee) as of the day of settlement. Any delinquent taxes should be paid by the seller at closing. Penalties and interest on delinquent taxes are established by law.

IN PRACTICE

Unpaid taxes are a lien on real property. The settlement agent must verify that prior years' taxes have been paid and ascertain the status of the current year's taxes. Any other information should be obtained from city or county tax offices.

Taxes are generally not payable in advance of the due date. However, each city and county has its own particular manner of assessing taxes and setting the due date. Real estate licensees should be aware of four phases of taxes:

1. Past-due taxes
2. Taxes currently due and payable
3. Taxes not yet due
4. Prepaid taxes

The taxes for the first two phases will be collected from the seller's proceeds and paid to the proper authority by the settlement attorney. In the third and fourth phases, there are no taxes to be paid at the time a sale is closed. The closer will prorate the taxes between buyer and seller.

In phase three, the seller will be charged with the portion of the taxes that represents the number of days the seller occupied the property. The buyer will be credited with the same amount.

In phase four, where the taxes have been prepaid, the seller will receive a credit for the amount of taxes already paid for the time that the seller will not be occupying the property. The buyer will be charged with the same amount.

Estimating Taxes

Sometimes, past-year taxes cannot be used to estimate current taxes. On occasion, a licensee may desire to prepare either a seller or buyer an illustration (through the use of a Net Sheet) of the costs associated with the transaction. If this occurs, the licensee should obtain tax information directly from the tax assessor's office or from the owner's records.

New Construction

In the case of new construction, the taxes on the land are prorated based on taxes for the past year. The licensee should alert the purchaser that the taxes for the previous year are artificially low because they are based on the value of the land only and not the improvement (new home) recently constructed on it. Taxes on the new improvements are estimated using the purchase price multiplied by the county or city assessment rate. Taxes are estimated from the date the certificate of occupancy is issued, or a partial assessment may be levied against new construction not yet completed. Any additional tax bills should be presented to the settlement agent for proper disposition and prorating of additional taxes to be paid. The settlement agent can address the finalization of tax costs at closing.

Leases

As a general rule, the landlord under any ordinary lease is responsible for the taxes on the property; however, this does not apply to a perpetual leaseholder who is, in effect, the owner of the property and is entitled to its use forever. In such a case, the burden of taxation is placed on the lessee. In the case of net leases, the tenant is usually responsible for payment of the taxes.

Tax Liens

Delinquent real property taxes are both a personal debt and a lien against the property. A tax lien on real property has priority over all other liens except court costs. A tax lien overrides a **vendor's lien**, even though the vendor's lien may have been first. A tax lien is also before the **landlord's lien** for rent. The Virginia statutes give real estate taxes priority over a deed of trust in the distribution of proceeds under a foreclosure sale. The foreclosing trustee must satisfy all outstanding deficiencies before distributing the remaining proceeds to other creditors. If the statute's requirements are not complied with, delinquent taxes remain a debt against the purchaser at the sale.

A lien in favor of the United States for unpaid taxes, interest, and penalties may arise against all real and personal property belonging to a taxpayer. The lien is perfected under Virginia law by filing a notice of tax lien in the circuit court for the jurisdiction in which the taxpayer resides. The tax lien remains in effect until the taxes are paid.

When taxes on real estate in a county, city, or town are delinquent on December 31 following the third anniversary of the date on which the taxes became due, the real estate may be sold to collect the tax.

E X A M P L E

An individual's property tax was due on June 10, 2012, but was never paid. If the tax is still delinquent on December 31, 2015, the property may be sold for taxes on January 1, 2016.

At least 30 days before taking any action to sell the property, the tax-collecting officer must send a notice to the last known address of the property owner. Notice of the sale must be published in a newspaper of general circulation in the area 30 to 60 days before the commencement of the sale proceedings.

The sale proceedings are initiated by filing a suit in the circuit court of the county or city where the real estate is located. Owners of real estate, or their heirs, successors, and assigns, have the right to redeem the real estate before the sale date by paying all taxes, penalties, and interest due, plus costs, including the cost of publication and a reasonable attorney's fee set by the court. The former owner of any real estate sold for delinquent real estate taxes is entitled to any receipts from the sale in excess of the taxes, penalties, interest, and costs.

Special Assessments

There is a distinction between **special assessments** and general tax levies for purposes of funding government services and operations. Special assessments are taxes levied against specific benefited properties to pay for limited local improvements. They are founded on the theory of benefits brought about by improvements to adjacent properties. This public improvement enhances the value of a specific property—a sidewalk, for example, or a repaved alley. A special assessment is distinguished from an improvement that benefits the entire community, such as a park.

The statute specifically provides that notice must be given to abutting landowners of the contemplated improvements before the ordinance authorizing the improvements is put into effect. This gives the landowner an opportunity to be heard concerning the adoption or rejection of such an ordinance. The statute provides for special assessments relating to sewers, street paving, and other local public improvements.

The only properties subject to special assessments are those of abutting landowners. Local improvements may be ordered by a town or city council (with costs to be defrayed by special assessment) following receipt of a petition from not less than three-fourths of the landowners who will be affected by the assessment. However, the council may issue such an improvement order without a petition.

The amount of special assessment for a local improvement constitutes a lien on the property benefited by the improvement, enforceable by a suit in court. Property owners have the right to appear before the municipal authorities and protest both the authorization of the improvements and the assessments.

Estate and Inheritance Tax

There is no Virginia estate tax for decedents whose death occurred on or after July 1, 2007.

For a complete discussion of real estate taxes, see Code of Virginia, Table of Contents, Title 58.1—Taxation, at http://leg1.state.va.us/lis.htm.

LIENS OTHER THAN TAXES

There are numerous other types of liens that may be filed against real property. The mere issuance of an attachment creates no lien on the real estate. To create a lien, it is necessary for the officer to show that levy (actual attachment or seizure) was made.

A **lis pendens**, or pending suit, does not bind or affect a subsequent purchaser of real estate unless a memorandum is properly recorded giving notice of the suit. The memorandum of notice states the title of the suit, its general object, and the court in which it is pending. The notice declares the amount of the claim, describes the property, and names the person whose estate is intended to be affected.

If the lis pendens is not docketed as provided by the statutes, a purchaser (without notice of the pending suit) takes good title, with no lien on the land by virtue of the pending suit.

Mechanic's Lien

One of the most common types of liens affecting the sale of real property is a **mechanic's lien**. Anyone who performs labor or furnishes material with a value of $150 or more for the construction, removal, repair, or improvement of any building or structure has a right of lien on both the land and the building. The object of the law is to give laborers and materialmen the security of a lien on the property to the extent that they have added to its value. No lien will attach to the property for repairs or improvements that were not ordered by the owner, or the owner's agent.

The Virginia Mechanics' Lien Disclosure Act, Code of Virginia, Title 43, Chapter 1, requires that the seller of property disclose in the sales contract a warning that an effective mechanic's lien may be filed against the real property even after settlement.

The act's purpose is to protect contractors, brokers, purchasers, title agents, and insurers from builders or owners who contracted for improvements, sold the property, and never paid the contractor. The act requires that each residential sales contract include the following:

> NOTICE Virginia law § 43.1 et seq. permits persons who have performed labor or furnished materials for the construction, removal, repair, or improvement of any building or structure to file a lien against the property. This lien may be filed at any time after the work is commenced or the material is furnished, but not later than the earlier of (1) 90 days from the last day of the month in which the lienor last performed work or furnished materials, or (2) 90 days from the time the construction, removal, repair, or improvement is terminated.

While inclusion of the statement is mandatory, failure to include it will not void the contract.

Perfecting the Lien

A general contractor or a subcontractor may perfect a mechanic's lien by filing a memorandum of mechanic's lien with the clerk of court in the jurisdiction in which the property or structure is located. The filing must be within 90 days of the last day of the month in which the contractor last performed labor or furnished materials. However, under no circumstances may filing occur later than 90 days from the time the building is completed or the work otherwise terminated.

Written notice must be given to the owner of the property. The notice memorandum must include

- the name of the owner of the property;
- the name of the claimant;
- the amount of the claim;
- the time when the amount is due and payable; and
- a brief description of the property.

A mechanic's lien is enforced by a suit filed within six months of recording the memorandum of lien or 60 days from the completion or termination of work on the structure, whichever is later. If the person who ordered the work owns less than the fee simple estate in the land, only his actual interest is subject to the lien.

When a buyer constructs a building or structure, or undertakes repairs to an existing building or structure before the transaction has closed, the owner's interest will be subject to any mechanic's lien if the owner knows about the activity.

When a lien, such as a deed of trust, is created on land before work is begun or materials furnished, the deed of trust is a first lien on the land and a second lien on the building or structure. A deed of trust that is recorded before the work began is entitled to priority to the extent of the estimated value of the property without improvements for which the lien is claimed.

Seller Affidavit

Typically, the seller must execute an affidavit at closing that declares no work has been performed or any materials furnished within 120 days before the date of closing. This declaration ensures that no mechanic can file a lien on the property after closing for labor performed or materials furnished before closing. Nonetheless, a buyer should be advised to obtain additional assurances that no mechanic's lien can be filed.

Closing agents are charged with the responsibility to advise buyers of possible mechanic's lien filings and must inform buyers about title insurance protection.

A lien waiver should be demanded for new construction stating that all amounts have been paid for labor performed and materials furnished in connection with the construction. The waiver should be executed by the general contractor and all subcontractors. However, no waiver is required if affirmative mechanic's lien coverage is provided by a title insurance company.

Judgments

Every money judgment rendered in Virginia by any court, or by confession of judgment, constitutes a lien on any real estate the judgment debtor owns or may own in the future. The lien is effective from the date the judgment is docketed, that is, indexed by the clerk of court. It is prudent to docket the judgment in the city or county in which the debtor's property is located. If the debtor currently has no property, it is wise to docket the judgment wherever property is located that may become the debtor's in the future (for example, property owned by family members).

A **writ of execution** may be issued and the judgment enforced within 20 years from the date the judgment was rendered. A judgment may be extended beyond its 20-year life by a motion made in the circuit court, following notice to the judgment debtor and redocketing of the judgment.

If the real estate is conveyed to a grantee for value subject to a **money judgment lien**, the judgment creditor must bring the suit to enforce the judgment lien within 10 years from the date the grantee's deed was recorded.

If the judgment is for recovery of specific real property, a **writ of possession** is needed. If the judgment debtor owns real estate outside Virginia, the debtor may be required to convey it to a sheriff.

Within 30 days of the satisfaction, that is, payment of a judgment, a judgment creditor must release the judgment wherever it is docketed. Failure to do so within 10 days of demand by the judgment debtor makes the creditor subject to a fine.

Miscellaneous

Vendor's Lien

In Virginia, if any person conveys any real estate and the purchase money remains unpaid at the time of the conveyance, the vendor will not have a lien for the unpaid purchase money unless the lien is expressly reserved on the face of the deed. The object of this statute is to make the lien a matter of record, putting all persons who deal with the property on notice of all liens and encumbrances. The extent of the vendor's lien does not depend on the extent of the vendor's interest in the land conveyed but on the contract of the parties as gathered from the deed itself.

Landlord's Lien

The Virginia statutes give a landlord a right of lien. It exists independently of the right to hold property for payment of rent. When the landlord's lien for rent is obtained, it relates back to the very beginning of the tenancy and takes precedence over any lien that any other person has obtained or created against goods (personal property) on the leased premises since the tenancy began. A lien legally attaches to all property on the premises when it is asserted or on the premises within 30 days before attachment of lien. The landlord can seize the tenant's goods only to the extent necessary to satisfy the rent justly believed to be due.

See Unit 9 for more information on landlord and tenant rights and obligations.

Commercial Broker's Lien

A commercial real estate broker has a **broker's lien** on the rent paid by the tenant in the amount of the compensation (commission) agreed on by the owner and the broker.

SUMMARY

Real estate taxes in Virginia are levied according to the provisions of Article X of the Virginia Constitution. All property is levied at fair market value and must be uniform in the same class of subjects (i.e., residential, commercial). Title 58.1 of the Code of Virginia contains the general laws regarding taxation. There are numerous exemptions from taxation, the most recent being for the surviving spouse of a soldier killed in action. The governing body of any county, city, or town may provide exemption for the elderly or disabled. Buildings on the Virginia Landmarks Register may be levied at a different rate.

Recent legislation clarified the vested rights of owners of properties that were built before current zoning regulations were in effect or where permits can no longer be located and extend protection for business owners. The 2013 Transportation Funding and Reform Package is generating funds by changing the gasoline tax and sales tax. It also provided for regional self-help provisions.

In Virginia, taxes "run with the land," meaning the owner is responsible for paying taxes from the date of closing to the end of the year. Taxes on new construction are based on the value of the land only and may be artificially low for the first year. A tax lien on real property has priority over all other liens and will be paid first after deducting court costs. Special assessments are levied to pay for limited local improvements with notice given to abutting landowners.

A mechanic's lien may be filed by anyone who performs labor or furnishes material with a value of $150 or more for construction, removal, repair, or improvement of a building. Filing of the lien must be within 90 days of the last day of the month in which the work was performed. The seller of a property must disclose in the sales contract that a mechanic's file could be filed after settlement. The seller must then execute an affidavit at closing that declares no work has been performed or materials furnished within 120 days before closing.

Every money judgment rendered by a court constitutes a lien on real estate. A judgment must be enforced within 20 years. A vendor's lien refers to unpaid purchase money. A landlord's lien attaches to personal property. A commercial broker's lien is for unpaid commission.

UNIT 4 QUIZ

1. Which of the following is *TRUE* of uniform real estate taxation in Virginia?
   A. Tax rates and assessments must be uniformly applied to similar properties.
   B. All properties pay the same amount of tax.
   C. Only the tax rate needs to be uniform.
   D. Uniformity is a common law principle.

2. A single-family house is located near the end of a block right next to a bakery shop. How must these properties be treated for real estate tax purposes?
   A. There can be no difference between them.
   B. They will be classified differently, according to use.
   C. The bakery will not be subject to taxation because it is for public use.
   D. Because the bakery abuts a residential zone, it must be treated as a residence.

3. All of the following types of real property are exempt from real property taxation *EXCEPT*
   A. a for-profit cemetery.
   B. government-owned land.
   C. land owned by nonprofit educational institutions.
   D. land owned by a totally disabled veteran.

4. Which of the following statements is *FALSE* regarding taxes on new construction?
   A. Taxes are prorated based on the previous year's taxes.
   B. Taxes are estimated from the date of the certificate of occupancy.
   C. The first year taxes may be artificially low.
   D. Taxes are estimated based on comparable values for the area.

5. In Virginia, the owner of property on the date of sale is
   A. the buyer.
   B. the seller.
   C. the buyer and seller, divided evenly.
   D. either, depending on negotiation.

6. Which of the following liens would have first priority?
   A. Deed of trust
   B. Mechanic's lien
   C. Property tax lien
   D. Landlord's lien

7. How long after the work is done may a mechanic wait before filing a mechanic's lien?
   A. No more than 30 days
   B. No more than 60 days
   C. No more than 90 days
   D. No more than 6 months

8. How soon after filing the lien must the mechanic enforce it by filing suit?
   A. Within three months
   B. Within six months
   C. Within nine months
   D. Within one year

9. Based on the Virginia Mechanic's Lien Disclosure Act, disclosure of the possibility for a mechanic's lien must be made
   A. as part of the sales contract exactly as written in the act.
   B. as an addendum to the contract.
   C. any time before settlement.
   D. within three days after ratification of the contract.

10. A creditor on a judgment must enforce the judgment once it is rendered within
    A. six months.
    B. one year.
    C. five years.
    D. twenty years.

11. If a lien against the property of a decedent is made, it remains enforceable for
    A. 6 months.
    B. 18 months.
    C. 2 years.
    D. 10 years.

12. A lis pendens notice must declare all of the following *EXCEPT*
    A. the amount of the claim.
    B. the description of the property.
    C. the name of prospective purchaser.
    D. the name of the person whose estate is affected.

UNIT 5

Real Estate Contracts

LEARNING OBJECTIVES

When you have completed this unit, you will be able to

> **identify** methods of describing real estate in Virginia;
> **list** items found in a sales contract, including contingencies and statutory inclusion;
> **discuss** other contract procedures, including warranties; and
> **define** the following key terms:

as-built survey	house location survey	Statute of Frauds
attorney-in-fact	land surveyor	structural defect
boundary survey	lot-and-block method	subdivision plat
caveat emptor	metes-and-bounds method	walk-through inspection
equitable title	parol evidence	
four-corners doctrine	power of attorney	

OVERVIEW

The Code of Virginia allows real estate licensees—brokers and salespersons—to prepare written contracts for the sale, purchase, option, exchange, or rental of real estate as long as the contract is incidental to a specific real estate transaction and there is no additional charge for preparing the contract. (§ 54.1-2101.1) In some states, brokers and salespersons are not authorized to prepare contracts. In Virginia, the operative word is *incidental.*

EXAMPLE

While a licensee assists a buyer in a variety of functions, such as locating property, arranging financing, selecting a settlement agent, and so on, the preparation of the sales contract is incidental to the variety of services provided. In the situation of a seller who hires the licensee, the licensee performs a variety of services, such as marketing the property, advertising, showing the property to buyers, and so on. As in the case of the buyer example, the preparation of the sales contract is incidental to the transaction.

STATUTE OF FRAUDS

The English law passed in 1667 called the **Statute of Frauds** requires that the transfer of real estate be in writing. Virginia contract law prevents the enforcement of an oral contract or promise. (§ 11-1 and 11-2) The statute does not invalidate oral contracts; rather, it addresses the contract's enforceability. The statute bars any action concerning a contract for the sale of real estate or for a lease on real property for more than one year unless the document is in writing. Although an oral lease for a term of more than one year is unenforceable and the parties cannot be compelled to perform, they are nonetheless free to make and comply with such an agreement. Further discussion of the statute of frauds may be found in the Code of Virginia, Title 8.2A-201 (Commercial Code).

The actual contract used for the purchase and sale of real property may take any form. The only requirement is that it be in enough detail to clearly state the agreement between the parties. One important point of clarification is an accurate legal description.

Legal Descriptions

The most common method of describing real estate in Virginia is a combination of the **metes-and-bounds method** and the **lot-and-block method**.

Licensees should use great care in describing property. Both the real estate plat map and county or city tax records, as well as at least one deed by which the land was conveyed in the past, may be checked to verify that the proper legal description is being used. The description should enable the parties or a court to determine exactly what land the parties intended to convey.

Although the street address is usually given on a purchase contract, this is not an adequate legal description due to the fact that street addresses are frequently changed.

Methods of Description

The description of land by any of the following methods is legally sufficient, if the county or city and state are included:

- By courses and distances with an identifiable starting point (metes-and-bounds method)

- As bounded by natural or artificial objects or by the land of named persons (monuments method)

- By reference to a recorded map, plat, survey, deed, or other writing (lot-and-block method)

- By number or code on a recorded subdivision (subdivision method)

- By geodetic survey of townships, ranges, meridians, and so forth (rectangular government survey method)

- By house number and named street, where there is an established system of numbering (in many cases, this is not considered to be an adequate legal description because house numbers and street names are frequently subject to change)

- By any name by which the land is generally known and identifiable

- As occupied or acquired by a named person at a definite time

- As being all the land of the grantor in a designated way or acquired in a specific way

EXAMPLE

This is a common property description:

"All those certain lots, pieces, or parcels of land, situated in the city of Norfolk, Virginia, known, numbered, and designated on the Plat of Estabrook Corporation, made by S.W. Armistead, C.E., February, 1920, and recorded in the clerk's office of the Circuit Court of the City of Chesapeake, Virginia, in Map Book 17, page 4, as Lots No. 35 and 36, located on the north side of Amherst Street in Block 'E' in said subdivision called Estabrook, and appurtenances thereunto belonging said lots being 25 × 100 feet each."

A shortened form is frequently used in listing agreements and sales contracts:

"Lots 35 and 36, Block E, Plat of Estabrook, Norfolk, Virginia 23513, also known and described as 36 Amherst Street."

The following would also be an acceptable description:

"All that land called Warrens Crossing, as purchased by Nicholas Lilly on June 17, 1984, and bounded on the north by Richmond Hwy., on the south by Muddy Run, on the east by the farm belonging to John Evans, and on the south by the Redly Estate owned by Elizabeth Davies."

A false description does not invalidate the deed if, after rejecting the false description, enough information remains to permit reliable identification of the land to be conveyed. A complete description can be found in the deed that conveyed the property to the seller. The identical description should be used to convey the land to the buyer.

Disputed boundaries between two adjoining lands may be settled by express agreement. Virginia law provides for a court proceeding to establish boundaries. In conflicts concerning true boundaries, Virginia law gives preference to methods of description in the following order:

1. Natural monuments or landmarks

2. Artificial monuments and established lines

3. Adjacent boundaries or lines of adjoining tracts

4. Calls for courses and distances

5. Designation of quantity, such as "approximately 3.5 acres"

This preference will not be applied where it would frustrate the intent of the parties.

In disputes among purchasers of a lot shown on a plat, the metes and bounds established accurate survey, and corresponding calls of courses and distances that are noted on the plat will supersede errors in the plat and will control dimensions and configuration of the lots.

SURVEYING AND SURVEYS

To engage in the practice of land surveying in Virginia, a person must hold a valid surveyor's license, unless exempt by the statute (i.e., a licensed architect or engineer when surveying is incidental to a particular project). A **land surveyor** must pass a board examination and complete a minimum of 16 hours of continuing education per biennium.

Lenders are not allowed to require that a particular surveyor perform the survey in connection with making a loan to purchase real property. Surveys are recorded in the clerk's office of the circuit court where the land is located.

Four Types of Surveys

The following are four types of surveys commonly used in Virginia:

- A **subdivision plat** is a map of each parcel of land. The plat shows subdivided lots, streets, and similar features. The plat is generally created from a tract of land to subdivide it. The subdivided lots may or may not be staked on the ground once the plat has been created.

- A **boundary survey**, as opposed to a subdivision plat, shows the boundary or perimeter of the parcel as taken from and applied to the ground. Corner stakes or other physical landmarks appear.

- A **house location survey** is a boundary survey with the location of the house shown.

- An **as-built survey** (also called a *physical survey*) is a house location survey with all other physical features of the subject property shown, including water courses, utility lines, fence lines, outbuildings, and similar features.

A recently recorded survey of a subject property may reveal matters not shown in the record.

The attorney is primarily the person obligated to examine the survey. The following conditions suggest that potential problems may exist and should be brought to the attention of an attorney:

- Property boundaries that do not conform with the recorded plat
- Structural encroachments by the property onto neighboring properties, or by neighboring structures onto the subject property
- Fences that are not on the boundary line
- Party walls
- Riparian rights of others in streams, lakes, and other bodies of water
- Utilities that service other properties
- Old roadways
- Cemeteries
- Violation of setback, side, or rear building lines
- Property that may be landlocked

Any defect shown on the survey should be reported and corrective action taken where necessary.

Plat Maps

In areas of Virginia where recorded plat maps are used in lieu of individual surveys, the appropriate lot must be identified and lot dimensions must be legibly shown. Necessary endorsements to the title insurance policy must be issued pertaining to easements, deed restrictions, and property identification. The closing lawyer is responsible for obtaining the endorsements.

Subdivision Plat

In Virginia, a subdivision plat must contain all the necessary approvals of county or city officials. In addition, the dedications or consents of all owners, trustees, and other similar parties must be properly recorded. The law provides that the mere recordation of a plat transfers the streets, alleys, and other areas set aside for public use to the county or municipality in fee simple.

THE CONTRACT

The actual contract used for the purchase and sale of real property may take any form. The only requirement is that it be in enough detail to clearly state the agreement between the parties.

When two parties agree to form a contract, they attempt to write down all of the specific terms of the agreement (drafting the contract). Occasionally, however, one party later feels that all the terms of the agreement were not included in the written document and wishes to introduce evidence of prior oral agreements to alter the terms of the existing contract.

Parol evidence, that is, evidence of facts and circumstances not included in the deed or contract, is admissible in a court proceeding if the facts were well known in the community at the time the deed was made.

Parol evidence should not be confused with the statute of frauds, which requires that any contract for the sale of real estate be in writing in order to be enforceable.

Contract Provisions

Typically, a sales contract contains information covering the following:

- Real property
  - Personal property, fixtures, and utilities
  - Equipment, maintenance, and condition
- Legal description
- Price and financing
  - Deposit
  - Down payment
  - Loan application, approval, and appraisal

- Inspections
  - Access to property
  - Well and septic system inspection
  - Termite and wood-destroying pest inspection
  - Repairs
- Damage or loss
- Title and settlement
  - Conveyances, deed(s) of trust
  - Possession date
  - Settlement
  - Fees: broker's, attorney's, adjustments
- Disclosures and notices
- Contingencies or other Addenda

Earnest Money Deposit (EMD)

$ Deposit business 5 days From ratified contract

Although not legally required as part of a contract for the purchase of real estate, an earnest money deposit (EMD) is usually submitted along with the original offer to purchase. The earnest money serves to show that the potential buyer is indeed "in earnest" about going through with the purchase. No specific amount is recommended, but the larger the EMD, the most risk there is for the buyer; a large EMD should provide some assurance for a seller that the buyer will not back out.

IN PRACTICE

An all-cash offer often includes a large EMD because there is no third party involved in confirming the financial status of the purchaser.

The Virginia REB regulations are very specific about the disposition of any EMD:

- The money must be deposited in the broker's escrow account within five business days of ratification of the contract.

- The EMD may not be released from the escrow account until

  Closing — it is credited toward the sales price at settlement,

  Agreement — the seller and the purchaser agree in writing as to its disposition,

  Courts — a court orders a disbursement of the funds, or

  Disposal — it is disposed of in any other manner authorized by the REB. *Broker Letter to give $ to seller*

If the EMD is to be placed in an interest-bearing account, the contract must state who is to receive the interest.

Contract Forms

Local real estate associations often have standard sales contract forms to be used by their members. As business practices change and regulations increase, contract documentation and forms change to meet these new requirements. Because a sales contract often contains information specific to a given geographic area, you should contact your local real estate association or MLS for information on how to obtain up-to-date contract forms.

It is customary for real estate licensees to assist buyers and sellers with the preparation of the contract by filling in the blanks on the form. As with any printed form, all blanks should be filled in. If the item does not apply, the notation N/A (not applicable) should be inserted. Licensees should be careful when striking out whole paragraphs or sections of a contract because important beneficial language often can be inadvertently deleted. Licensees should use a proper addendum of clauses or amendments to alter terms specifically spelled out in the contract.

IN PRACTICE

As with all legal matters, real estate brokers and salespersons should refrain from trying to explain the legal technicalities. Improper or misunderstood explanations could subject the licensee to legal action later.

Though the word *contract* may imply the use of a single document, in actual practice, the average real estate contract for a given transaction is a series of documents, the most important of which is the actual sales agreement between the seller and the purchaser. Other documents and forms are typically added to the basic sales contract forms to meet compliance with federal, state, and local requirements for the sale and transfer of property. It is not uncommon for these pages of the transaction contract to exceed the number of pages in the standard sales contract. For example, Virginia has a Residential Property Disclosure Law, which requires that a disclosure be made as a part of the contract. The Environmental Protection Agency (EPA) requires a disclosure on all properties constructed before 1978 when lead-based paint was used in construction.

Builder Contracts

When new construction is involved, the entire contract package is typically provided by the builder, although some associations have published New Homes Sales Contracts. In a transaction that involves the sale of land, a contract specifically designated for that purpose should be used.

Builder negotiation on contract terms is rare when there are multiple buyers interested in one property. Things to be aware of when dealing with a builder contract include the following:

- *Substitutions*—The contract may allow the builder to make substitutions. If the purchaser wants certain specifications, they should be noted in the contract with a right to terminate the contract if substitutions are not acceptable.

- *Warranties*—Section 55-70.1 provides a solid warranty for new homes, but homebuyers may be asked to waive that warranty. Any such waiver should be conspicuous, all caps and large type in order to be easily identified. The standard warranty may be replaced by a third-party warranty only covering specific items.

- *Deposits and Advance Payments*—Any such payments must be placed in a separate escrow account, with no accessibility by the builder. A builder having financial difficulties could result in an uncompleted house with unpaid liens against it.

- *Four-Corner Doctrine*—Virginia abides by the four-corner doctrine that says all agreements must be present within the "**four corners**" of the contract in order to be valid. An oral agreement between builder and buyer is not valid. The best advice to give a new homebuyer client is to suggest seeking legal counsel to review the contract.

drafted by attorney to cover builder

While it is impractical to include every scenario in which a particular form is required, Figure 5.1 provides an approximation of how certain forms might be included in a total contract package.

FIGURE 5.1: Contract Form

Standard Form	# of Pages
Agency Disclosure: An appropriate disclosure for the type of agency used in the transaction is included	1
Sales Contract: Contains the basics of the sales transaction between the purchaser and the seller	10
Jurisdictional Addendum: Some contracts may require the use of a regional addendum for the appropriate jurisdiction	3
Contingencies and Clauses Addendum: Special contingencies (e.g., home inspections, radon inspection, third-party approval, short sale, sale of home, or post-occupancy agreements) and optional standard paragraph clauses are far too numerous to include in the standard sales contract	3-4
Property Disclosure: Virginia Residential Property Disclosure Additional disclosures where needed (military air noise, septic, drywall, methamphetamine) Condominium and Property Owners' Association Disclosure where applicable	2-4
Lead-Based Paint Disclosure: Required by EPA if the property was constructed before 1978	1
FHA Home Inspection Notice: If FHA financing is used, a notice of information on a home inspection is required	1
Approximate Total Pages (minimum)	24

STATUTORY INCLUSIONS

Federal and state laws require that certain disclosures be made during the course of a real estate transaction. Although brokerage relationship disclosures were covered in Unit 2, the information is reiterated here because it is in the actual assembly of a sales contract that these documents again come into play. The average sales contract will contain the required statutory disclosures as proof that they were actually made to the parties to the contract as required by law. Additionally, many firms and brokers require stricter standards than those required by laws of the state. These practices by some firms and brokers help to ensure maximum compliance with state regulations.

Disclosure of Brokerage Relationship

According to Virginia REB regulations, a disclosure of brokerage relationship must be made to nonrepresented buyers on the first substantive discussion about a specific property. Good real estate practice dictates this be done before showing any property to a nonrepresented buyer.

Disclosed Dual Representation (§ 54.1-2139)

In Virginia, a licensee may represent both parties in the same real estate transaction—seller and buyer or landlord and tenant—only with the written consent of all clients in the transaction. The client's signature on the written disclosure form is presumptive evidence of the brokerage relationship. The disclosure must be substantially in the same form as shown in Unit 2.

A dual standard agent does not terminate any brokerage relationship by making the required disclosures of dual representation. (§ 54.1-2139F) As mentioned previously, a licensee may withdraw from representing a client who refuses to consent to disclosed dual agency. The licensee may continue to represent in other transactions the client who refused dual representation. (§ 54.1-2139G)

Designated Representation

A principal or supervising broker may assign different affiliated licensees as designated standard agents to represent different clients in the same transaction. The appointment of designated representatives excludes other licensees in the firm from involvement in the transaction. The use of designated representatives does not constitute dual representation if each designee represents only one client in a particular real estate transaction. The designated representatives are pledged to maintain all confidential information received from their clients. Such information may be shared with the principal or supervising broker, who remains in the position of a dual representative with equal responsibilities to both clients. The disclosure must be made in writing and must be similar to the form shown in Unit 2. See Code of Virginia § 54.1-2139.1 for more detail.

Limited Services Agency

A licensee may act as a limited service agent only pursuant to a written brokerage agreement. Limited service agents must disclose their status as a limited services agent and present the client with a written disclosure that compares the services to be provided with the duties and services required of a standard agent that the licensee will not perform.

Residential Property Disclosure Documentation

The Virginia Residential Property Disclosure Act requires that the owner of residential real property consisting of one- to four-dwelling units furnish a purchaser with a residential property disclosure statement. This requirement is effective whether or not the transaction is with the assistance of a licensed real estate broker or salesperson. A complete discussion of the act was covered in Unit 1.

IN PRACTICE

A licensee must make sure that a Property Disclosure Statement and a Rights and Obligations Form are given to a buyer before ratification of a contract. The purchaser is directed to a DPOR website maintained by the REB with a full list of seller representations.

Lead-Based Paint Disclosure Requirements

Since 1996, the EPA has required that all prospective buyers and tenants receive an EPA pamphlet describing the hazards of lead-based paint for any property built before 1978. A lead-based paint disclosure form must be a part of all contracts and leases for such properties (see Figure 5.2). In July 2008, the EPA passed a rule requiring that all repairs, renovations, and painting projects affecting more than six square feet of interior space or 20 square feet of exterior on properties built before 1978 be done by an EPA-certified contractor. This rule went into effect April 2010.

FIGURE 5.2: Sale: Disclosure and Acknowledgement of Information on Lead-Based Paint and Lead-Based Paint Hazards

---

Disclosure of Information on Lead-Based Paint and/or Lead-Based Paint Hazards

Lead Warning Statement

Every purchaser of any interest in residential real property on which a residential dwelling was built prior to 1978 is notified that such property may present exposure to lead from lead-based paint that may place young children at risk of developing lead poisoning. Lead poisoning in young children may produce permanent neurological damage, including learning disabilities, reduced intelligence quotient, behavioral problems, and impaired memory. Lead poisoning also poses a particular risk to pregnant women. The seller of any interest in residential real property is required to provide the buyer with any information on lead-based paint hazards from risk assessments or inspections in the seller's possession and notify the buyer of any known lead-based paint hazards. A risk assessment or inspection for possible lead-based paint hazards is recommended prior to purchase.

Seller's Disclosure

(a) Presence of lead-based paint and/or lead-based paint hazards (check (i) or (ii) below):

    (i) _____ Known lead-based paint and/or lead-based paint hazards are present in the housing (explain).

_____

    (ii) _____ Seller has no knowledge of lead-based paint and/or lead-based paint hazards in the housing.

(b) Records and reports available to the seller (check (i) or (ii) below):

    (i) _____ Seller has provided the purchaser with all available records and reports pertaining to lead-based paint and/or lead-based paint hazards in the housing (list documents below).

_____

    (ii) _____ Seller has no reports or records pertaining to lead-based paint and/or lead-based paint hazards in the housing.

Purchaser's Acknowledgment (initial)

(c) _____ Purchaser has received copies of all information listed above.

(d) _____ Purchaser has received the pamphlet *Protect Your Family from Lead in Your Home.*

(e) Purchaser has (check (i) or (ii) below):

    (i) _____ received a 10-day opportunity (or mutually agreed upon period) to conduct a risk assessment or inspection for the presence of lead-based paint and/or lead-based paint hazards; or

    (ii) _____ waived the opportunity to conduct a risk assessment or inspection for the presence of lead-based paint and/or lead-based paint hazards.

Agent's Acknowledgment (initial)

(f) _____ Agent has informed the seller of the seller's obligations under 42 U.S.C. 4852d and is aware of his/her responsibility to ensure compliance.

Certification of Accuracy

The following parties have reviewed the information above and certify, to the best of their knowledge, that the information they have provided is true and accurate.

Seller	Date	Seller	Date
Purchaser	Date	Purchaser	Date
Agent	Date	Agent	Date

Contingencies

Once a contract is prepared for presentation to the seller, certain conditions of the purchase can appear in the form of contingencies to contract on ratification. Typical contingencies include a home inspection or a well and septic system inspection. These contingencies, while important, are generated by the wishes of the purchaser or as a requirement of the lender. There are other contingencies, however, that are generated by statute. If a property is a condominium or is in a subdivision bound by a POA, the seller must provide the purchaser with an opportunity to review the condominium resale packet or POA disclosure packet regarding the referenced property. This requirement of the law automatically creates a contingency to the contract and must be afforded to the purchaser exclusive of any other terms or conditions of the contract.

Request for Property Owners' Association Disclosure Packet

The Virginia POA Act requires that the seller request and furnish the disclosure packet regarding the referenced property. By the provisions of Virginia Code Section § 55-512, this packet must be delivered to the seller within 14 days of the request. Payment by seller is currently required to be made at settlement.

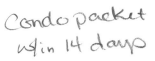

POA delivered (HOA) w/in 14 days of request

Request for Condominium Disclosure

The Virginia Condominium Act requires that the seller request the condominium resale packet regarding the referenced property and furnish it to the buyer. By the provisions of Virginia Code Section 55-79.97, this packet must be delivered within 14 days of the request. Payment by seller is made at settlement.

Condo packet w/in 14 days

Contingencies, Addenda, and Amendments

Sometimes additional conditions must be met before a sales contract becomes in full force. The contingency may be a part of the original contract or can be attached as an addendum or an amendment. In all cases, the signatures (or initials) of all parties are required in order for the contingency to be enforceable. A contingency should always include

- reference to the original contract with names of all parties and the correct date,
- a clear statement of what action is to be performed,
- any changes clearly marked with a cross-hatch for initials of all parties, and
- copies provided for all parties.

An addendum is new information that is to be included as part of the original contract. An amendment is a change to information that is already a part of the original contract. An addendum or amendment is usually prepared sometime after the original contract has been ratified. It requires the approval of all parties before it can become enforceable as part of the sales contract.

A contingency to a contract must be satisfied, removed, or approved before the parties can move forward with the other terms of the contract.

EXAMPLE

A home inspection contingency typically permits the purchaser to inspect the property with the aid of a certified or licensed professional. The contract is then said to be contingent on a mutual resolution between the purchaser and the seller of the outcome of the inspection. If a mutual resolution cannot be reached, typically the contract dies (becomes void). For a contingency to be enforceable, it must contain an expiration date and time plus a list or description of options available to the parties.

CONTRACT PROCEDURES

Use of a standard form does not excuse the licensee from pointing out to both parties that the contract is a legally binding document and that legal advice should be sought if either party has legal questions. The parties may make the agreement contingent on review and approval by an attorney.

Power of Attorney

Sometimes a party cannot be present at the closing and must be represented by an **attorney-in-fact** acting under a **power of attorney**. In Virginia, a specific power of attorney specifying the transaction and the parties involved, is generally preferred, rather than a general power of attorney. The power of attorney must be notarized and recorded with the deed.

It is not a good business practice and perhaps may even be a conflict of interest for licensees to perform as attorneys-in-fact for their seller or buyer clients. It is best to suggest that the client engage a licensed attorney to serve as an attorney-in-fact. Additionally, if a buyer is using a power of attorney, the buyer should be counseled to consult with the lender and the settlement company to ensure that the power of attorney document will be acceptable for loan purposes.

IN PRACTICE

Many military notaries are from outside Virginia and may not comply with the requirements of the Virginia Code. Most settlement companies use their own form of power of attorney; always check with them first.

Spousal Consent

If property is owned in severalty and the owner is married, it is generally recommended that the seller's spouse join in the contract to avoid any possibility of later claims. If one or the other spouse does not sign, it is possible the court may not order specific performance on the contract unless the buyer is willing to accept a deed that remains subject to the spousal interest. If the seller is not able to convey the property with a clear title, the contract could possibly be in jeopardy. Licensees should not attempt to resolve any legal issues, but should refer the client to appropriate legal counsel.

IN PRACTICE

There was an infamous court case in Northern Virginia many years ago where the seller of a large tract of property sold the property without the signature of his estranged spouse. When the property was later developed into a multi-million dollar project, the wife suddenly reappeared, claiming to have a share in the property. Risk management advice to brokers is to have all spouses sign the listing agreement and any contract for sale of the property to avoid the possibility of later court action.

The capacity in which each signer executes the contract should be clearly stated. The contract should indicate whether the signer is an individual, a married couple, a partnership, a corporation, a limited liability company, or any other legal entity.

TITLE

The buyer under a real estate sales contract expects to receive marketable title to the property from the seller. Marketable title and insurable title are not necessarily the same because a title insurance policy may list exceptions against which it does not insure.

Equitable Title

When the buyer and seller have ratified, that is, signed, the sales contract, the buyer's interest is called **equitable title**. A buyer's equitable title gives the buyer an insurable interest in the property. While Virginia law places the risk of damage to the property during this period on the buyer, most sales contracts in Virginia provide that the seller bears the risk of loss. Licensees should ensure that this point is addressed in the contract.

WARRANTIES

The principle of **caveat emptor** (Latin for "let the buyer beware") is still the law in Virginia regarding previously owned homes.

Responsibility of Inspections is on buyer

Consumer Protection

Buyers and sellers should ensure that the sales contract is sufficiently complete in order to provide for the identification and resolution of deficient items for which they may have concern. These actions may include, but are not limited to, property inspection contingencies, such as lead-based paint, radon, or mold inspections; exterior insulation finishing system (EIFS) or defective drywall; wood-destroying pests and moisture inspections, and other appropriate property reviews, such as well and septic inspection; and a final **walk-through inspection**. Many real estate jurisdictions have local consumer disclosure forms that alert the buyer to issues that may be pertinent to the locale, such as a Megan's Law disclosure. If in doubt, buyers should insist on a study period (contingency) in the sales contract to provide sufficient time to investigate various issues.

Contracted requests completed by the walkthrough 7-10 days prior to close

Existing Homes

In most areas, the seller will warrant that the heating, plumbing, electrical, and air-conditioning systems are in normal working order at the time of settlement. The buyer usually has the opportunity for a walk-through inspection before settlement to verify that no material changes have occurred since the signing of the sales contract (such as storm damage, vandalism, or the removal of fixtures). If there have been any changes, the seller must inform the buyer of them, regardless of whether a walk-through is to be performed. It is a buyer's responsibility to determine what conditions beyond the property's boundaries may affect its value.

New Construction

For new homes, the builder normally supplies a detailed warranty, primarily to limit liability, which includes either a 5-year or 10-year warranty against foundation defects. At the time of closing, there is an implied warranty that the dwelling and its fixtures (to the seller's best actual knowledge) are free from **structural defects** and constructed in a professional manner. A structural defect is a flaw that reduces the stability or safety of the structure below accepted standards or that restricts the normal use of the structure. The implied warranties continue for one year after the date of transfer of title or the buyer's taking possession, whichever occurs first.

Builder is required to give 1 yr warranty by law

Homeowner Warranty

Several companies offer a homeowner warranty that allows for repair or replacement of various systems and appliances within the home for a one-year period. The warranty may be purchased by either the seller or the buyer and does not require an inspection.

IN PRACTICE

The listing agent can provide information on different home warranty plans that the seller might choose to include as part of the listing package as an incentive to potential buyers. This sometimes relieves concern on the part of the buyer as to the condition of existing systems and appliances, especially in an older home. The buyer agent can also present the home warranty information to the buyer as a form of insurance against needed repairs in the first year.

SUMMARY

The Code of Virginia allows real estate licensees—brokers and salespersons—to prepare written contracts for the sale, purchase, option, exchange, or rental of real estate as long as the contract is incidental to a specific real estate transaction and there is no additional charge for preparing the contract the English law passed in 1667 called the Statute of Frauds requires that the transfer of real estate be in writing. Virginia contract law prevents the enforcement of an oral contract.

A legal description is included in a sales contract. The most common method of describing real estate in Virginia is a combination of the metes-and-bounds method and the lot-and-block method. Although the street address is usually given on a purchase contract, this is not an adequate legal description. There are four types of surveys commonly used in Virginia. In areas where recorded plat maps are used in lieu of individual surveys, the appropriate lot must be identified and lot dimensions must be legibly shown.

There are many other provisions typically included in a sales contract including price and financing, necessary inspections, title and settlement information, required disclosures, and any contingencies or other addenda. Although not legally required as part of a contract for the purchase of real estate, an EMD is usually submitted along with the original offer to purchase. There are no standard contracts although local associations may make them available. New home builders usually have their own contract packages.

Required disclosures include disclosure of brokerage relationship, residential property disclosure, lead-based paint, and condominium or POA disclosures. Contingencies and other addenda may deal with any number of topics, depending on the client's requests.

In most areas, the seller will warrant that the heating, plumbing, electrical, and air-conditioning systems are in normal working order at the time of settlement. The buyer usually has the opportunity for a walk-through inspection before settlement. For new homes, builders normally supply a detailed warranty. Some sellers provide a homeowner warranty or it may be purchased by the buyer.

UNIT 5 QUIZ

1. All of the following are satisfactory legal descriptions in Virginia *EXCEPT*
   A. "Lot 7, Block D, Plat of Red Valley, Martin County, Virginia"
   B. "The entire 77.5 acres purchased by Edna Kelly on June 20, 1991, and called Seaside Neck, Roanoke"
   C. "727 Olean Drive, Fletcherton, Virginia"
   D. "Proceeding 120 feet due west of the intersection of the east line of J Street and the north line of 11th Street to a point; thence north 10 degrees 31 minutes west 100 feet"

2. A deed contains the following description: "Lots 7 and 8, Block F, Section 3, Plat of Greydon, otherwise called 14 Havers Drive, Venus, Virginia." In fact, Block F has only six lots, and the street address is Lot 5. Is this deed valid?
   A. No, a false element in a description invalidates the deed.
   B. No, because the lot description is faulty, a new deed is needed.
   C. Yes, it's valid if the buyer knows which property is meant.
   D. Yes, enough correct information remains to permit identification.

3. A lender wishes to use the services of only licensed surveyors and says he will *NOT* accept the surveys of unlicensed or nonexempt surveyors. Is this practice legal?
   A. Yes, a lender may require the services of either licensed or exempt surveyors, but the lender cannot require that a particular surveyor conduct the survey.
   B. Yes, as long as the lender always uses the same surveyor, this practice is legal.
   C. No, surveyors are selected by the clerk's office.
   D. Yes, the lender can require that a particular surveyor conduct the survey.

4. The survey for a property shows the location of the house, the garage, the fence, utility lines, and the children's playhouse in the backyard. This is *MOST* likely which type of survey?
   A. Subdivision plat
   B. Boundary survey
   C. House location survey
   D. As-built survey

5. The buyer and seller agree to the sale of a home for $150,000. No written contract is signed, but the seller accepts payment in full from the buyer and delivers the deed. Which of the following statements is *TRUE*?
   A. The sale is without legal effect; the seller continues to own the home.
   B. The sale violates the statute of frauds' maximum amount for oral contracts.
   C. The sale is enforceable in a court of law under the statute of frauds, due to the parties' compliance.
   D. The sale is unenforceable under the statute of frauds, but the parties are free to comply with its terms.

6. An actual contract used for the purchase and sale of real property
   A. must be on a form approved by the REB.
   B. must be drafted by an attorney licensed to practice in the Commonwealth of Virginia.
   C. may take any form.
   D. does not need enough detail to clearly state the agreement between the parties.

7. A sales contract contains all of the following information *EXCEPT* the
   A. type of sewage system.
   B. amount of the down payment.
   C. age of the parties to the contract.
   D. the possession date.

8. All of the following are statutory contingencies required by law *EXCEPT*
   A. review of the condominium resale packet.
   B. review of the POA disclosure packet.
   C. well and septic system inspection.
   D. review of property disclosure.

9. The disclosure of lead-based paint and lead-based paint hazards is required on all
   A. sales contracts.
   B. residential sale contracts.
   C. residential contracts for properties constructed before 1978.
   D. residential contracts for sale to purchasers with small children.

10. All of the following are required disclosure forms that must be included with a sales contract *EXCEPT*
    A. brokerage relationship.
    B. property disclosure.
    C. home inspection disclosure.
    D. lead-based paint disclosure.

11. Two weeks after a buyer and seller signed a sales contract on a house, the house burned to the ground. If the contract is <u>silent</u> on the issue, which party is liable?
    A. Only the buyer is liable according to Virginia law.
    B. The buyer and seller share the risk of loss equally.
    C. The seller is liable because she continues to possess title to the property.
    D. The seller is liable under the implied condition of good faith.

12. During construction of a new house, the foundation cracked and the builder decided to build the bearing walls of a lighter material to keep the entire structure from collapsing. A structural engineer told him that a strong wind would probably blow the house down. Nonetheless, the cracked foundation and structural shortcuts were easily covered over, and the house was sold to a first-time homebuyer without mentioning the defects. Two weeks after closing, the house collapsed in a thunderstorm. Is the builder liable?
    A. No, under caveat emptor
    B. No, because the buyer never asked about specific defects
    C. Yes, due to the implied warranty against foundation defects
    D. Yes, due to the failure to have the property inspected

13. Do *marketable title* and *insurable title* mean virtually the same thing?
    A. Yes, they are synonymous.
    B. Yes, if it is marketable, it is insurable.
    C. No, insurable title lists exceptions for which it will not insure.
    D. No, insurable title is the same as equitable title.

14. A homeowner warranty is *MOST* similar to
    A. a home inspection contingency.
    B. insurable title.
    C. a builder warranty.
    D. a walk-through inspection.

15. The sellers of a property have already moved to another state where they are living in an assisted-living home and are not healthy enough to travel. Their best choice for a power of attorney to attend settlement on their behalf would be
    A. their listing agent.
    B. the selling agent.
    C. the listing broker.
    D. the seller's brother who is an attorney.

Never the agent

UNIT
6

Real Estate Financing

LEARNING OBJECTIVES

When you have completed this unit, you will be able to

> **explain** the use of a note and deed of trust in financing home mortgage loans;
> **discuss** the impact of the Consumer Financial Protection Bureau (CFPB) on home mortgage lending;
> **explain** the purpose and actions of the Virginia Housing Development Authority (VHDA);
> **review** the process for foreclosing on a deed of trust; and
> **define** the following key terms:

alienation clause	grantor	promissory note
beneficiary	home equity line of credit	purchase-money financing
deed of trust	(HELOC)	qualified residential mortgage
deferred purchase money	judicial foreclosure	(QRM)
due-on-sale clause	loan origination fee	short sale
government-sponsored	mixed-use development	title theory
enterprise (GSE)	nonjudicial foreclosure	trustee
grace period	power of sale clause	usury

OVERVIEW

This unit briefly discusses the financing of single-family residential real estate in Virginia. It does not address commercial or more sophisticated transactions, but many of the concepts addressed will apply to such transactions.

PURCHASE CONTRACTS AND FINANCING

A licensed real estate broker or agent who has negotiated a sale may prepare a routine contract for the transaction. If a first **deed of trust** loan is to be obtained, the contract usually is made contingent on the purchaser's obtaining the loan. The real estate licensee must be careful in describing the loan because of the complexity of the terms. The seller may add the provision that the purchaser must apply for the loan promptly; should the purchaser not notify the seller by a certain date that loan approval has been obtained, the contingency will be deemed waived. Typically, preprinted real estate contracts provide that the purchaser has a specified number of days from the date of the contract in which to apply for financing. The contract should specifically state what type of financing is contemplated: cash, assumption, seller financed, FHA, VA, or conventional loan obtained through an institutional lender.

The contract should provide a ceiling on the interest rate the borrower will accept. If this condition is not included, the purchaser could be bound by the contract even if the interest rate rises several percentage points between the date the contract is ratified and the date the purchaser locks in the interest rate with a lender. The lack of an interest rate cap could end up significantly increasing the cost of the home for the buyer.

If an existing loan is to remain on the property, the contract should specify whether it will be assumed or whether title will be taken subject to the existing loan.

Institutional Financing

In Virginia, a deed of trust, rather than a mortgage, is the instrument used to establish collateral in a residential sales transaction. Three parties are involved in a deed of trust: the borrower, the lender (**beneficiary**), and a **trustee** (a neutral third party) who holds the deed of trust for both the borrower and the lender. By signing the note and deed of trust, the borrower waives various rights, including the right to a court hearing in case of foreclosure. It is extremely important that the borrower fully understands the nature of the note and deed of trust. The **promissory note** defines the amount of debt and method of repayment. Even though collateral for the loan is established by a deed of trust, the term *mortgage* is still used generically when referring to a mortgage loan, obtaining a mortgage, mortgage payment, mortgage broker, and so on. The note and deed of trust give the lender, in the event the borrower should default, the right to declare the entire debt due and payable. In that situation, the **power of sale clause** in the deed of trust gives the trustee the right to sell the property (foreclose) without going to court. This is called a **nonjudicial foreclosure**. Some states require the use of a mortgage that takes a court action to foreclose and is called a **judicial foreclosure**.

The Note and Deed of Trust

The note and deed of trust are generally prepared by the lender. Standard forms are available for specialized loans, such as those insured (e.g., FHA) or guaranteed (e.g., VA) by the government. The note is not usually recorded although the deed of trust should always be promptly recorded.

The note and deed of trust should be signed in the exact manner and in the same name as the title is held. No witnesses are necessary. The deed of trust must be acknowledged (notarized) to permit its recordation in the land records of the circuit court where the property is located. Further, VA and FHA notes and notes to be sold out of state require notarization with a seal. Good sources of information on residential financing are available at the following locations:

■ FHA: www.hud.gov

■ VA: www.va.gov

■ Fannie Mae: www.fanniemae.com

■ Freddie Mac: www.freddiemac.com

Due-On-Sale Clause

Loans that contain a **due-on-sale clause**, also called an **alienation clause**, are not assumable unless the lender chooses to waive the due-on-sale clause. Due-on-sale clauses are enforceable in Virginia. When a loan containing a due-on-sale clause is made on real property comprising not more than four residential dwelling units, the deed of trust generally includes a statement like the following:

> In the event the Property or any part thereof or any interest therein is sold, conveyed or alienated by the trustor, whether voluntarily or involuntarily, except as prohibited by law, all obligation secured by this instrument, irrespective of the maturity dates express therein, at the option of the holder hereof and without demand or notice, shall immediately become due and payable.

(Sample from the U.S. Securities and Exchange Commission)

[handwritten: Loan due upon sale of property]

Releases

Whenever the borrower pays off any note, a marginal release is made on the face of the instrument wherever the document is recorded. Alternatively, a certificate of satisfaction or a partial satisfaction form is filed in the deed books in the clerk's office in the county where the land is located.

Lender Charges

Many conventional first deeds of trust loans contain a provision for a late charge if a monthly payment is not made within a certain period after the due date (called a **grace period**). The fact that a late charge may be collected must be disclosed in the loan's Truth in Lending statement. In Virginia, late charges may not exceed 5% of the installment due and cannot be collected unless the payment is not made within seven calendar days after the due date. Most lenders permit 15 days. The late charge must be specified in the contract between the lender and the borrower. Late charges in excess of the statutory amount are void only with regard to the excess amount; an inflated late charge does not affect the underlying obligation.

[handwritten: -5% or less late fee]

In addition to such charges as points, late charges, and escrows, Virginia law permits lenders to charge a **loan origination fee** for granting a loan, which is often combined with the points charged for the loan as 2 points plus origination fee = 3 points.

[handwritten: 1% of loan]

Other allowable closing costs are the fees charged for title examination, title insurance, recording charges, taxes, hazard insurance, mortgage guarantee insurance, appraisals, credit reports, surveys, document preparation, real estate tax service fees, lender inspection, and attorney or settlement agent charges for closing the loan and settlement on the property. Lenders may require flood insurance coverage for any property located in a FEMA designated flood hazard area. However, lenders may not require flood insurance coverage exceeding the replacement value of the property's improvements. The lender generally requires a house location survey. The survey must be current (within the past six months), and the survey must be done by a certified land surveyor.

[handwritten: Lenders - require Flood Ins. - Survey]

HOME MORTGAGE LOANS

Home loans generally fall into two categories: conventional and government. Conventional loans are those that conform to standards set by Fannie Mae and Freddie Mac. Non-conforming loans do not meet the Fannie/Freddie standards and will not be purchased by them (e.g., a jumbo loan that exceeds the current Fannie/Freddie loan limit).

Fannie Mae and Freddie Mac

In the past, Fannie Mae and Freddie Mac were independent agencies called **government-sponsored enterprises** (GSEs). In 2008, regulation of Fannie Mae and Freddie Mac was given to the Federal Housing Finance Administration (FHFA), which also has the authority to establish conforming mortgage loan limits. The loan limit for 2017 is $424,100 in most of the country, with some increased amounts for high-cost areas. For current loan limits by county for one to four units visit www.fhfa.gov and select *Conforming Loan Limits*.

For more information on Fannie Mae loans see www.fanniemae.com, for Freddie Mac loans, see www.freddiemac.com.

Government loans include FHA, VA, Rural Housing Service (RHS), and certain loans provided by local or state financing authorities. FHA loans are insured by the Federal Housing Administration; VA loans are guaranteed by the Department of Veterans Affairs.

FHA Financing

Many Virginians obtain FHA-insured mortgage loans for either first-time or subsequent purchases of a home. Both current loan limits (based on geographic area) and FHA mortgage insurance premiums are subject to frequent change. As of January 1, 2017, the standard mortgage limit for a one-unit dwelling is $275,665. In an FHA-considered high-cost area, the limit is $636,150. The loan limits for two-, three-, or four-unit dwellings can be found at www.fha.com or www.hud.gov.

FHA mortgage insurance premiums (MIPs) undergo frequent changes. As of January 1, 2017, the upfront MIP is 1.75% of the loan amount, except for some special loan programs. The annual premium as of January 1, 2017, for a 30-year mortgage is .80% of loan amount for loans with more than 5% down and .85% for loans with less than 5% down. The upfront MIP is amortized over the term of the loan (usually 30 years) and has less impact on the monthly payment. The annual fee, however, is divided by 12 and added to the monthly payment, which can make a significant difference in the amount due each month. The MIP rates for 15-year loans are lower and may be canceled after 11 years.

Changes Regarding Condominiums

In the past, it has often been difficult to obtain FHA financing for condominiums because of the limitations on the percentage of investor owners. An FHA mortgagee letter issued September 13, 2012, focused on four major concerns:

- Treatment of delinquent dues
- Property certification requirements
- Owner-occupancy requirements
- Treatment of commercial space

Changes covered in this letter to lenders included the following:

- A developer or a single investor may own up to 50% of the total units at the time of project approval.

- **Mixed-use developments** are defined as developments with a combination of any of the following: commercial, residential, retail, office, or parking space (half of the space may be devoted to commercial use as long as the commercial space does not have a negative impact on the residential character of the project).

- No more than 15% of the total units can be in arrears (more than 60 days past due) on condominium association fee payments.

- The Project Owner's Certification document has been revised. For more details, see www.hud.gov.

The Modernization Act of 2016 made some changes to the rules for condominium financing, lowering the owner-occupancy requirements on certain condo developments. Under the new rule, the requirement would be lowered to 35% owner occupied provided the project meets certain conditions proscribed by FHA (e.g., higher reserves, low percentage of association dues in arrears, and evidence of long-term financial stability). The condo development must be more than 12 months old, have no more than 10% of the total units in arrears, and three years of acceptable financial documents must be provided.

A major change for 2017 was that any investor or entity (single or multiple owner entities) may own up to 50% of the total units *if* at least 50% of the units are owner occupied as principal residences. (The previous limit was 10%.)

Assistance for Disaster Areas

Homeowners with FHA-insured mortgages struggling to repair or rebuild homes in the wake of major disasters like Hurricanes Sandy or Hermine may be helped by the following provisions:

- A 90-day moratorium of foreclosures on properties located in presidentially declared disaster areas is outlined.

- Servicers must consider a full range of benefits for affected borrowers, including mortgage modifications, partial claims, use of FHA, HAMP, or other refinance options, and a waiver of late charges.

- Lenders are to release homeowners' insurance proceeds to the borrower rather than retaining such proceeds to make up for missed payments.

- HUD's Section 203(h) mortgage insurance product to assist disaster victims is summarized, and reference is made to HUD's Section 203(k) rehabilitation mortgage insurance product.

VA Loans

The Department of Veterans Affairs (VA) guarantees loans for eligible active-duty military and veterans, including an adjustable-rate mortgage (ARM) that was made a permanent loan product in August 2012. The current VA loan limit for most counties in Virginia is $424,100, but may be as high as $636,150 in high-cost areas such as Northern Virginia. The current VA entitlement is $36,000. Lenders will generally loan up to four times that amount with no money down because the first 25% of the loan is guaranteed by the government. Veterans can borrow over that amount by making a down payment for the amount that exceeds the limit. For more details on VA eligibility, see www.va.gov.

Consumer Financial Protection Bureau (CFPB)

The Consumer Financial Protection Bureau (CFPB) was created as part of the Dodd-Frank legislation in 2010. The CFPB goal is to issue regulations that protect consumers and promote fair, transparent, and competitive markets. The CFPB established new rules for mortgage servicers that went into effect January 10, 2014. Despite concern in the mortgage lending industry regarding the thousands of pages of rules and new processes that would now be required, lenders were able to develop coping strategies and to implement the new regulations in a timely fashion.

The CFPB rules require the servicer to maintain policies and procedures to include, but are not limited to:

- provide billing information in writing;
- provide at least two months' warning if there is going to be a change in an ARM interest rate that means payments are about to change;
- promptly credit mortgage payments;
- respond quickly when asked about paying off a loan;
- not charge for insurance that is not needed, or overcharge for force-placed insurance;
- quickly resolve complaints and share information;
- have and follow good customer service policies and procedures;
- contact the borrower to help when the borrower is having trouble making payments;
- work with the borrower who is having trouble paying the mortgage, before starting or continuing foreclosure; and
- allow the borrower to seek review of the mortgage servicer's decision about a loan workout request.

This information is available in the CFPB brochure, *What the New Mortgage Servicing Rules Mean for Consumers*. The brochure also provides contact information for any consumer who does not believe that the lender is following the mortgage servicing rules.

An updated 2016 Mortgage Servicing Rule was issued on August 4, 2016 that added additional protections for borrowers:

- Provides foreclosure protections more than once over the life of the loan (particularly helpful for borrowers who obtain a permanent loan modification and later suffer an unrelated hardship)
- Clarifies borrower protections when the servicing of a loan is transferred (referred to as *successors in interest* (ensures that surviving family members or others who inherit have the same protections as the original borrower)
- Provides important loan information to borrowers in bankruptcy

The CFPB issued a Compliance Bulletin on November 28 2016 entitled, *Detecting and Preventing Consumer Harm from Production Incentives*. Twice a year, the CFPB publishes an agenda of its upcoming planned rulemaking activities. You can view all of the CFPB Final Rules, Compliance Bulletins, and consumer brochures on the CFPB website at www .consumerfinance.gov.

Qualified Residential Mortgage (QRM)

After three years of deliberations, the six regulators finalized the **Qualified Residential Mortgage** (QRM) rule in October, 2014. The final rule aligns the QRM with the Qualified Mortgage standard implemented earlier in 2014. A major concern for future borrowers in the original QRM proposal was the requirement for a 20% down payment. Under the new rule, the loan is considered to be qualified if the borrower's debt-to-income ratio is not more than 43 percent and no onerous down payment is required. Another part of the original rule would have required the lender to retain 5% of the loan amount for loans that did not meet the QRM standards. Because the QRM loan now comes without the risk-retention requirement, it is hoped that this will help open up the lending market.

[handwritten margin note: Used to require 20% down   Now qualified if debt : income less than 43%]

TILA-RESPA Integrated Disclosures (TRID)

Rulemaking authority for the Truth in Lending Act (TILA)—Regulation Z and the Real Estate Settlement Procedures Act (RESPA)—Regulation X was transferred to the CFPB in July 2011. After four years of study, research, and revisions, TILA-RESPA Integrated Disclosures (TRID) was made mandatory on October 3, 2015. Under TRID, the Loan Estimate (LE) that replaced the initial Truth in Lending statement and Good Faith Estimate must be delivered to a borrower within three days of application. The other new form created by the CFPB is the Closing Disclosure (CD) which must be delivered to the borrower at least three days before settlement and which has very little tolerance for any changes from the original LE. The CD replaces the final TILA statement and the HUD-1 Settlement Statement.

[handwritten margin note: LE = within 3 days of application   CD = in 3 days before settlement]

TRID is triggered by an application for a federally related mortgage loan. Construction-only loans, vacant land, and properties with 25 acres or more did not fall under RESPA, but are now subject to TRID. Business, commercial, and agricultural loans are still exempt.

VIRGINIA HOUSING DEVELOPMENT AUTHORITY (VHDA)

The Virginia Housing Development Authority (VHDA) was created in 1972 by the Virginia General Assembly. Its purpose is to make housing more affordable for those with low or moderate incomes. VHDA is self-supporting, and funding for its programs is provided by the private sector through the sales of VHDA bonds. Federal and state tax dollars are not used to fund VHDA lending programs. Basic VHDA services include the following:

[handwritten margin note: VHDA :   ▲ 1972   ▪ affordable housing for ↓ incomes   ▪ self-supporting thru bond sales]

- Single-family loan programs—creative and lower interest rate loans for low-income to moderate-income homebuyers who have not had an ownership interest in their primary residences during the three years before making application for the loan

- Multifamily loan products—mortgage loans to developers of multifamily projects (primarily for rentals for low-income and moderate-income tenants)

- Administration of the federal low-income housing Tax Credit Program

- Administration of the federal Section 8 and Section 236 rent subsidy programs

- Virginia Housing Fund—loans for multifamily housing that will serve low-income and moderate-income residents in difficult situations or locations

Administration of some functions of the Virginia Housing Partnership Fund VHDA also builds and operates residential housing, nursing care facilities, and nursing homes providing medical and related facilities for the residence and care of the elderly.

VHDA offers a variety of different loan programs, including those made in conjunction with FHA, VA, and RHS. A homeownership education course is required of first-time buyers. As of 2015, VHDA offers a Mortgage Credit Certificate that allows a dollar-for-dollar reduction in federal income taxes up to 20% of the annual interest paid on the mortgage. The remaining 80% of the interest is still eligible for the usual itemized deduction.

Specific guidelines for the various VHDA loan products may be obtained from a local lender or by contacting VHDA headquarters in Richmond or online at www.vhda.com.

Virginia Housing Partnership Fund

The Virginia Housing Partnership (Revolving) Fund was created to address the serious shortage in the Commonwealth of safe and decent residential housing at prices that persons and families of low and moderate incomes can afford. Housing developments and housing projects funded through the fund are intended to provide additional affordable housing opportunities for low-income and moderate-income Virginians by preserving existing housing units, by producing new housing units, and by assisting persons with special needs with obtaining adequate housing.

This fund was renamed the Virginia Housing Trust Fund by the 2013 General Assembly, and $7 million was allocated to the fund to be administered by the VHDA along with the Department of Housing and Community Development (DHCD). Eighty percent of the money is to be used for low-interest loans made through eligible organizations, with the remaining 20% directed to reducing homelessness in the Commonwealth.

FIGURE 6.1: Loan Estimate

Save this Loan Estimate to compare with your Closing Disclosure.

Loan Estimate

	LOAN TERM
	PURPOSE
DATE ISSUED	**PRODUCT**
APPLICANTS	**LOAN TYPE** ☐ Conventional ☐ FHA ☐ VA ☐ _____
	LOAN ID #
	RATE LOCK ☐ NO ☐ YES, until
PROPERTY	*Before closing, your interest rate, points, and lender credits can*
SALE PRICE	*change unless you lock the interest rate. All other estimated closing costs expire on*

Loan Terms

	Can this amount increase after closing?
Loan Amount	
Interest Rate	
Monthly Principal & Interest *See Projected Payments below for your Estimated Total Monthly Payment*	
	Does the loan have these features?
Prepayment Penalty	
Balloon Payment	

Projected Payments

Payment Calculation	
Principal & Interest	
Mortgage Insurance	
Estimated Escrow *Amount can increase over time*	
Estimated Total Monthly Payment	
Estimated Taxes, Insurance & Assessments *Amount can increase over time*	**This estimate includes** **In escrow?** ☐ Property Taxes ☐ Homeowner's Insurance ☐ Other: *See Section G on page 2 for escrowed property costs. You must pay for other property costs separately.*

Costs at Closing

Estimated Closing Costs	Includes in Loan Costs + in Other Costs – in Lender Credits. *See page 2 for details.*
Estimated Cash to Close	Includes Closing Costs. *See Calculating Cash to Close on page 2 for details.*

Visit **www.consumerfinance.gov/mortgage-estimate** for general information and tools.

LOAN ESTIMATE   PAGE 1 OF 3 · LOAN ID #

FIGURE 6.1: Loan Estimate (continued)

Closing Cost Details

Loan Costs

A. Origination Charges

   % of Loan Amount (Points)

B. Services You Cannot Shop For

C. Services You Can Shop For

D. TOTAL LOAN COSTS (A + B + C)

Other Costs

E. Taxes and Other Government Fees

Recording Fees and Other Taxes
Transfer Taxes

F. Prepaids

Homeowner's Insurance Premium (months)
Mortgage Insurance Premium (months)
Prepaid Interest (per day for   days @   )
Property Taxes (months)

G. Initial Escrow Payment at Closing

Homeowner's Insurance	per month for	mo.
Mortgage Insurance	per month for	mo.
Property Taxes	per month for	mo.

H. Other

I. TOTAL OTHER COSTS (E + F + G + H)

J. TOTAL CLOSING COSTS

D + I
Lender Credits

Calculating Cash to Close

Total Closing Costs (J)

Closing Costs Financed (Paid from your Loan Amount)

Down Payment/Funds from Borrower

Deposit

Funds for Borrower

Seller Credits

Adjustments and Other Credits

Estimated Cash to Close

Adjustable Payment (AP) Table

Interest Only Payments?	
Optional Payments?	
Step Payments?	
Seasonal Payments?	
Monthly Principal and Interest Payments	
First Change/Amount	
Subsequent Changes	
Maximum Payment	

Adjustable Interest Rate (AIR) Table

Index + Margin	
Initial Interest Rate	
Minimum/Maximum Interest Rate	
Change Frequency	
First Change	
Subsequent Changes	
Limits on Interest Rate Changes	
First Change	
Subsequent Changes	

FIGURE 6.1: Loan Estimate (continued)

Additional Information About This Loan

LENDER	**MORTGAGE BROKER**
NMLS/___ LICENSE ID	**NMLS/___ LICENSE ID**
LOAN OFFICER	**LOAN OFFICER**
NMLS/___ LICENSE ID	**NMLS/___ LICENSE ID**
EMAIL	**EMAIL**
PHONE	**PHONE**

Comparisons	Use these measures to compare this loan with other loans.
In 5 Years	Total you will have paid in principal, interest, mortgage insurance, and loan costs. Principal you will have paid off.
Annual Percentage Rate (APR)	Your costs over the loan term expressed as a rate. This is not your interest rate.
Total Interest Percentage (TIP)	The total amount of interest that you will pay over the loan term as a percentage of your loan amount.

Other Considerations	
Appraisal	We may order an appraisal to determine the property's value and charge you for this appraisal. We will promptly give you a copy of any appraisal, even if your loan does not close. You can pay for an additional appraisal for your own use at your own cost.
Assumption	If you sell or transfer this property to another person, we ☐ will allow, under certain conditions, this person to assume this loan on the original terms. ☐ will not allow assumption of this loan on the original terms.
Homeowner's Insurance	This loan requires homeowner's insurance on the property, which you may obtain from a company of your choice that we find acceptable.
Late Payment	If your payment is more than ___ days late, we will charge a late fee of _____
Refinance	Refinancing this loan will depend on your future financial situation, the property value, and market conditions. You may not be able to refinance this loan.
Servicing	We intend ☐ to service your loan. If so, you will make your payments to us. ☐ to transfer servicing of your loan.

Confirm Receipt
By signing, you are only confirming that you have received this form. You do not have to accept this loan because you have signed or received this form.

_____   _____   _____   _____
Applicant Signature   Date   Co-Applicant Signature   Date

LOAN ESTIMATE   PAGE 3 OF 3 · LOAN ID #

FIGURE 6.2: Closing Disclosure

Closing Disclosure

This form is a statement of final loan terms and closing costs. Compare this document with your Loan Estimate.

Closing Information		Transaction Information		Loan Information	
Date Issued	4/15/2013	**Borrower**	Michael Jones and Mary Stone	**Loan Term**	30 years
Closing Date	4/15/2013		123 Anywhere Street	**Purpose**	Purchase
Disbursement Date	4/15/2013		Anytown, ST 12345	**Product**	Fixed Rate
Settlement Agent	Epsilon Title Co.	**Seller**	Steve Cole and Amy Doe		
File #	12-3456		321 Somewhere Drive	**Loan Type**	☒ Conventional ☐ FHA
Property	456 Somewhere Ave		Anytown, ST 12345		☐ VA ☐ _____
	Anytown, ST 12345	**Lender**	Ficus Bank	**Loan ID #**	123456789
Sale Price	$180,000			**MIC #**	000654321

Loan Terms

		Can this amount increase after closing?
Loan Amount	$162,000	**NO**
Interest Rate	3.875%	**NO**
Monthly Principal & Interest *See Projected Payments below for your Estimated Total Monthly Payment*	$761.78	**NO**
		Does the loan have these features?
Prepayment Penalty		**YES** • **As high as $3,240** if you pay off the loan during the first 2 years
Balloon Payment		**NO**

Projected Payments

Payment Calculation	Years 1-7		Years 8-30	
Principal & Interest		$761.78		$761.78
Mortgage Insurance	+	82.35	+	—
Estimated Escrow *Amount can increase over time*	+	206.13	+	206.13
Estimated Total **Monthly Payment**	**$1,050.26**		**$967.91**	

Estimated Taxes, Insurance & Assessments *Amount can increase over time* *See page 4 for details*	**$356.13** a month	**This estimate includes** **In escrow?** ☒ Property Taxes **YES** ☒ Homeowner's Insurance **YES** ☒ Other: Homeowner's Association Dues **NO** *See Escrow Account on page 4 for details. You must pay for other property costs separately.*

Costs at Closing

Closing Costs	$9,712.10	Includes $4,694.05 in Loan Costs + $5,018.05 in Other Costs – $0 in Lender Credits. *See page 2 for details.*
Cash to Close	$14,147.26	Includes Closing Costs. *See Calculating Cash to Close on page 3 for details.*

FIGURE 6.2:   Closing Disclosure (continued)

Closing Cost Details

Loan Costs		Borrower-Paid		Seller-Paid		Paid by Others
		At Closing	Before Closing	At Closing	Before Closing	
A. Origination Charges		**$1,802.00**				
01 0.25 % of Loan Amount (Points)		$405.00				
02 Application Fee		$300.00				
03 Underwriting Fee		$1,097.00				
04						
05						
06						
07						
08						
B. Services Borrower Did Not Shop For		**$236.55**				
01 Appraisal Fee	to John Smith Appraisers Inc.					$405.00
02 Credit Report Fee	to Information Inc.		$29.80			
03 Flood Determination Fee	to Info Co.	$20.00				
04 Flood Monitoring Fee	to Info Co.	$31.75				
05 Tax Monitoring Fee	to Info Co.	$75.00				
06 Tax Status Research Fee	to Info Co.	$80.00				
07						
08						
09						
10						
C. Services Borrower Did Shop For		**$2,655.50**				
01 Pest Inspection Fee	to Pests Co.	$120.50				
02 Survey Fee	to Surveys Co.	$85.00				
03 Title – Insurance Binder	to Epsilon Title Co.	$650.00				
04 Title – Lender's Title Insurance	to Epsilon Title Co.	$500.00				
05 Title – Settlement Agent Fee	to Epsilon Title Co.	$500.00				
06 Title – Title Search	to Epsilon Title Co.	$800.00				
07						
08						
D. TOTAL LOAN COSTS (Borrower-Paid)		**$4,694.05**				
Loan Costs Subtotals (A + B + C)		$4,664.25	$29.80			

Other Costs						
E. Taxes and Other Government Fees		**$85.00**				
01 Recording Fees	Deed: $40.00 Mortgage: $45.00	$85.00				
02 Transfer Tax	to Any State			$950.00		
F. Prepaids		**$2,120.80**				
01 Homeowner's Insurance Premium (12 mo.) to Insurance Co.		$1,209.96				
02 Mortgage Insurance Premium (mo.)						
03 Prepaid Interest ($17.44 per day from 4/15/13 to 5/1/13)		$279.04				
04 Property Taxes (6 mo.) to Any County USA		$631.80				
05						
G. Initial Escrow Payment at Closing		**$412.25**				
01 Homeowner's Insurance $100.83 per month for 2 mo.		$201.66				
02 Mortgage Insurance per month for mo.						
03 Property Taxes $105.30 per month for 2 mo.		$210.60				
04						
05						
06						
07						
08 Aggregate Adjustment		– 0.01				
H. Other		**$2,400.00**				
01 HOA Capital Contribution	to HOA Acre Inc.	$500.00				
02 HOA Processing Fee	to HOA Acre Inc.	$150.00				
03 Home Inspection Fee	to Engineers Inc.	$750.00			$750.00	
04 Home Warranty Fee	to XYZ Warranty Inc.			$450.00		
05 Real Estate Commission	to Alpha Real Estate Broker			$5,700.00		
06 Real Estate Commission	to Omega Real Estate Broker			$5,700.00		
07 Title – Owner's Title Insurance (optional) to Epsilon Title Co.		$1,000.00				
08						
I. TOTAL OTHER COSTS (Borrower-Paid)		**$5,018.05**				
Other Costs Subtotals (E + F + G + H)		$5,018.05				

J. TOTAL CLOSING COSTS (Borrower-Paid)		**$9,712.10**				
Closing Costs Subtotals (D + I)		$9,682.30	$29.80	$12,800.00	$750.00	$405.00
Lender Credits						

CLOSING DISCLOSURE

FIGURE 6.2:   Closing Disclosure (continued)

Calculating Cash to Close

Use this table to see what has changed from your Loan Estimate.

	Loan Estimate	Final	Did this change?
Total Closing Costs (J)	$8,054.00	$9,712.10	**YES** • See **Total Loan Costs (D)** and **Total Other Costs (I)**
Closing Costs Paid Before Closing	$0	− $29.80	**YES** • You paid these Closing Costs **before closing**
Closing Costs Financed (Paid from your Loan Amount)	$0	$0	**NO**
Down Payment/Funds from Borrower	$18,000.00	$18,000.00	**NO**
Deposit	− $10,000.00	− $10,000.00	**NO**
Funds for Borrower	$0	$0	**NO**
Seller Credits	$0	− $2,500.00	**YES** • See Seller Credits in **Section L**
Adjustments and Other Credits	$0	− $1,035.04	**YES** • See details in **Sections K and L**
Cash to Close	$16,054.00	$14,147.26	

Summaries of Transactions

Use this table to see a summary of your transaction.

BORROWER'S TRANSACTION

K. Due from Borrower at Closing	$189,762.30
01 Sale Price of Property	$180,000.00
02 Sale Price of Any Personal Property Included in Sale	
03 Closing Costs Paid at Closing (J)	$9,682.30
04	
Adjustments	
05	
06	
07	

Adjustments for Items Paid by Seller in Advance

08	City/Town Taxes	to	
09	County Taxes	to	
10	Assessments	to	
11	HOA Dues	4/15/13 to 4/30/13	$80.00
12			
13			
14			
15			

L. Paid Already by or on Behalf of Borrower at Closing	$175,615.04
01 Deposit	$10,000.00
02 Loan Amount	$162,000.00
03 Existing Loan(s) Assumed or Taken Subject to	
04	
05 Seller Credit	$2,500.00
Other Credits	
06 Rebate from Epsilon Title Co.	$750.00
07	
Adjustments	
08	
09	
10	
11	

Adjustments for Items Unpaid by Seller

12	City/Town Taxes	1/1/13 to 4/14/13	$365.04
13	County Taxes	to	
14	Assessments	to	
15			
16			
17			

CALCULATION

Total Due from Borrower at Closing (K)	$189,762.30
Total Paid Already by or on Behalf of Borrower at Closing (L)	− $175,615.04
Cash to Close ☒ **From** ☐ **To Borrower**	**$14,147.26**

SELLER'S TRANSACTION

M. Due to Seller at Closing	$180,080.00
01 Sale Price of Property	$180,000.00
02 Sale Price of Any Personal Property Included in Sale	
03	
04	
05	
06	
07	
08	

Adjustments for Items Paid by Seller in Advance

09	City/Town Taxes	to	
10	County Taxes	to	
11	Assessments	to	
12	HOA Dues	4/15/13 to 4/30/13	$80.00
13			
14			
15			
16			

N. Due from Seller at Closing	$115,665.04
01 Excess Deposit	
02 Closing Costs Paid at Closing (J)	$12,800.00
03 Existing Loan(s) Assumed or Taken Subject to	
04 Payoff of First Mortgage Loan	$100,000.00
05 Payoff of Second Mortgage Loan	
06	
07	
08 Seller Credit	$2,500.00
09	
10	
11	
12	
13	

Adjustments for Items Unpaid by Seller

14	City/Town Taxes	1/1/13 to 4/14/13	$365.04
15	County Taxes	to	
16	Assessments	to	
17			
18			
19			

CALCULATION

Total Due to Seller at Closing (M)	$180,080.00
Total Due from Seller at Closing (N)	− $115,665.04
Cash ☐ **From** ☒ **To Seller**	**$64,414.96**

FIGURE 6.2:   Closing Disclosure (continued)

Additional Information About This Loan

Loan Disclosures

Assumption
If you sell or transfer this property to another person, your lender
☐ will allow, under certain conditions, this person to assume this loan on the original terms.
☒ will not allow assumption of this loan on the original terms.

Demand Feature
Your loan
☐ has a demand feature, which permits your lender to require early repayment of the loan. You should review your note for details.
☒ does not have a demand feature.

Late Payment
If your payment is more than *15* days late, your lender will charge a late fee of *5% of the monthly principal and interest payment.*

Negative Amortization (Increase in Loan Amount)
Under your loan terms, you
☐ are scheduled to make monthly payments that do not pay all of the interest due that month. As a result, your loan amount will increase (negatively amortize), and your loan amount will likely become larger than your original loan amount. Increases in your loan amount lower the equity you have in this property.
☐ may have monthly payments that do not pay all of the interest due that month. If you do, your loan amount will increase (negatively amortize), and, as a result, your loan amount may become larger than your original loan amount. Increases in your loan amount lower the equity you have in this property.
☒ do not have a negative amortization feature.

Partial Payments
Your lender
☒ may accept payments that are less than the full amount due (partial payments) and apply them to your loan.
☐ may hold them in a separate account until you pay the rest of the payment, and then apply the full payment to your loan.
☐ does not accept any partial payments.
If this loan is sold, your new lender may have a different policy.

Security Interest
You are granting a security interest in
456 Somewhere Ave., Anytown, ST 12345

You may lose this property if you do not make your payments or satisfy other obligations for this loan.

Escrow Account
For now, your loan
☒ will have an escrow account (also called an "impound" or "trust" account) to pay the property costs listed below. Without an escrow account, you would pay them directly, possibly in one or two large payments a year. Your lender may be liable for penalties and interest for failing to make a payment.

Escrow		
Escrowed Property Costs over Year 1	$2,473.56	Estimated total amount over year 1 for your escrowed property costs: *Homeowner's Insurance Property Taxes*
Non-Escrowed Property Costs over Year 1	$1,800.00	Estimated total amount over year 1 for your non-escrowed property costs: *Homeowner's Association Dues* You may have other property costs.
Initial Escrow Payment	$412.25	A cushion for the escrow account you pay at closing. See Section G on page 2.
Monthly Escrow Payment	$206.13	The amount included in your total monthly payment.

☐ will not have an escrow account because ☐ you declined it ☐ your lender does not offer one. You must directly pay your property costs, such as taxes and homeowner's insurance. Contact your lender to ask if your loan can have an escrow account.

No Escrow		
Estimated Property Costs over Year 1		Estimated total amount over year 1. You must pay these costs directly, possibly in one or two large payments a year.
Escrow Waiver Fee		

In the future,
Your property costs may change and, as a result, your escrow payment may change. You may be able to cancel your escrow account, but if you do, you must pay your property costs directly. If you fail to pay your property taxes, your state or local government may (1) impose fines and penalties or (2) place a tax lien on this property. If you fail to pay any of your property costs, your lender may (1) add the amounts to your loan balance, (2) add an escrow account to your loan, or (3) require you to pay for property insurance that the lender buys on your behalf, which likely would cost more and provide fewer benefits than what you could buy on your own.

FIGURE 6.2: Closing Disclosure (continued)

Loan Calculations

Total of Payments. Total you will have paid after you make all payments of principal, interest, mortgage insurance, and loan costs, as scheduled.	$285,803.36
Finance Charge. The dollar amount the loan will cost you.	$118,830.27
Amount Financed. The loan amount available after paying your upfront finance charge.	$162,000.00
Annual Percentage Rate (APR). Your costs over the loan term expressed as a rate. This is not your interest rate.	4.174%
Total Interest Percentage (TIP). The total amount of interest that you will pay over the loan term as a percentage of your loan amount.	69.46%

Questions? If you have questions about the loan terms or costs on this form, use the contact information below. To get more information or make a complaint, contact the Consumer Financial Protection Bureau at **www.consumerfinance.gov/mortgage-closing**

Other Disclosures

Appraisal
If the property was appraised for your loan, your lender is required to give you a copy at no additional cost at least 3 days before closing. If you have not yet received it, please contact your lender at the information listed below.

Contract Details
See your note and security instrument for information about
- what happens if you fail to make your payments,
- what is a default on the loan,
- situations in which your lender can require early repayment of the loan, and
- the rules for making payments before they are due.

Liability after Foreclosure
If your lender forecloses on this property and the foreclosure does not cover the amount of unpaid balance on this loan,
☒ state law may protect you from liability for the unpaid balance. If you refinance or take on any additional debt on this property, you may lose this protection and have to pay any debt remaining even after foreclosure. You may want to consult a lawyer for more information.
☐ state law does not protect you from liability for the unpaid balance.

Refinance
Refinancing this loan will depend on your future financial situation, the property value, and market conditions. You may not be able to refinance this loan.

Tax Deductions
If you borrow more than this property is worth, the interest on the loan amount above this property's fair market value is not deductible from your federal income taxes. You should consult a tax advisor for more information.

Contact Information

	Lender	Mortgage Broker	Real Estate Broker (B)	Real Estate Broker (S)	Settlement Agent
Name	Ficus Bank		Omega Real Estate Broker Inc.	Alpha Real Estate Broker Co.	Epsilon Title Co.
Address	4321 Random Blvd. Somecity, ST 12340		789 Local Lane Sometown, ST 12345	987 Suburb Ct. Someplace, ST 12340	123 Commerce Pl. Somecity, ST 12344
NMLS ID					
ST License ID			Z765416	Z61456	Z61616
Contact	Joe Smith		Samuel Green	Joseph Cain	Sarah Arnold
Contact NMLS ID	12345				
Contact ST License ID			P16415	P51461	PT1234
Email	joesmith@ficusbank.com		sam@omegare.biz	joe@alphare.biz	sarah@epsilontitle.com
Phone	123-456-7890		123-555-1717	321-555-7171	987-555-4321

Confirm Receipt

By signing, you are only confirming that you have received this form. You do not have to accept this loan because you have signed or received this form.

_____ _____   _____ _____
Applicant Signature　　　Date　　　Co-Applicant Signature　　　Date

PURCHASE-MONEY FINANCING AND SELLER FINANCING

Purchase-money financing occurs when a mortgage or deed of trust is given as part of the purchaser's consideration for the purchase of real property. Purchase-money financing may be provided by a third party, such as an institutional lender or the seller. When provided by the seller, it commonly refers to a seller taking back a second trust in lieu of cash to make up the difference between the first trust from the institutional lender and the selling price for the property.

"owner- financing"

EXAMPLE

A seller wants $100,000 for his property. The purchasers are able to secure a $70,000 loan secured by a first deed of trust from an institutional lender. Because they have only $10,000 in cash available for a down payment, they ask the seller to accept a purchase-money deed of trust (seller financing) for $20,000. The rate and terms must be agreed on between the seller and the purchasers.

A purchase-money deed of trust has priority over other claims or liens against the purchaser except for property tax or IRS tax liens.

Purchase $ Deed ↑ priority but not over taxes

Deferred Purchase-Money Deed of Trust

Sellers with no immediate need for cash from the proceeds of a sale may choose to defer the income of the sale and obtain an installment tax treatment by creating an annuity in the form of a **deferred purchase money** deed of trust, held by the seller. One advantage to sellers is that they usually receive a substantial down payment. Such an arrangement may be prohibited, however, if there is to be a first deed of trust to an outside (institutional) lender. A purchase-money deed of trust held by the seller should state that it is granted to secure deferred purchase money, while a purchase-money deed of trust to a third (institutional lender) party states that it is granted to secure purchase money. If it is a second deed of trust, it can be for a short term with a balloon payment at the end. The first lender's guidelines must be followed. If it is subordinated, the purchase-money second deed of trust should include a provision that any default in a senior encumbrance or lien will also be considered a default on a second deed of trust.

EXAMPLE

A seller wants $400,000 for her property but does not want to take the proceeds of the sale in one tax year. She offers to take back financing in the form of a deferred purchase-money deed of trust. She will accept a $20,000 down payment from the purchasers and hold a note for $380,000 that balloons in 10 years. The rate and terms must be agreed on between the seller and the purchasers.

HELOCs OR CREDIT LINE DEEDS OF TRUST

Sometimes called credit line deeds of trust, a **home equity line of credit** (HELOC) permits the note holder to make advances from time to time secured by the real estate described in the deed. Most HELOCs are second trusts and are sometimes made at the same time as the first trust with the same lender. The total amount of advances may not exceed the maximum credit line extended to the borrower. Virginia law permits credit line deeds of trust, subject to certain rules. The trust document must identify itself as a credit line deed of trust on the front page in capital letters and underscored type. The phrase, "this is a credit line deed of

Must be paid off

trust," gives notice that the note holder named in the deed of trust and the **grantors** and other borrowers identified in the deed have an agreement.

From the date of the recording of a credit line deed of trust, the lien has priority over all other deeds, conveyances, and other instruments or contracts in writing that are unrecorded at that time and of which the note holder has no knowledge. The credit line deed of trust also has priority over judgment liens subsequently docketed. However, if a judgment creditor gives notice to the note holder at the address indicated on the credit line deed of trust, the deed of trust has no priority over the judgment for any advances or extensions of credit subsequently made under the deed of trust.

Usury

Usury is the loan of money at a greater rate of interest than allowed by law. Virginia law provides that loans secured by a first deed of trust on real estate may be lawfully enforced with no limitation on the amount of interest, if that arrangement is properly stated in the instrument or separate agreement. The contract generally is considered to be the promissory note. Most prudent lenders insert the rate in the note.

The law provides that disclosure of charges may be contained in an interest disclosure statement if such disclosure is not otherwise specified in the note. It further provides that an interest rate that varies in accordance with any exterior standard or that cannot be ascertained from the contract without reference to exterior circumstances or documents is enforceable as agreed in the signed contract. For example, a note providing for an interest rate of 3% above the stated prime rate of a specific bank is enforceable.

Allowable Interest Rates

When the seller in a bona fide real estate transaction takes back a purchase-money deed of trust, the promissory note may provide for any rate of interest agreed to by the parties. Usury is not applicable to such a transaction because the interest rate is considered a part of the purchase price.

FORECLOSURE IN VIRGINIA

There are three ways to foreclose a deed of trust in Virginia:

- Decree of court (strict foreclosure)
- Conveyance of the property by the grantors and the trustees to the beneficiary in consideration of the debt (deed in lieu of foreclosure)
- Sale by the trustee pursuant to a power of sale (trustee sale—most common)

Although an exhaustive discussion of foreclosure procedures is not included here, it is important for licensees to be aware that bankruptcy of the mortgagor is an automatic stay of foreclosure. If a lien is foreclosed, that is, no bankruptcy was granted, the lien and all inferior liens are wiped out. Superior liens, however—those that have priority over the foreclosed lien—are not affected. A purchaser takes the property subject to any prior liens.

Foreclosure of VA and FHA loans is subject to certain additional requirements. For example, the loan must have been in default for three months before the commencement of foreclosure; notices must be given to both the debtor and the insuring agency; and the lender must take affirmative steps to avoid foreclosure, including personal interviews and acceptance of partial payments.

Trustee's Powers and Duties

Virginia is a **title theory** state. Legal title to the property conveyed by the deed of trust is vested in the trustee for the benefit of the note holder. The trustee can act only in a manner authorized by statute or the express or implied terms of the trust.

The trustee is the agent for both the grantor (the homeowner) and the beneficiary (the lender) and is bound to act impartially between them. The trustee is obliged to seek every possible advantage to the trust in the course of any sale. This includes using all reasonable diligence to obtain the best price possible. The trustee may adjourn the sale from time to time to meet any unexpected occurrences, but the re-advertisement of the sale must be in the same manner as the original advertisement.

The terms of the deed of trust will determine how the property is advertised. Even if the number of advertisements meets the terms, Virginia law provides that the sale may take place no earlier than the eighth day after the first advertisement and no later than 30 days after the last advertisement.

If it is clear at the sale that the property will be sold for a grossly inadequate or sacrificial price, it is the trustee's duty to adjourn the sale. In addition, if the trustee knows of facts that might keep bidding low, such as a cloud on title, he must adjourn the sale and remove the hindrance.

By statute, the trustee must ascertain whether there are any real estate tax liens against the property being sold. The trustee is obligated to pay the taxes out of the proceeds of sale and give the tax lien priority over the deed of trust. In addition, the purchaser must see that the taxes are paid. If the taxes are not paid, the trustee may be liable personally and the purchaser takes the land subject to the tax lien (though not personally liable for its payment). The trustee should also pay the prorated portion of the current year's real estate taxes.

Potential Conflict of Interest

A trustee may not purchase the property held in trust without written permission from the trustor. The trustee is bound by law to secure the highest possible price for the property, while a purchaser seeks to procure the property at the lowest possible price. The trustee's duty to the trust transcends any potential personal interest the trustee may have or acquire in the property.

The sale must be held in accordance with the terms of the deed of trust, which specifies the time, manner, and place of sale. Unless the deed of trust states otherwise, the sale is held at the property itself, near the circuit court building, or at some other place selected by the trustee in the city or county in which the property is located.

At the sale, the trustee sells the property to the highest bidder, and the successful purchaser executes a memorandum of sale. The trustee obtains the deposit from the purchaser.

The trustee cannot convey a greater interest than the deed of trust gives authority to sell. The sale is subject to encumbrances that have priority over the deed of trust. Accordingly, the trustee's deed should contain only a special warranty of title. However, the form of the deed and the title conveyed must conform to the manner in which the property was advertised.

Disbursement of Proceeds

The trustee must apply the proceeds of sale in the following order:

- Fees

Taxes + levies

Remaining liens

left over to grantor

1. Discharge the expenses of executing the trust, including a commission to the trustee of 5% of the gross proceeds

2. Discharge all taxes, levies, and assessments with costs and interest, if they have priority over the deed of trust

3. Discharge, in the order of their priority, any remaining debts and obligations secured by the deed of trust and any liens of record inferior to the deed of trust, with interest

4. Render the residue of the proceeds to the grantor (foreclosed mortgagor) or his assigns

When the sale is made under any recorded deed of trust, the trustee must file a report and accounting with the commissioner of accounts within four months of the sale.

Short Sales

In an effort to avoid foreclosure, some homeowners are able to reach an agreement with their mortgage loan lender to accept a **short sale**, an amount that is less than what is actually due on the mortgage loan. The federal government has prepared standardized rules and forms for short sales. At the present time, the borrower has no tax liability for the amount of debt forgiven, based on the Mortgage Debt Relief Act.

Fannie Mae and Freddie Mac issued guidelines to enhance and streamline the short sale process. Hardship eligibility has been increased and improvements have been made to the valuation process. Many homeowners who were delinquent in their mortgage payments found it beneficial to participate in a short sale. Initially, lenders were reluctant to accept less than the amount actually due on the mortgage note, but eventually came to realize that their loss could be less with a short sale than if they proceeded with an actual foreclosure.

IN PRACTICE

The REB advises licensees who perform or intend to perform transactions involving foreclosures or short sales to complete adequate training before offering their service to the public.

The rule of caveat emptor (let the buyer beware) applies in foreclosure sales, with regard to both the quality of title and the condition of the property.

Loan Modification Programs

Since 2008, the government has taken steps to help at-risk homeowners avoid foreclosure. The Home Affordable Modification Program (HAMP) was created in March 2009 as part of the Making Home Affordable initiative. All lenders participating in the government's program agreed to follow very specific procedures and formulas. The HAMP program gave some homeowners an opportunity to modify or refinance their mortgage in order to make the monthly payments affordable and avoid foreclosure. The HAMP program was discontinued in December of 2016. The companion program, Home Affordable Refinance Program (HARP) remains in place until September, 2017. More information is available on the Making Home Affordable website, www.mha.gov.

HARP made refinancing available for many homeowners regardless of hardship conditions.

SUMMARY

In Virginia, a deed of trust, rather than a mortgage, is the instrument used to establish collateral in a residential sales transaction. Three parties are involved in a deed of trust: the borrower, the lender (beneficiary), and a trustee (a neutral third party) who holds the deed of trust for both the borrower and the lender. By signing the note and deed of trust, the borrower waives the right to a court hearing in case of foreclosure. The note and deed of trust are generally prepared by the lender.

Loans that contain a due-on-sale clause are generally not assumable. In addition to such charges as points, late charges, and escrows, Virginia law permits lenders to charge a loan origination fee. Late charges may not exceed 5% of the payment due. Other allowable closing costs are the fees charged for title examination, title insurance, recording charges, taxes, hazard insurance, mortgage guarantee insurance, appraisals, credit reports, surveys, document preparation, real estate tax service fees, lender inspection, and attorney or settlement agent charges for closing the loan and settlement on the property. Lenders may require flood insurance coverage for any property located in a FEMA designated flood hazard area. These fees are collected at closing.

Home loans fall in two categories: conforming to Fannie Mae and Freddie Mac guidelines and non-conforming in which guidelines are set by the lender. Fannie Mae and Freddie Mac are regulated by the FHFA. The FHFA sets the conforming loan limits. Many Virginians obtain FHA-insured mortgage loans for either first-time or subsequent purchases of a home. Both current loan limits (based on geographic area) and FHA MIPs are subject to frequent change. The VA guarantees loans for eligible active-duty military and veterans, including an ARM.

The CFPB issues regulations to protect consumers. New rules for mortgage servicers went into effect in January of 2014 and were further updated in 2016. After three years of deliberations, the six regulators finalized the QRM rule in October, 2014, aligning the QRM with the Qualified Mortgage standard already in place. The earlier QRM proposal that would have required a 20% down payment was dropped. After much research and study, the CFPB released the TRID effective October 3, 2015. The new LE replaced the initial TILA statement and the GFE. The new CD replaced the final TILA statement and the HUD-1 Settlement Statement.

The VHDA was created in 1972 by the Virginia General Assembly to make housing more affordable for those with low or moderate incomes. VHDA is self-supporting through the sale of VHDA bonds. VHDA also administers the Virginia Housing Trust Fund.

Purchase-money financing provided by the seller commonly refers to a seller taking back a second trust to make up the difference between the first trust from the institutional lender and the selling price of the property. A purchase-money deed of trust has priority over other claims or liens against the purchaser except for property taxes or IRS tax liens. Sometimes called *credit line deeds of trust*, a HELOC permits the note holder to make advances from time to time secured by the real estate described in the deed. The usury law does not apply to home loans as long as the interest rate is stated in the agreement.

There are three ways to foreclose a deed of trust in Virginia:

- Decree of court (strict foreclosure)
- Conveyance of the property by the grantors and the trustees to the beneficiary in consideration of the debt (deed in lieu of foreclosure)
- Sale by the trustee pursuant to a power of sale (trustee sale- this is the most common.)

Virginia is a title theory state. Legal title to the property is conveyed by the deed of trust to the trustee for the benefit of the lender. The trustee is the agent for both the grantor (the homeowner) and the beneficiary (the lender) and is bound to act impartially between them. The trustee must apply the proceeds of sale in the following order:

1. Discharge the expenses of executing the trust, including the trustee commission

2. Discharge all taxes, levies, and assessments with costs and interest

3. Discharge, in the order of their priority, any remaining debts and obligations or liens of record

4. Render the residue of the proceeds to the grantor (foreclosed mortgagor) or his assigns

In an effort to avoid foreclosure, some homeowners are able to reach an agreement with their lender to accept a short sale, an amount that is less than what is actually due on the mortgage loan. At the present time, the borrower has no tax liability for the amount of debt forgiven, based on the Mortgage Debt Relief Act.

The government's HAMP was discontinued in December of 2016. The companion program, HARP remains in place until September, 2017.

UNIT 6 QUIZ

1. When borrowers sign a note and deed of trust, they are giving the lender the right to
   A. request a court hearing within 30 days of default.
   B. set the time and place of the court hearing.
   C. initiate a nonjudicial foreclosure.
   D. initiate a judicial foreclosure.

2. What is the maximum late charge that may be assessed on a mortgage loan payment in Virginia?
   A. No limit if the charge is stated in the loan contract
   B. 5%
   C. 10%
   D. 15%

3. The responsibility for preparing the note and deed of trust involved in a closing belongs to
   A. the seller's broker.
   B. the lender.
   C. the buyer.
   D. the settlement attorney.

4. FHA and VA loans are classified as
   A. conventional conforming loans.
   B. conventional non-conforming loans.
   C. government loans.
   D. specialized loans.

5. Fannie Mae and Freddie Mac were independent agencies referred to as government-sponsored enterprises (GSEs). In 2008, they were both placed under the regulation of
   A. the FHA.
   B. the FHFA.
   C. Congress.
   D. the HUD.

6. Which of the following statements with regard to FHA MIPs is _NOT_ true?
   A. FHA MIPs are subject to frequent changes.
   B. As of January 1, 2017, the upfront MIP is 1.75% of the loan amount.
   C. The upfront MIP is amortized over the life of the loan.
   D. The annual MIP is amortized over the life of the loan.

7. The CFPB was created to
   A. protect the financial interests of the consumer.
   B. regulate the FHA.
   C. oversee Fannie Mae and Freddie Mac.
   D. administer the Virginia Housing Trust Fund.

8. The new rules for mortgage servicers established by the CFPB include all of the following _EXCEPT_
   A. provide two month's warning for any rate increase.
   B. promptly credit mortgage payments.
   C. work with the borrower before starting foreclosure proceedings.
   D. allow a six month's moratorium for delinquent loans.

9. All of the following statements with regard to the Qualified Residential Mortgage (QRM) are true _EXCEPT_
   A. The QRM is now aligned with the Qualified Mortgage standard implemented in 2014.
   B. The QRM requires a down payment of 20% of the sales price.
   C. A QRM loan is qualified if the borrower's debt-to-income ratio is not more than 43%.
   D. The lender is no longer required to retain 5% of the loan amount.

10. The TILA-RESPA Integrated Disclosures (TRID) that was made mandatory on October 3, 2015 includes the new form called the Loan Estimate (LE) which replaced
    A. the GFE.
    B. the Truth in Lending statement.
    C. the HUD-1 Settlement Statement.
    D. both the GFE and the initial Truth in Lending statement

11. The primary purpose of the Virginia Housing Development Authority (VHDA) is to
    A. encourage more housing development in Virginia.
    B. make housing more affordable for low-income and moderate-income buyers.
    C. obtain funds from state tax dollars.
    D. replace VA and FHA funding in Virginia.

12. The VHDA is funded by
    A. HUD.
    B. Virginia income tax.
    C. sale of bonds in the private sector.
    D. federal subsidy programs.

13. In addition to providing loans for affordable housing, VHDA also builds and operates all of the following *EXCEPT*
    A. schools.
    B. nursing care facilities.
    C. nursing homes providing medical facilities for the elderly.
    D. residential housing for the elderly.

14. Basic VHDA services include all of the following *EXCEPT*
    A. administration of the federal Section 8 rent subsidy program.
    B. administration of the Virginia Residential Landlord and Tenant Act.
    C. Virginia Housing Fund loans.
    D. administration of some functions of the Virginia Housing Partnership Fund.

15. Who or what is paid first from a sale at foreclosure?
    A. The expenses of executing the trust, including 5% commission to the trustee
    B. All taxes, levies, and assessments with costs and interest, if they have priority over the deed of trust
    C. Any remaining debts and obligations secured by the deed of trust
    D. The foreclosed mortgagor

16. A deed of trust can be foreclosed on in Virginia in any of the ways listed *EXCEPT*
    A. decree of court (strict foreclosure).
    B. deed in lieu of foreclosure.
    C. sale by a trustee under the power of sale.
    D. bankruptcy.

17. The trustee's responsibilities include all of the following *EXCEPT*
    A. purchase the property.
    B. act as agent for both grantor (homeowner) and beneficiary (lender).
    C. adjourn the sale if property will be sold at an inadequate price.
    D. determine if there are any real estate taxes due.

18. Which of the following statement regarding a short sale is *TRUE*?
    A. A short sale is one that goes to settlement in less than two weeks.
    B. A short sale is one where the lender agrees to accept less than the full amount due.
    C. A short sale is a non-conforming conventional loan.
    D. A short sale always results in a tax liability for the seller.

UNIT 7

Transfer of Title

LEARNING OBJECTIVES

When you have completed this unit, you will be able to

> **describe** the requirements for a valid conveyance of title;
> **explain** transfer of title by adverse possession and by will;
> **review** the responsibilities of a settlement agent;
> **define** title examination and title insurance and the procedures involved; and
> **define** the following key terms:

adverse possession	judgment	testator
chain of title	nuncupative will	title examination
cloud on the title	recordation tax	title insurance
grantor tax	settlement agent	will
holographic will	specific power of attorney	

OVERVIEW

This unit covers the requirements for a valid deed in Virginia, including who may execute the deed, as well as the attendant transfer taxes and fees, last wills and testaments, real estate settlement agents, titles and title examinations, and the specific laws pertaining to such matters.

REQUIREMENTS FOR A VALID CONVEYANCE

In Virginia, the requirements for a valid deed are as follows:

- Grantor who has the legal capacity to execute the deed
- Grantee
- Consideration
- Granting clause

- Accurate legal description of the property
- Any relevant exceptions or reservations
- Signature of the grantor, sometimes with acknowledgment
- Delivery and acceptance of the deed

Virginia law allows the same person to be both the grantor and grantee in a deed.

 EXAMPLE

An individual can convey the deed to his farm to himself and his granddaughter.

The grantee named to receive a deed to real property should be legally competent to receive the property. The grantee's full name should be used in preparing the deed. A deed to a nonexistent person is a valid conveyance to the intended but misnamed grantee if the intended grantee exists and the intention of the parties can be determined.

The grantor is presumed to have been competent at the time a deed was executed. The test of legal capacity is the party's mental ability to understand the nature and consequences of the transaction at the time it is entered into. The burden of proving incompetence is on the party who attacks the validity of the deed.

In Virginia, a conveyance of land by a minor is a valid transfer of title, unless it is repudiated by the minor after attaining majority. Repudiation may occur even though the grantee has already conveyed the property to another purchaser without notice that a minor was the grantor in the previous transaction.

Power of Attorney

If a seller or buyer is unable to attend the closing, there are two options:

- Prepare all papers to be signed in advance of the closing
- Use a power of attorney

A power of attorney must be signed by the seller with the same formalities as a deed. Although a power of attorney can be general or specific, a **specific power of attorney** is strongly recommended to convey real property in Virginia. In reviewing a power of attorney, the licensee should have a lawyer verify that it specifically authorizes performance of all necessary acts and that the attorney-in-fact performs in accordance with the authority granted in the power of attorney.

Affidavits and other sworn statements cannot be signed by the attorney-in-fact. These must be signed by the principal before the closing. The deed or other instrument to be signed must indicate that it is being signed by an attorney-in-fact. Normally, this is accomplished by a recital in the body of the instrument or under the signature line.

If an institutional lender is making a new loan, the lender's permission should be obtained for a borrower to execute a power of attorney. The lender may not allow the use of an attorney-in-fact, especially if the loan is subject to truth-in-lending requirements.

A power of attorney must be recorded, and the recording fees are charged to the party using the attorney-in-fact. If the power of attorney is not recorded, it is as though the deed were unsigned by the party being represented by the attorney-in-fact.

TRANSFER TAXES AND FEES

Chapter 8 of Title 58.1—Taxation, of the Code of Virginia, sets the tax on the transfer of property as levied on the seller and the purchaser individually. The seller pays a **grantor tax** and the purchaser pays a **recordation tax**. In some adjoining jurisdictions, the transaction is taxed as a whole and the tax liability is shared in some formula agreed on by the seller and the purchaser.

With certain exceptions, all deeds are subject to state and city or county recordation tax. The state recordation tax is currently $0.25 per $100 (or a fraction of $100) of the consideration paid or the value of the property, whichever is greater. A more direct mathematical representation is 0.0025 × the sales price. The county or city may charge up to one-third of that amount, which in the case of Fairfax County, for example, is an additional 0.0008 × the sales price. County/city tax rates may differ.

Recordation taxes are usually paid by the buyer and collected at closing. Payment of these taxes is a prerequisite to having the deed recorded. There is also a transfer fee of $1.00 charged.

IN PRACTICE

The state recordation tax is $0.25 per $100, or $0.0025 per $1. If the sales price of a home is $475,000, then the state recordation tax is $475,000 × 0.0025 = $1,187.50. For Fairfax County, the recordation tax is $475,000 × 0.0008 = $380. Recording fees are subject to change. Licensees should always be aware of the most current tax rates and fees.

In addition to the recordation taxes, all deeds are subject to a grantor's tax of $0.50 per $500 (or a fraction of $500) of the purchase price or the value of the grantor's equity in the property being transferred, in the case of assumption. (In many areas of Virginia, the rate is quoted as $1 per $1,000.) The grantor's tax is paid by the seller and is collected at closing and paid to the clerk of the county where the deed is recorded.

Congestion Relief Fee

As of July 1, 2013, a regional congestion relief fee is imposed on the recording of any deed or instrument conveying real property that is located in the Northern Virginia Region. The fee is paid by the seller (grantor) at the rate of $0.15 per $100 (or fraction thereof). Localities affected are the cities of Alexandria, Fairfax, Falls Church, Manassas, and Manassas Park, and the counties of Arlington, Fairfax, Loudoun, and Prince William.

C A L C U L A T E Calculating Virginia Transfer Taxes

A home is purchased in Fairfax County for $675,600. The state recordation tax rate is $0.25 and the Fairfax County tax rate is $0.08.

1. State and County or City Recordation Tax

$675,600 ÷ 100 = 6,756 recordation tax units

Purchaser will pay $1,689.00 in state recordation taxes (6,756 × $0.25 = $1,689.00) and $540.48 in county or city recordation tax (6,756 × $0.08 = $540.48)

2. Grantor Tax

$675,600 ÷ 500 = 1,351.2 grantor tax units

Round up to 1,352 grantor tax units

Seller's grantor tax is 1,352 grantor tax units × $0.50 = $676.00

Taxes and Fees on Mortgage Documents

Unless exempt, deeds of trust and mortgages are taxed on a sliding scale according to the amount of the obligation (i.e., the debt) that the instrument secures. If the amount is not ascertainable, the tax is based on the fair market value of the property, including the value of any improvements as of the date of the deed. Deeds of trust are also subject to city or county recordation taxes, clerk's fees, and any plat recordation fees. Deeds of trust that secure both construction loans and permanent loans are normally subject to tax.

For each document admitted to record, the clerk of court collects a transfer fee that is generally paid by the buyer. In addition to the transfer fee, the clerk of court collects a clerk fee for recording plats, powers of attorney, certificates of satisfaction, and release of **judgments**. The amount of the fee is usually based on the number of pages that must be recorded.

The buyer generally pays the fees to record the new items, and the seller pays for the release of the old items. The payment of fees may be negotiated between the parties.

ADVERSE POSSESSION

Establishing title to land by **adverse possession** is somewhat similar to an easement by prescription, which is described earlier in Unit 3.

To establish title to land by adverse possession in Virginia, it is necessary to show actual, hostile, exclusive, visible, and continuous possession of property for the statutory period of 15 years. The possession by the defendant must be actual and continuous; that is, more than just a sporadic taking of timber or occasional camping is required. The adverse possession must be exclusive to constitute an ousting of the true owner.

When several persons enter upon land in succession, these possessions cannot be tacked to preserve the essential continuity unless there is a privity of estate between them. In other words, the intent to establish a continuous succession of adverse possessors must be proven.

Adverse possession cannot be claimed if the possession has been abandoned by the claimant during the required time period. The occupancy necessary to support a claim of title of adverse possession must be hostile and without the true owner's permission.

TRANSFER OF DECEASED PERSON'S PROPERTY

When any person with title to real estate that may be inherited dies testate, that is, having executed a legal **will**, the real estate will pass according to the terms of the instrument.

In Virginia, circuit courts serve as probate courts. Normally there is a probate section in the clerk's office where wills, lists of heirs, affidavits, and other documents related to probate are located. A probate tax is charged on all estates exceeding $15,000 in value. As with other documents, a will index is located in the circuit courts.

IN PRACTICE

When listing a property that is part of a decedent's estate, a licensee should establish that the rate of commission to be paid has been approved by the court handling the probate.

Until probate, the will is only the legal declaration of a person's intended disposition. A will may be revoked at any time after execution, while a deed cannot be revoked after it has been delivered to the grantee. The rule of construction in determining whether an instrument is a will or a contract is that if it passes a present interest, it is a deed or contract; but, if its rights or interests do not convey until the death of the maker, it is a testamentary paper, or will.

Legislation passed in 2013 allows landowners to name a beneficiary on their deeds, either on the initial filing or any subsequent revision. This allows a property to be transferred directly to heirs without going through the probate process and incurring recordation taxes.

Last Will and Testament

The person creating a will is called a **testator**. A testator can have only one last will and testament. A will may be set aside for fraud, undue influence, force, or coercion.

No person of unsound mind or under the age of 18 years is considered to be capable of making a valid will. Virginia law requires only testamentary capacity at the time the will is made; the testator's subsequent capacity is not relevant.

Neither the testator's poor health nor impaired intellect is sufficient, standing alone, to render a will invalid.

No will is valid unless it is in writing. A valid will must be signed by the testator or by some other person in the testator's presence and by the testator's direction in such a way as to make it clear that the name is intended as the testator's signature. A will is also valid that is wholly in the testator's handwriting (a **holographic will**) if the testator signs the will and acknowledges it in the presence of at least two competent witnesses who are both present at the same time. These witnesses also must sign the will in the presence of the testator. The testamentary intent must appear on the face of the paper itself. Virginia law is silent on the subject of oral or **nuncupative (deathbed) wills**.

IN PRACTICE

When representing the purchaser of property from a decedent's estate or in taking a listing of estate property, it is wise for a real estate licensee to request a certified copy of the will and determine whether the executor under the will has the power of sale. Where the executor does not have the power of sale, or in dealing with an intestate's property, all the heirs and their spouses must execute a deed as grantors conveying the property to the grantee.

SETTLEMENT AGENT

Real Estate Settlement Agents

The Real Estate Settlement Agents (RESA) Act (replaced the earlier CRESPA law) requires that persons who perform escrow, closing, or settlement services comply with consumer protection safeguards with respect to licensing, financial responsibility, and the handling of settlement funds.

RESA also provides specific language that is to be included in all contracts for the purchase of real estate containing not more than four residential dwelling units. The specific language is included here:

> Choice of Settlement Agent: Chapter 27.3 (§ 55-525.16 et seq.) of Title 55 of the Code of Virginia provides that the purchaser or borrower has the right to select the **settlement agent** to handle the closing of this transaction. The settlement agent's role in closing this transaction involves the coordination of numerous administrative and clerical functions relating to the collection of documents and the collection and disbursement of funds required to carry out the terms of the contract between the parties. If part of the purchase price is financed, the lender for the purchaser will instruct the settlement agent as to the signing and recording of loan documents and the disbursement of loan proceeds. No settlement agent can provide legal advice to any party to the transaction except a settlement agent who is engaged in the private practice of law in Virginia and who has been retained or engaged by a party to the transaction for the purpose of providing legal services to that party.

The provisions of Chapter 27.3 may not be varied by agreement, and rights conferred by this chapter may not be waived. In some cases, a builder may request the purchaser to use the builder's attorney because much of the preliminary work involved with the sale of a new property is already in the possession of that attorney. However, the law is very clear that the seller may not require the use of a particular settlement agent as a condition of the sale of the property. The choice of settlement agent is left up to the purchaser or borrower.

Settlement agents cannot practice law or provide legal advice unless they are practicing lawyers in Virginia. A settlement agent who is an attorney practicing in Virginia may be retained by a party to the transaction for the purpose of providing legal services to that party.

A person licensed under Chapter 21 (§ 54.1-2100 et seq.) of Title 54.1, or such licensee's employees or independent contractors, may perform escrow, closing, or settlement services, as defined by RESA, to facilitate the settlement of a transaction in which the licensee is involved so long as the licensee, the licensee's employees, or independent contractors are not named as the settlement agent on the settlement statement and the licensee is otherwise not prohibited from performing such services by law or regulation.

IN PRACTICE

Even though a real estate broker can legally conduct a settlement, most choose not to in order to avoid any conflict of interest.

The settlement agent will usually be either an attorney or a title company and must be registered with the Virginia State Bar, carry errors and omissions (E&O) or malpractice insurance at a minimum of $250,000, and maintain a surety bond of not less than $200,000.

In addition to the surety bond, a settlement agent is required to carry a blanket fidelity bond or employee dishonesty insurance policy covering persons employed by the settlement agent and providing a minimum of $100,000 in coverage. When the settlement agent has no employees except the owners, partners, shareholders, or members, the settlement agent may apply to the appropriate licensing authority for a waiver of this fidelity bond or employee dishonesty requirement.

If any interest is to be earned on funds deposited in connection with any escrow, settlement, or closing, this must be disclosed in the purchaser contract along with the future disposition of the interest earned. The settlement agent is usually provided a copy of the purchase agreement by the buyer's broker.

Settlement Services

The escrow, closing, or settlement services include placing orders for **title insurance**, receiving and issuing receipts for money received from the parties, ordering loan checks and payoffs, ordering surveys and inspections, preparing settlement statements, determining that all closing documents conform to the parties' contract requirements, setting the closing appointment, following up with the parties to ensure that the transaction progresses to closing, ascertaining that the lender's instructions have been satisfied, conducting a closing conference at which the documents are executed, receiving and disbursing funds, completing form documents and instruments selected by and in accordance with instructions of the parties to the transaction, handling or arranging for the recording of documents, sending recorded documents to the lender, sending the recorded deed and the title policy to the buyer, and when required, reporting federal income tax information for the real estate sale to the Internal Revenue Service (IRS) (§ 6.1-2.20). For further information about the IRS, visit www.irs.gov.

For many years, the settlement agent was responsible for preparing the HUD-1 Settlement Form. This form was replaced by the CD Form as required by the TRID regulations prepared by the CFPB. In 2016, a new term *closing disclosure* was added to provisions relating to RESAs. The term is defined as the combined mortgage loan disclosure statement of final loan terms and closing costs prescribed under RESPA and the CFPB.

Recordation and Disbursement of Funds

The first piece of legislation designed to deal with the problem of delayed disbursements after settlement was enacted in 1978. This was repealed in 1980 due to ambiguous wording and replaced with the Wet Settlement Act, which was revised several times over the years. The most recent legislation is found in the Code at Section 55-525.11—Duties of Settlement Agents, and states that the settlement agent must cause recordation of the deed, the deed of trust, or mortgage, or other documents required to be recorded and must cause disbursement of settlement proceeds within two business days of settlement.

A settlement agent may not disburse any or all loan funds or other funds coming into its possession before the recordation of any instrument except (i) funds received that are overpayments to be returned to the provider of such funds, (ii) funds necessary to effect the recordation of instruments, or (iii) funds that the provider has by separate written instrument directed to be disbursed before recordation of any instrument. Additionally, in any transaction involving the purchase or sale of an interest in residential real property, the settlement agent must provide notification to the purchaser of the availability of owner's title insurance as required under Section 38.2-4616.

TITLE

Title Examination

An important function of the settlement agent is to obtain a **title examination**. The seller should be asked to provide the settlement agent with any information specific to the title condition of the property, such as any unrealized deeds, existing title insurance policies, and any known unrecorded deed, lien, or encumbrance information. The seller must have marketable title at the time of settlement and must be given a reasonable time to correct any title defects found before settlement. If title defects are found, the seller should be formally notified and then take whatever actions are necessary to correct the defects. Defects are referred to as a " **cloud on the title**." The real estate licensee is not specifically involved with the title examination but can facilitate communication between the settlement agent and the seller or buyer.

In a title examination, the prospective seller's **chain of title** is developed by searching through the grantee index backward in time to some predetermined point to establish the source of title for each owner in the chain. Then, for each grantor in the chain of title, the examiner searches the grantor's index from the date the grantor acquired title to the date it was transferred to the next grantor in the chain. This process is called *adversing the title* and is done to determine whether any person not in the seller's direct chain of title might have some adverse claim or interest recorded against the property to be conveyed.

Finally, the examiner will search other indexes to determine whether there are any unrecorded claims against the property, such as judgment liens, mechanics' liens, or tax liens. While real estate licensees do not perform a title search in the normal course of taking a listing, they should alert the parties' attorneys in the event of even the slightest hint of title issues.

Title examinations may be classified as full or limited searches. In a full search, the seller's title must be established for at least 60 years. A limited search is a title examination that goes back fewer than 60 years. Limited searches are appropriate for some loan assumptions and second mortgage closings, unless the second mortgagee requires lender's title insurance.

A chain of title consists of consecutive terms of ownership; a gap in the chain could be caused by an unrecorded deed, a name change, an unadministered estate, a foreign divorce decree, or some other circumstance. Unless the missing link can be reconstructed from reliable sources, the defect could terminate the contract.

Errors, such as an erroneous legal description, a misspelled name, or an improper execution, in a prior recorded deed in the seller's chain of title, must be corrected before the closing can proceed. Where possible, these problems can be cured by a correction deed from the same grantor to the same grantee; the correction deed must be recorded. A correction deed may not be used to change a greater estate to a lesser estate, nor can it be used to change the identity of the grantor altogether. It is the responsibility of the seller to locate the parties, then to correct the deed. More serious defects may require filing an action to quiet title, which involves time and can delay the closing.

At a minimum, the title report should reveal

- title holder of record;
- legal description of property;
- existing lenders;
- other lienholders (such as mechanics' lienors, judgment lienors, and tax lienors);
- status of taxes;
- easements, covenants, and other restrictions;
- objections to marketability;
- other matters affecting title; and
- requirements for vesting marketable title in the purchaser.

Title Insurance

Settlement agents are required by Virginia law to advise purchasers and borrowers of the availability of owner title insurance and of the benefits of acquiring it. It is to the benefit of the purchaser to have title insurance because the premium paid is nominal compared with the potential cost an owner could incur in connection with a suit to quiet title or other litigation regarding a defect in title.

If the purchaser is obtaining a loan secured by a deed of trust on the property, the lender will require that a lender's title insurance policy be provided. This policy protects only the lender's interest and will diminish in protection as the loan is paid down. The additional charge to obtain an owner's policy that protects the owner for the full value of the property is minimal compared with the amount of protection provided.

Title insurance is offered by many companies. The purchaser should contact the title insurance provider (usually through the settlement company) to obtain an advance copy of the types of policies, their costs, and options offered.

Full disclosure is required if the settlement agent has any ownership interest in the title insurance company offering title insurance on the transaction.

Title Issues

Judgments constitute liens against all real property that the defendant owns or subsequently acquires. If the seller denies being named in the judgment, and it is not certain that the judgment is against the seller, an affidavit to this effect may be sufficient to protect the purchaser.

Judgments against prior owners of property may remain as valid liens against the property despite the fact that the property has been subsequently conveyed. The purchaser should require that the seller satisfy all judgments against the property because they remain as liens against the property for 20 years and are subject to execution.

Unreleased Deed of Trust

A real estate licensee should be aware that it is not unusual for a title examiner to discover an unreleased deed of trust on the property. Most often, this is due to the failure of the lender or closer to have a certificate of satisfaction or deed of release signed by the beneficiary and recorded in a timely manner. Unreleased deeds of trust often go unnoticed until the seller attempts to sell the property. When the lender was a bank or mortgage company and the lien was in fact paid off, it is relatively easy to have a certificate of satisfaction executed and recorded before closing. However, if an individual or private lender was involved, these situations can cause delays in the closing, primarily owing to the problems associated with locating the individual.

Mechanics' or Materialmen's Liens

Reported mechanics' or materialmen's liens must be treated as adverse claims against the property. The purchaser should require that these liens be paid and satisfied of record or discharged by the filing of a proper bond at or before closing. Unreported liens are also of concern to the purchaser, who will take the property subject to all mechanics' and materialmen's liens for work or materials furnished within the last 90 days. For this reason, the purchaser should require that the seller provide an affidavit that there have been no improvements performed or materials supplied within the 90 days before the date of closing. This affidavit, commonly called a 90-day letter, is required by all lenders and title insurance companies.

Mechanics' liens are generally not covered by standard title insurance. However, insurance carriers will provide this coverage for an additional premium.

IN PRACTICE

A seller is closing on the sale of a property in Virginia on Tuesday and expects to close on his new purchase in Maryland on Wednesday using the proceeds from the Tuesday closing in Virginia. He might not have access to the proceeds of Tuesday's Virginia closing in time for Wednesday's closing in Maryland because no disbursements can be made at the settlement table (closing) in Virginia until the transaction is recorded. The licensee should make sure that all parties are aware of the potential problem in time for special arrangements to be made.

SUMMARY

The requirements for a valid deed in Virginia are the following:

- Grantor who has the legal capacity to execute the deed
- Grantee
- Consideration
- Granting clause
- Accurate legal description of the property
- Any relevant exceptions or reservations
- Signature of the grantor, sometimes with acknowledgment
- Delivery and acceptance of the deed

If a seller or buyer is unable to attend the closing they can either prepare all papers to be signed in advance of the closing or use a power of attorney. A specific power of attorney is strongly recommended to convey real property in Virginia.

Transfer taxes are levied on both seller and purchaser; seller pays a grantor tax, and purchaser pays a recordation tax. Deeds are also subject to local recordation tax. A regional congestion relief fee may also be imposed in certain areas.

Title to property can be established through adverse possession (similar to an easement by prescription). It is necessary to show actual, hostile, exclusive, visible, and continuous possession of the property for 15 years.

Title to property may be inherited through a legal will processed in probate court. The will must be in writing and the testator of sound mind and over the age of 18. Handwritten (holographic) wills may be valid if acknowledged by at least two witnesses.

The old CRESPA law was recodified as RESA and still requires specific language in the contract giving the right to choose a settlement agent to the purchaser. The settlement agent no longer prepares the HUD-1 Settlement Statement. Under the TRID regulations, the lender prepares the CD.

The requirements of the old Wet Settlement Act are now included in the Duties of Settlement Agents. The agent must disburse settlement proceeds within two business days, but may not disburse until all documents are recorded. The agent must also provide the purchaser of the availability of title insurance.

An important function of the settlement agent is to obtain a title examination, going back at least 60 years. The seller's chain of title is searched along with other indexes to discover any unrecorded claims against the property. Minor errors can be corrected with a correction deed. More serious errors may require court action to quiet title. Common title issues include outstanding judgments, unreleased deed of trust, and mechanic's liens.

UNIT 7 QUIZ

1. An heir was to have inherited real property under his uncle's will. However, the uncle sold the property shortly before he died. The heir now wants to have the sale rescinded on grounds of the uncle's incompetence. Will the heir win?
   A. Yes, any such pleading by a close relative will prevail in court.
   B. Yes, the grantor would have had to prove competence in court during his lifetime.
   C. No, a deed can be invalidated due to incompetence only during the grantor's lifetime.
   D. No, a person is presumed competent unless a court has ruled otherwise.

2. The seller in a transaction was called out of town on business the day before the closing. Any affidavits or sworn statements the seller is required to deliver at the closing must be signed by
   A. the seller.
   B. the seller's attorney-in-fact.
   C. the buyer's attorney-in-fact.
   D. the seller's real estate agent.

3. The seller is expected to pay which of the following?
   A. Recordation tax for recording of the deed
   B. Recordation tax for recording of the deed of trust
   C. Grantor tax of $0.50 per $500 of purchase price
   D. Transfer fee for each document admitted to record

4. All of the following are entitled to prevail on a claim of title by adverse possession *EXCEPT*
   A. a person who has been in possession of the property for 19 years.
   B. a person who held the property for 5 years after inheriting it from a parent, who was in adverse possession for 10 years.
   C. a person who has been entering an orchard and taking apples every October for 15 years.
   D. a person who has erected a stall on and has been using a neighbor's property to sell produce for 20 years without permission.

5. An elderly woman was very ill, and she wrote a will in her own handwriting, leaving all her property to her niece. Three witnesses heard her say, "This is my will." The witnesses watched the woman's friend sign the woman's name to the document because she was too exhausted to do it herself. "That's as good as my signature," she said weakly. The witnesses signed the will. What is the status of this document?
   A. The will is invalid because Virginia does not recognize holographic wills.
   B. The will is valid.
   C. The will is invalid because *she* did not sign it herself.
   D. The will is valid, but cannot be enforced because it is a nuncupative will.

6. All of the following statements with regard to a will are true *EXCEPT*
   A. No person under the age of 18 years is considered to be capable of making a valid will.
   B. No will is valid unless it is in writing.
   C. Handwritten wills are never valid.
   D. Poor health is not sufficient to render a will invalid.

7. According to Real Estate Settlement Agents (RESA) law, the selection of a settlement agent is made by
   A. the seller.
   B. the buyer.
   C. either the buyer or the seller.
   D. either the buyer's or the seller's agent.

8. The settlement agent is responsible for all of the following *EXCEPT*
   A. preparing the HUD-1 Statement.
   B. placing orders for title insurance.
   C. ordering loan payoffs.
   D. setting the closing appointment.

9. A settlement agent is usually either an attorney or a title company and must do all of the following *EXCEPT*
   A. register with the Virginia State Bar.
   B. carry E&O or malpractice insurance.
   C. maintain a surety bond.
   D. provide legal advice to the parties to the transaction.

10. A full title search goes back how many years?
    A. 20 years
    B. 40 years
    C. 60 years
    D. 80 years

11. Which of the following changes may *NOT* be accomplished by using a correction deed?
    A. A change from a fee simple to a life estate
    B. Correction of an erroneous legal description
    C. Respelling of a misspelled name
    D. Correcting an improperly executed deed

12. In cases where title must be cleared by having correction deeds signed, the person responsible for locating the parties who must sign is
    A. the buyer.
    B. the seller.
    C. the settlement attorney.
    D. the real estate licensee who represents the owner.

13. The seller of real property must have marketable title
    A. at the time the listing is taken.
    B. when a sales contract is signed.
    C. by the time the buyer's loan is approved.
    D. at settlement.

14. At a minimum, the title report should reveal all of the following *EXCEPT*
    A. title holder of record.
    B. existing lienholders.
    C. list of names in the chain of title.
    D. easements, covenants, and restrictions.

15. In preparing for the settlement on a sale of property, it was discovered that an unreleased deed of trust is still shown on the county records. This *MOST* likely occurred because
    A. the seller never paid off the deed of trust.
    B. the lender neglected to have a deed of release signed and recorded.
    C. the original settlement attorney absconded with the funds.
    D. the seller still owes for county property taxes.

UNIT
8

Virginia Real Estate License Law

LEARNING OBJECTIVES

When you have completed this unit, you will be able to

› **define** Real Estate Board (REB) and important statutory words and phrases;
› **list** the requirements for licensure and renewal;
› **review** the rights and responsibilities of a broker;
› **discuss** the procedure for making a complaint; and
› **define** the following key terms:

actively engaged	continuing education	place of business
active license	inactive license	post-licensing education
concurrent license	Informal Fact-Finding	referral agent
conflict of interest	Conference (IFFC)	
consent order		

OVERVIEW

This unit discusses the specific authorities of the REB, individuals and businesses exempt from license law, and the most recent revision of the Real Estate Regulations, in effect since 2015, in all its four parts: General, Entry, Renewal, and Schools.

CODE OF VIRGINIA AND VIRGINIA ADMINISTRATIVE CODE (VAC)

The Code of Virginia 54.1, Chapter 21, is the section of the statute that governs the practice of real estate professionals. The purpose of the law is to protect the public interest against fraud, misrepresentation, dishonesty, and incompetence in real estate transactions.

The law designates the Real Estate Board (REB) as the authority with the power to enforce, amend, and promulgate rules and regulations for implementing the law.

References are made in this chapter to both the Code of Virginia statutes under Title 54.1, Chapter 21, and to Real Estate Regulations under the Virginia Administrative Code (VAC), Agency 135. The most recent update of the Regulations is November 1, 2015. A copy of the regulations can be found online or ordered from the DPOR office at 9960 Mayland Drive, Suite 102, Richmond, VA, 23233.

THE REAL ESTATE BOARD (REB) (§ 54.1-2104, 2105)

The REB is 1 of 19 boards that regulate more than 30 occupations and professions as part of the DPOR.

The REB is composed of nine members. Seven members may be either brokers or salespersons with at least five consecutive years' experience immediately before appointment, and two are citizen (consumer) members. Appointments are made by the governor for a term of four years. Sitting members may be reappointed for one additional four-year term. Members of the REB select the chairperson.

REB Authority

The REB, by statute, may do all things necessary and convenient for carrying into effect the provisions of the law. REB's authority includes

- issuing and renewing real estate licenses;
- enforcing the license law;
- taking disciplinary action for violations of license law or rules and regulations by
    - suspending or revoking a license,
    - levying fines, or
    - denying license renewal;
- establishing requirements for real estate licensing and renewal;
- approving schools for teaching authorized courses for real estate brokers and salespersons;
- determining license fees; and
- waiving all or part of the prelicensing requirements if an applicant for licensure is currently licensed in another state or the District of Columbia.

In addition to administering the real estate license law, the REB has the responsibility of administering the Virginia Fair Housing Act and the Virginia Real Estate Transaction Recovery Fund. The Virginia Condominium Act, the Virginia Time-Share Act, the Virginia Cooperative Act, and the Virginia Property Owners Association Act are now administered by the Common Interest Community (CIC) Board discussed in Unit 1.

The REB also sends out notices from time to time regarding important state issues or services, such as the Broker Price Opinion Guidance document that was approved in 2009. More recent guidance documents are, "Necessity for Brokerage Agreements," Sept. 6, 2012; "Transfer of Active Licenses," May 9, 2013; and, "Reasonable Accommodation Requests for Assistance Animals," Oct. 26, 2016.

There are some aspects of real estate practice with which the REB does not become involved. For example, the REB does not

- arbitrate disputes between salespersons and brokers;

- become involved in disputes between brokers;

- establish commission rates or commission splits; or

- standardize listing agreements, sales contracts, or many other forms used in the industry although from time to time the REB may be charged with development of specific forms, such as the disclosure forms required by the Virginia Residential Property Disclosure Act.

The REB could become involved in any of these matters in case of a violation of the license law or the rules and regulations.

If the REB is aware of someone who is engaging in acts of real estate brokerage without a license, it will investigate the matter. If the suspicion is true, the REB may issue a cease and desist order from acting as a real estate broker and impose a civil penalty for up to $1,000 for each transaction or the commission received, whichever is greater. The REB may also refer the matter to the Commonwealth attorney for further action. Operating without a license is considered to be a Class 1 misdemeanor with a penalty of up to $1,000 per violation. A third or subsequent violation within a single three-year period constitutes a Class 6 felony. The civil penalties against one person or business entity cannot exceed $10,000 per year. The DPOR also has the authority to investigate unlicensed activity and to enforce licensure and regulatory provisions of Title 54.1 by instituting proceedings in general district or circuit courts.

The REB newsletter, *VREB Speaking*, is published four times a year and is available online at www.dpor.virginia.gov/boards/real-estate/. It is a valuable source of current information from the REB.

Exemptions From License Law (§ 54.1-2103)

The law recognizes that under certain circumstances, individuals or business operations engaging in what could be considered an act of real estate brokerage may be entitled to exemption from the requirements of licensure. Those conditions include, but are not limited to, the following:

- Owners, lessors, and their employees dealing with their own property

- Persons acting as attorneys-in-fact under a power of attorney for final consummation of contracts for sale, lease, or exchange of real estate

- Attorneys-at-law in the performance of duties as an attorney-at-law to include the sale of real estate, condemnation proceedings, and so forth

- Receivers, trustees in bankruptcy, administrators, executors, or other persons acting under court order

- Trustees under trust agreements, deeds of trust, or wills or their employees

- Corporations managing rental housing when officers, directors, and members in the ownership corporation and the management corporation are the same persons and the management corporation manages no property for others

- Any existing tenant of a residential dwelling who refers a prospective tenant to the owner of the unit or to the owner's agent or employee and receives, or is offered, a referral fee from the owner, agent, or employee

- Auctioneers selling real estate at public auction when employed by the owner (an auctioneer cannot advertise that he is authorized to sell real estate)

Unit 8

- Any person licensed and in good standing as a real estate broker or salesperson in another state who assists a prospective purchaser, tenant, optionee, or licensee located in another state to purchase, lease, option, or license an interest in commercial real estate in the Commonwealth—the licensee from another state may be compensated by a real estate broker in the Commonwealth

Real estate licensees are always required to comply with the REB regulations, even though they may also be in one of the exempt categories.

REAL ESTATE REGULATIONS

The latest revision of the Real Estate Regulations became effective November 1, 2015. The regulations are provided here in their entirety in order to help candidates prepare for the state portion of the license exam and also to provide a resource for future reference. Significant changes are shown in bold with occasional additional comments.

Part I General

Definitions (18 VAC 135-20-10)

- Certain words and phrases are used throughout both the License Law and the Real Estate Regulations of the REB. These words and phrases have specific, statutory meanings separate and apart from any definition they might have outside the real estate profession. Several of these definitions were addressed in Unit 1 but are repeated here for emphasis. Some definitions included here do not appear in the 2015 revisions but are retained here for general information.

- *Active*—Any broker or salesperson under the supervision of a principal or supervising broker performing real estate brokerage activities defined in Sections 54.1-2100 and 54.1-2101 of the Code of Virginia.

- **Actively engaged**—A broker or salesperson having active licensure with a licensed real estate firm or sole proprietorship and active for an average of at least 40 hours per week. The REB may waive the 40-hour-per-week requirement at its discretion.

- *Associate broker*—Any individual holding a broker's license other than the one designated as the principal broker.

- *Client*—An individual who has entered into a brokerage relationship with a licensee as defined by Section 54.1-2130 of the Code of Virginia.

- *Customer*—An individual who has not entered into a brokerage relationship with a licensee but for whom a licensee may perform ministerial acts. (This definition is not included in the November 2015 revisions.)

- *Firm*—Any sole proprietorship (non-broker-owner), partnership, association, limited liability company (LLC), or corporation, other than a sole proprietorship (principal-broker-owned), that is required by regulation to obtain a separate brokerage firm license. The firm's licensed name may be any assumed or fictitious name properly filed with the board.

- *Inactive status*—Any broker or salesperson who is not under the supervision of a principal broker or supervising broker, who is not affiliated with a firm or sole proprietorship, or who is not performing any real estate activities defined in Sections 54.1-2100 and 54.1-2101 of the Code of Virginia.

- *Independent contractor*—A licensee who acts for or represents a client other than as a standard agent and whose duties and obligations are governed by a written contract between licensee and the client.

- *Licensee*—real estate brokers and salespersons as defined in Chapter 21 (§ 54.1-2100 et seq.) of Title 54.1 of Code of Virginia or real estate firms.

- *Limited service agent*—A licensee who acts for or represents a client pursuant to a brokerage agreement that provides that the limited service agent will not provide one or more of the duties of a standard agent. (Definition not included in 2015 revisions.)

- *Principal broker*—The individual broker designated by each firm to ensure compliance with Chapter 21 of Title 54.1 of the Code of Virginia and this chapter and to receive all communications and notices from the REB that may affect the firm or its licensees. In the case of a sole proprietorship, the licensed broker who is the sole proprietor has the responsibilities of the principal broker. The principal broker will have responsibility for the activities of the firm and all of its licensees. The principal broker will have signatory authority on all escrow accounts maintained by the firm.

- *Principal to a transaction*—Any party to a real estate transaction including without limitation a seller, buyer, landlord or tenant, optionor or optionee, or licensor or licensee. The listing and selling brokers are not, by virtue of their brokerage relationship, principals to the transaction.

- *Real estate*—As defined in the Virginia law, real estate includes condominiums, leaseholds, time-sharing, and any other interest in real property. Ownership of a cooperative apartment is also considered real estate ownership, even though the shares held by members of the co-op are construed as personal property. (Not included in 2015 revisions.)

- *Sole proprietor*—Any individual, not a corporation, LLC partnership, or association, who is trading under the individual's name or under an assumed or fictitious name, pursuant to the provisions of Chapter 5 of the Code of Virginia.

- *Standard agent*—A licensee who acts for or represents a client in an agency relationship. A standard agent will have the obligations as provided in Article 3 (§ 54.1-2130 et seq.) of Chapter 21 of Title 54.1 of the Code of Virginia.

- *Supervising broker*—Means (i) the individual broker designated by the principal broker to supervise the provision of real estate brokerage services by associate brokers and salespersons assigned to branch offices or (ii) the broker, who may be the principal broker, designated by the principal broker to supervise a designated agent as stated in Section 54.1-2130 of the Code of Virginia.

Part II Entry

Necessity for License (18 VAC 135-20-20) (Refer to § 54.1-2106.1 of the Code of Virginia)

A. Sole proprietor (principal broker owner). A real estate broker's license shall be issued to an individual trading under an assumed or fictitious name, that is, a name other than the individual's full name, only after the individual signs and acknowledges a certificate provided by the board, setting forth the name under which the business is to be organized and conducted, the address of the individual's residence, and the address of the individual's **place of business**. Each certificate must be attested by the clerk of court of the county or jurisdiction wherein the business is to be conducted. The attention of all applicants and licensees is directed to §§ 59.1-69 through 59.1-76 of the Code of Virginia.

B. Sole proprietor (nonbroker owner), partnership, association, limited liability company, or corporation. Every sole proprietor (nonbroker owner), partnership, association, limited liability company, or corporation must secure a real estate license for its firm before transacting real estate business. This license is separate and distinct from the individual broker license required of each partner, associate, manager of a limited liability company, and officer of a corporation who is active in the firm's brokerage business. Each applicant for such license shall disclose, and the license shall be issued to, the name under which the applicant intends to do or does business and holds itself out to the public. Each applicant shall also disclose the business address of the firm. The board will consider the application of any partnership, association, corporation or limited liability company only after the entity is authorized to conduct business in accordance with §§ 59.1-69 through 59.1-76 of the Code of Virginia.

C. Each real estate firm is required to have a principal broker whose license is in good standing with the board in order to transact real estate business.

D. Branch office license. If a real estate broker maintains more than one place of business within the state, a branch office license shall be issued for each place of business maintained. Application for the license shall be made on forms provided by the board and shall reveal the name of the firm, the location of the branch office, and the name of the supervising broker for that branch office. The branch office license shall be maintained at the branch office location.

Qualifications for Licensure (18 VAC 135-20-30)

Every applicant to the Real Estate Board for an individual salesperson's or broker's license shall have the following qualifications:

1. The applicant shall have a good reputation for honesty, truthfulness, and fair dealing, and be competent to transact the business of a real estate broker or a real estate salesperson in such a manner as to safeguard the interests of the public.

2. The applicant shall meet the current educational requirements by achieving a passing grade in all required courses of § 54.1-2105 of the Code of Virginia prior to the time the applicant sits for the licensing examination and applies for licensure.

3. The applicant shall be in good standing as a licensed real estate broker or salesperson in every jurisdiction where licensed and the applicant shall not have had a license as a real estate broker or real estate salesperson which was suspended, revoked or surrendered in connection with a disciplinary action or which has been the subject of discipline in any jurisdiction prior to applying for licensure in Virginia. The applicant shall be in compliance with all the terms of all board orders, including but not limited to paying imposed monetary penalties and costs, plus any accrued interest and other fees, and completing imposed education.

4. In accordance with § 54.1-204 of the Code of Virginia, each applicant shall submit to fingerprinting and shall disclose the following information:

   a. All misdemeanor convictions involving moral turpitude, sexual offense, drug distribution or physical injury within five years of the date of the application; and

    b. All felony convictions during his lifetime.

       Any plea of nolo contendere shall be considered a conviction for purposes of this subsection. The record of a conviction received from a court shall be accepted as prima facie evidence of a conviction or finding of guilt. The board, in its discretion, may deny licensure to any applicant in accordance with § 54.1-2104 of the Code of Virginia.

5. The applicant shall be at least 18 years old.

6. The applicant shall have a high school diploma or its equivalent.

7. The applicant, within 12 months prior to submitting a complete application for a license, shall have passed a written examination provided by the board or by a testing service acting on behalf of the board.

8. The applicant shall follow all procedures established with regard to conduct at the examination. Failure to comply with all procedures established with regard to conduct at the examination may be grounds for denial of application.

9. Applicants for licensure who do not meet the requirements set forth in subdivisions 3 and 4 of this section may be approved for licensure following consideration by the board.

Additional Qualifications for Brokers (18 VAC 135-20-40)

An applicant for an individual license as a real estate broker shall meet the following requirements in addition to those set forth in 18 VAC 135-20-30:

1. The applicant shall meet the current educational requirements of § 54.1-2105 of the Code of Virginia.

2. The applicant shall have been actively engaged as defined in 18 VAC 135-20-10 as a real estate salesperson for a period of 36 of the 48 months immediately preceding application. This requirement may be waived at the discretion of the board in accordance with § 54.1-2105 of the Code of Virginia.

3. The applicant's experience must be verified by the principal or supervising broker for whom the licensee worked at the time of obtaining that experience.

Additional Qualifications for Salesperson's or Broker's License as a Business Entity (18 VAC 135-20-45)

An applicant for a salesperson's license as a business entity shall meet the following requirements in addition to those set forth in 18 VAC 135-20-30:

1. Every owner or officer who actively participates in the real estate business shall hold a license as a salesperson or broker. The business entity license does not replace the individual license. More than one licensee may be a participant of the business entity.

2. When one licensee is the owner or officer, the business entity shall be named in accordance with § 54.1-2106.1 C of the Code of Virginia.

3. The board will consider the application of any partnership, association, corporation or limited liability company only after the entity is authorized to do business in accordance with §§ 59.1-69 through 59.1-76 of the Code of Virginia.

Concurrent Licenses (18 VAC 135-20-50)

Concurrent licenses shall be issued by the board to brokers active in more than one firm upon receipt of a concurrent license form and written statements verifying that written notice of the applicant's concurrent licensure status has been provided to the principal broker of each firm with which the applicant is and will be associated. Payment is required for each license. A concurrent license will not be issued to an individual applying to be associated with a firm if that individual has an expired license associated with the same firm and the expired license may be reinstated.

Exchange to Salesperson's License (18 VAC 135-20-55)

A broker who wants to exchange his license(s) for that of a salesperson must submit a complete application with appropriate fee. When exchanging the license(s), the licensee agrees his current broker's license(s) ceases to exist, and if he chooses to become licensed as a broker again, he must pass the current broker examination and must meet the current education and experience requirements in effect at the time of application.

Qualifications for Licensure by Reciprocity (18 VAC 135-20-60)

An individual who is currently licensed as a real estate salesperson or broker in another jurisdiction may obtain a Virginia real estate license by meeting the following requirements:

1. The applicant shall be at least 18 years of age.

2. The applicant shall have a high school diploma or its equivalent.

3. The applicant shall have received the salesperson's or broker's license by virtue of having passed in the jurisdiction of licensure a written examination deemed to be substantially equivalent to the Virginia examination.

4. The applicant shall sign a statement verifying that he has read and understands the provisions of this chapter and Chapter 21 (§ 54.1-2100 et seq.) of Title 54.1 of the Code of Virginia.

5. The applicant, within 12 months prior to submitting a complete application for a license, shall have passed a written examination provided by the board or by a testing service acting on behalf of the board covering Virginia real estate license law and regulations of the Real Estate Board.

6. The applicant shall follow all procedures established with regard to conduct at the examination. Failure to comply with all procedures established by the board with regard to conduct at the examination may be grounds for denial of application.

7. The applicant shall be in good standing as a licensed real estate broker or salesperson in every jurisdiction where licensed and the applicant shall not have had a license as a real estate broker or real estate salesperson which was suspended, revoked, or surrendered in connection with a disciplinary action or which has been the subject of discipline in any jurisdiction prior to applying for licensure in Virginia. The applicant shall be in compliance with all the terms of all board orders, including but not limited to paying imposed monetary penalties and costs, plus any accrued interest and other fees, and completing imposed education.

8. At the time of application for a salesperson's license, the applicant must have met educational requirements that are substantially equivalent to those required in Virginia. At the time of application for a broker's license, the applicant must have met educational requirements that are substantially equivalent to those required in

Virginia, and the applicant must have been actively engaged as defined by 18 VAC 135-20-10 for 36 of the preceding 48 months. The broker applicant's experience must be verified by an individual who has direct knowledge of the applicant's activities as defined in §§ 54.1-2100 and 54.1-2101 of the Code of Virginia. These requirements may be waived at the discretion of the board in accordance with § 54.1-2105 of the Code of Virginia.

9. The applicant shall have a good reputation for honesty, truthfulness, and fair dealing, and be competent to transact the business of a real estate salesperson or broker in such a manner as to safeguard the interests of the public.

10. In accordance with § 54.1-2104 of the Code of Virginia, each applicant shall submit to fingerprinting and shall disclose the following information:

 a. All misdemeanor convictions involving moral turpitude, sexual offense, drug distribution or physical injury within five years of the date of the application; and

 b. All felony convictions during his lifetime.

 Any plea of nolo contendere shall be considered a conviction for purposes of this subsection. The record of a conviction received from a court shall be accepted as prima facie evidence of a conviction or finding of guilt. The board, in its discretion, may deny licensure to any applicant in accordance with § 54.1-204 of the Code of Virginia.

11. Applicants for licensure who do not meet the requirements set forth in subdivisions 7 and 10 of this section may be approved for licensure following consideration by the board.

Activation or Transfer of License (18 VAC 135-20-70)

A. Any inactive licensee may activate that license with a licensed real estate firm or sole proprietorship by completing an activate form prescribed by the board. A licensee who submits an activate application to the board shall not conduct business with the real estate firm or sole proprietorship set forth in the application until the application is processed and the license is issued by the board. **Continuing education** pursuant to § 54.1-2105.03 of the Code of Virginia shall be completed within two years prior to activation of a license when the license has been inactive for more than 30 days. Any licensee who has not been active with a licensed real estate firm or sole proprietorship for a period of greater than three years shall be required to meet the existing prelicense educational requirements.

B. Any licensee may transfer from one licensed real estate firm or sole proprietorship to another by completing and submitting to the board a transfer application and the fee as set forth in 18 VAC 135-20-80. The transfer application shall include the signature of the new principal broker or supervising broker with signature authority who will be responsible for the licensee's real estate activities and shall be effective upon the principal broker or supervising broker's execution of the transfer application.

Application Fees (18 VAC 135-20-80)

A. All application fees for licenses are nonrefundable and the date of receipt by the board or its agent is the date that will be used to determine whether it is on time.

B. Application fees are as follows:

Salesperson by education and examination	$150
Salesperson by reciprocity	$150
Salesperson's or broker's license as a business entity	$190
Broker by education and examination	$190
Broker by reciprocity	$190
Broker concurrent license	$140
Firm license	$250
Branch office license	$190
Transfer application	$60
Activate application	$60

C. The fee for examination or reexamination is subject to contracted charges to the board by an outside vendor. These contracts are competitively negotiated and bargained for in compliance with the Virginia Public Procurement Act (§ 2.2-4300 et seq. of the Code of Virginia). Fees may be adjusted and charged to the candidate in accordance with these contracts.

Part III Renewal of License

Renewal Required (18 VAC 135-20-90)

Licenses issued under this chapter for salespersons, brokers, and firms shall expire two years from the last day of the month in which they were issued, as indicated on the license, except concurrent broker licenses which shall expire on the same date as the original broker license.

Qualification for Renewal; Continuing Education Requirements (18 VAC 135-20-101)

As a condition of renewal, and pursuant to § 54.1-2105.03 of the Code of Virginia, all active salespersons, resident or nonresident, except those called to active duty in the Armed Forces of the United States, shall be required to satisfactorily complete a course or courses of not less than a total of 16 classroom, correspondence, or other distance learning instruction hours during each licensing term, except for salespersons who are renewing for the first time and are required to complete 30 hours of **post-license education** in their first year of licensure regardless of whether their licenses are active or inactive. All active brokers, resident or nonresident, except those called to active duty in the Armed Forces of the United States, shall be required to satisfactorily complete a course or courses of not less than a total of 24 classroom, correspondence, or other distance learning instruction hours during each licensing term. Active licensees called to active duty in the Armed Forces of the United States may complete these courses within six months of their release from active duty. Inactive brokers and salespersons are not required to complete the continuing education course as a condition of renewal (see 18 VAC 135-20-70, Activation or transfer of license).

Legislation enacted in 2016 allows the REB to grant waivers or exemptions for reasons of certified illness or undue hardship.

1. Providers shall be those as defined in 18 VAC 135-20-350;

2. Effective January 1, 2016, for salespersons, eight of the required 16 hours shall include two hours in fair housing laws, three hours in ethics and standards of conduct, and a minimum of one hour each in legal updates and emerging trends, to include flood zone areas and the National Flood Insurance Program, real estate agency and real estate contracts. For brokers, 16 of the 24 required hours shall include eight hours in supervision and management of real estate agents and the management of real estate brokerage firms, two hours in fair housing laws, three hours in ethics and standards of conduct, and a minimum of one hour each in legal updates and emerging trends, to include flood zone areas and the National Flood Insurance Program, real estate agency and real estate contracts. If the licensee submits a notarized affidavit to the board that certifies that he does not practice residential real estate brokerage, residential management or residential leasing and shall not do so during the licensing term, training in fair housing shall not be required; instead such licensee shall receive training in other applicable federal and state discrimination laws and regulations. The remaining hours shall be on subjects from the following list:

   a. Property rights;

   b. Contracts;

   c. Deeds;

   d. Mortgages and deeds of trust;

   e. Types of mortgages;

   f. Leases;

   g. Liens;

   h. Real property and title insurance;

   i. Investment;

   j. Taxes in real estate;

   k. Real estate financing;

   l. Brokerage and agency contract responsibilities;

   m. Real property management;

   n. Search, examination and registration of title;

   o. Title closing;

   p. Appraisal of real property;

   q. Planning subdivision developments and condominiums;

   r. Regulatory statutes;

   s. Housing legislation;

   t. Fair housing;

   u. Real Estate Board regulations;

   v. Land use;

   w. Business law;

   x. Real estate economics;

   y. Real estate investments;

   z. Federal real estate law;

   aa. Commercial real estate;

      bb. Americans With Disabilities Act;

      cc. Environmental issues impacting real estate;

      dd. Building codes and design;

      ee. Local laws and zoning;

      ff. Escrow requirements;

      gg. Ethics and standards of conduct; and

      hh. Common interest ownership.

3. Effective January 1, 2016, salespersons holding licenses in other jurisdictions must complete eight hours, which shall include fair housing laws, legal updates and emerging trends, to include flood zone areas and the National Flood Insurance Program, ethics and standards of conduct, and real estate agency and real estate contracts and may substitute education completed in their jurisdiction for the remaining hours required by subdivision 2 of this section. Brokers holding licenses in other jurisdictions must complete 16 hours that shall include supervision and management of real estate agents and the management of real estate brokerage firms, fair housing laws, legal updates and emerging trends, to include flood zone areas and the National Flood Insurance Program, ethics and standards of conduct, and real estate agency and real estate contracts and may substitute education completed in their jurisdiction for the remaining hours required by subdivision 2 of this section.

4. The board may approve additional subjects at its discretion and in accordance with § 54.1-2105.03 of the Code of Virginia.

5. Credit for continuing education course completion is given for each class hour/clock hour as defined in 18 VAC 135-20-350.

6. Licensees are responsible for retaining for three years and providing proof of continuing education. Proof of course completion shall be made on a form prescribed by the board. Failure to provide documentation of completion as directed by the board will result in the license not being renewed and/or disciplinary action pursuant to this chapter.

7. Instructors who are also licensees of the board may earn continuing education credit for teaching continuing education courses.

8. Any continuing education credits completed by the licensee in excess of that required in the current license term that are obtained in the six months immediately prior to the license expiration date shall carry over into the next two-year renewal period.

On March 17, 2016 the REB determined that this would also apply to new licensees who have completed their 30 hours of post-license courses in the first year of licensure and wish to take additional courses in the six months before their renewal date.

Procedures for Renewal (18 VAC 135-20-110)

Prior to the expiration date shown on the license, each licensee desiring to renew the license shall return to the board the renewal application forms and the appropriate fee as outlined in 18 VAC 135-20-120. Failure to receive notices from the board regarding license renewal does not relieve the licensee of the obligation to renew.

Fees for Renewal (18 VAC 135-20-120)

A. All fees for renewals are nonrefundable, and the date of receipt by the board or its agent is the date that will be used to determine whether it is on time.

B. Renewal fees are as follows:

Salesperson	$65
Salesperson's or broker's license as a business entity	$90
Broker	$80
Concurrent broker	$80
Firm	$160
Branch office	$90

Board Discretion to Deny Renewal (18 VAC 135-20-130)

The board may deny renewal of a license for (i) the same reasons as it may refuse initial licensure or discipline a current licensee; (ii) failure to meet the terms of an agreement for licensure or other board order; or (iii) failure to fully pay monetary penalties and costs imposed by the board, plus any accrued interest.

Failure to Renew; Reinstatement Required (18 VAC 135-20-140)

A. All applicants for reinstatement must meet all requirements set forth in 18 VAC 135-20-101. Applicants for reinstatement who want to activate their license must have completed the continuing education requirement in order to reinstate and activate the license. Applicants for reinstatement of an **inactive license** are not required to complete the continuing education requirement for license reinstatement.

B. If the requirements for renewal of a license, including receipt of the fee by the board, are not completed by the licensee within 30 days of the expiration date noted on the license, a reinstatement fee is required as follows:

Salesperson	$100
Salesperson's or broker's license as a business entity	$135
Broker	$120
Concurrent Broker	$120
Firm	$245
Branch Office	$135

C. A license may be reinstated for up to one year following the expiration date with payment of the reinstatement fee. After one year, the license may not be reinstated under any circumstances and the applicant must meet all current educational and examination requirements and apply as a new applicant.

D. A licensee may not perform activities defined in §§ 54.1-2100 and 54.1-2101 of the Code of Virginia with an expired license. Any real estate activity conducted subsequent to the expiration date may constitute unlicensed activity and be subject to prosecution under Chapter 1 (§ 54.1-100 et seq.) of Title 54.1 of the Code of Virginia.

Board Discretion to Deny Reinstatement (18 VAC 135-20-150)

The board may deny reinstatement of a license for (i) the same reasons as it may refuse initial licensure or discipline a current licensee; (ii) failure to meet fully pay monetary penalties and costs imposed by the board, plus any accrued interest.

Grounds for Disciplinary Action (18 VAC 135-20-155)

The board has the power to fine any licensee or certificate holder and to suspend or revoke any license or certificate issued under the provisions of Chapter 21 (§ 54.1-2100 et seq.) of Title 54.1 of the Code of Virginia and this chapter in accordance with subdivision A 7 of § 54.1-201 and § 54.1-202 of the Code of Virginia and the provisions of the Administrative Process Act, Chapter 40 (§ 2.2-4000 et seq.) of Title 2.2 of the Code of Virginia, where the licensee or certificate holder has been found to have violated or cooperated with others in violating any provision of Chapters 1 (§ 54.1-100 et seq.), 2 (§ 54.1-200 et seq.), 3 (§ 54.1-300 et seq.), and 21 (§ 54.1-2100 et seq.) of Title 54.1 of the Code of Virginia, Chapter 27.3 (§ 55-525.16 et seq.) failing to comply with the provisions of Chapter 21 (§ 54.1-2100 et seq.) of Title 54.1 of the Code of Virginia or the regulations of the Real Estate Board in performing any acts covered by §§ 54.1-2100 and 54.1-2101 of the Code of Virginia may be charged with a violation, regardless of whether those acts are in the licensee's personal capacity or in his capacity as a real estate licensee.

Place of Business (18 VAC 135-20-160)

A. Within the meaning and intent of § 54.1-2110 of the Code of Virginia, a place of business shall be an office where:

1. The principal broker, either through his own efforts or through the efforts of his employees or associates, regularly transacts the business of a real estate broker as defined in § 54.1-2100 of the Code of Virginia; and

2. The principal broker and his employees or associates can receive business calls and direct business calls to be made.

B. No place of business shall be in a residence unless it is separate and distinct from the living quarters of the residence with its own entrance and is accessible by the public.

C. Every principal broker shall have readily available to the public in the main place of business the firm license, the principal broker license and the license of every salesperson and broker active with the firm. The branch office license and a roster of every salesperson or broker assigned to the branch office shall be posted in a conspicuous place in each branch office.

The section on Duties of Supervising Broker has been significantly updated to include supervisory responsibility for unlicensed assistants in an office.

Duties of Supervising Broker (18 VAC 135-20-165)

Each place of business and each branch office shall be supervised by a supervising broker. The supervising broker shall exercise reasonable and adequate supervision of the provision of real estate brokerage services by associate brokers and salespersons assigned to the branch office. The supervising broker may designate another broker to assist in administering the provisions of this section. The supervising broker does not relinquish overall responsibility for the supervision of the acts of all licensees assigned to the branch office. Factors to be considered in determining whether the supervision is reasonable and adequate include but are not limited to the following:

1. The availability of the supervising broker to all licensees under the supervision of the broker to review and approve all documents, including but not limited to leases, contracts affecting the firm's clients, brokerage agreements, and advertising;

2. The availability of training and written procedures and policies that provide, without limitation, clear guidance in the following areas:

   a. Proper handling of escrow deposits;

   b. Compliance with federal and state fair housing laws and regulations if the firm engages in residential brokerage, residential leasing, or residential property management;

   c. Advertising;

   d. Negotiating and drafting of contracts, leases, and brokerage agreements;

   e. Use of unlicensed individuals;

   f. Agency or independent contractor relationships;

   g. Distribution of information on new or changed statutory or regulatory requirements;

   h. Disclosure of matters relating to the condition of the property; and

   i. Such other matters as necessary to assure the competence of licensees to comply with this chapter and Chapter 21 (§ 54.1-2100 et seq.) of Title 54.1 of the Code of Virginia.

3. The availability of the supervising broker in a timely manner to supervise the management of the brokerage services;

4. The supervising broker ensures the brokerage services are carried out competently and in accordance with the provisions of this chapter and Chapter 21 (§ 54.1-2100 et seq.) of Title 54.1 of the Code of Virginia;

5. The supervising broker undertakes reasonable steps to ensure compliance by all licensees assigned to the branch office, including but not limited to ensuring the licensees have an active, current license; (See License Lookup Site at www.dpor .virginia.gov/LicenseLookup/)

6. The supervising broker undertakes reasonable steps to ensure only licensees undertake activities requiring a license, including but are not limited to:

   a. Show property;

   b. Hold an open house;

   c. Answer questions on listings, title, financing, closing, contracts, brokerage agreements, and legal documents;

   d. Discuss, explain, interpret, or negotiate a contract, listing, lease agreement, or property management agreement with anyone outside the firm; and

   e. Negotiate or agree to any commission, commission split, management fee, or referral fee.

7. The supervising broker shall provide adequate supervision over the unlicensed employees or assistants under the supervision of a broker as they perform the following permitted activities:

   a. Perform general clerical duties, including answering the phones, responding by electronic media, and providing information shown on the listing;

   b. Submit listings and changes to MLS;

   c. Follow up on loan commitments after contracts have been ratified;

   d. Have keys made for listings;

   e. Compute commission checks;

   f.   Place signs on properties;

   g.   Act as a courier service;

   h.   Schedule appointments;

   i.   Record and deposit earnest money deposits, security deposits, and advance rents;

   j.   Prepare contract forms for approval of the licensee and supervising broker;

   k.   Prepare promotional materials and advertisements for approval of the licensee and supervising broker;

   l.   Assemble closing documents;

   m.   Obtain required public information from governmental entities;

   n.   Monitor license and personnel files;

   o.   Order routine repairs as directed by licensee;

   p.   Are compensated for their work at a predetermined rate that is not contingent upon the occurrence of a real estate transaction; and

   q.   Perform any other activities undertaken in the regular course of business for which a license is not required.

8.   If a supervising broker is located more than 50 miles from the place of business or the branch office and there are licensees who regularly conduct business assigned to the branch office or at the place of business, the supervising broker must certify in writing on a quarterly basis on a form provided by the board that the supervising broker complied with the requirements of this section; and

9.   The supervising broker must maintain the records required in this section for three years. The records must be furnished to the board's agent upon request.

As of January 1, 2017, supervising brokers must provide the name and license number for each supervising broker of a branch office. Upon renewal or transfer of a licensee's license to a branch office, the supervising broker must inform the VREB of each licensee's name and license number.

Maintenance of Licenses (18 VAC 135-20-170)

A.   Name and address.

   1.   Salespersons and individual brokers shall at all times keep the board informed of their current name and home address. Changes of name and address must be reported to the board in writing within 30 calendar days of such change. The board shall not be responsible for the licensee's failure to receive notices, communications and correspondence caused by the licensee's failure to promptly notify the board of any change of address. A licensee may use a professional name other than a legal name if that professional name is filed with the board prior to its use. The professional name shall include the licensee's first or last name and shall not include any titles.

   2.   Salespersons and brokers shall be issued a license only to the place of business of the sole proprietorship or firm with which the salesperson or broker is active.

   3.   Principal brokers must at all times keep the board informed of their current firm and branch office name and addresses and changes of name and address must be reported to the board in writing within 30 calendar days of such change. A physical address is required. A post office box will not be accepted.

B. Discharge or termination of active status.

1. When any salesperson or broker is discharged or in any way terminates his active status with a sole proprietorship or firm, it shall be the duty of the sole proprietor or principal broker to return the license to the board so that it is received within 10 calendar days of the date of termination or being notified of the status change. The sole proprietor or principal broker shall indicate on the license the date of termination, and shall sign the license before returning it.

2. When any principal broker is discharged or in any way terminates his active status with a firm, it shall be the duty of the firm to notify the board and return the license to the board within three business days of termination or being notified of the status change. The firm shall indicate on the license the date of termination, and shall sign the license before returning it. See § 54.1-2109 of the Code of Virginia for termination relating to the death or disability of the principal broker.

Code of Virginia § 54.1-2109—Death or Disability of a Broker

Upon the death or disability of a licensed real estate broker who was engaged in a proprietorship or who was the only licensed broker in a corporation or partnership, the Real Estate Board shall grant approval to carry on the business of the deceased or disabled broker for 180 days following the death or disability of the broker solely for the purpose of concluding the business of the deceased or disabled broker in the following order:

1. A personal representative qualified by the court to administer the deceased broker's estate.

2. If there is no personal representative qualified pursuant to subdivision 1, then an agent designated under a power of attorney of the disabled or deceased broker, which designation expressly references this section.

3. If there is no agent designated pursuant to subdivision 2, the executor nominated in the deceased broker's will.

4. If there is no executor nominated pursuant to subdivision 3, then an adult family member of the disabled or deceased broker.

5. If there is no adult family member nominated pursuant to subdivision 4, then an employee of the disabled or deceased broker.

In the event none of the foregoing is available or suitable, the Board may appoint any other suitable person to terminate the business within 180 days.

This next section on the maintenance and management of escrow accounts is very important. The majority of cases of violations brought forward to the REB are the result of mismanagement of escrow accounts.

Maintenance and Management of Escrow Accounts (18 VAC 135-20-180)

A. Maintenance of escrow accounts.

1. If money is to be held in escrow, each firm or sole proprietorship shall maintain in the name by which it is licensed one or more federally insured separate escrow accounts in a federally insured depository into which all down payments, earnest money deposits, money received upon final settlement, application deposits as defined by § 55-248.4 of the Code of Virginia, rental

payments, rental security deposits, money advanced by a buyer or seller for the payment of expenses in connection with the closing of real estate transactions, money advanced by the broker's client or expended on behalf of the client, or other escrow funds received by him or his associates on behalf of his client or any other person shall be deposited unless all principals to the transaction have agreed otherwise in writing. The balance in the escrow accounts shall be sufficient at all times to account for all funds that are designated to be held by the firm or sole proprietorship. The principal broker shall be held responsible for these accounts, including having signatory authority on these accounts. The supervising broker and any other licensee with escrow account authority may be held responsible for these accounts. All such accounts, checks and bank statements shall be labeled "escrow" and the account(s) shall be designated as "escrow" accounts with the financial institution where such accounts are established.

2. Funds to be deposited in the escrow account may include moneys which shall ultimately belong to the licensee, but such moneys shall be separately identified in the escrow account records and shall be paid to the firm by a check drawn on the escrow account when the funds become due to the licensee. Funds in an escrow account shall not be paid directly to the licensees of the firm. The fact that an escrow account contains money which may ultimately belong to the licensee does not constitute "commingling of funds" as set forth by subdivision C 2 of this section, provided that there are periodic withdrawals of said funds at intervals of not more than six months, and that the licensee can at all times accurately identify the total funds in that account which belong to the licensee and the firm.

3. If escrow funds are used to purchase a certificate of deposit, the pledging or hypothecation of such certificate, or the absence of the original certificate from the direct control of the principal or supervising broker, shall constitute commingling as prohibited by subdivision C 2 of this section.

4. Lease transactions: application deposits. Any application deposit as defined by § 55-248.4 of the Code of Virginia paid by a prospective tenant for the purpose of being considered as a tenant for a dwelling unit to a licensee acting on behalf of a landlord client shall be placed in escrow by the end of the fifth business banking day following approval of the rental application by the landlord unless all principals to the lease transaction have agreed otherwise in writing.

B. Disbursement of funds from escrow accounts.

1. a. Purchase transactions. Upon the ratification of a contract, earnest money deposits and down payments received by the principal broker or supervising broker or his associates must be placed in an escrow account by the end of the fifth business banking day following ratification, unless otherwise agreed to in writing by the principals to the transaction, and shall remain in that account until the transaction has been consummated or terminated. In the event the transaction is not consummated (nonconsummation), the principal broker or supervising broker shall hold such funds in escrow until (i) all principals to the transaction have agreed in writing as to their disposition, and the funds shall be returned to the agreed upon principal within 20 days of the agreement, or (ii) a court of competent jurisdiction orders such disbursement of the funds, or (iii) the funds are successfully interpleaded into a court of competent jurisdiction pursuant to this section, or (iv) the broker can pay the funds to the

principal to the transaction who is entitled to receive them in accordance with the clear and explicit terms of the contract which established the deposit. In the latter event, prior to disbursement, the broker shall give written notice to the principal to the transaction not to receive the deposit by either (i) hand delivery receipted for by the addressee, or (ii) by certified mail return receipt requested, with a copy to the other party, that this payment will be made unless a written protest from that principal to the transaction is received by the broker within 30 days of the hand delivery or mailing, as appropriate, of that notice. If the notice is sent within 90 days of the date of nonconsummation, the broker may send the notice by receiptable email or facsimile if such email address or facsimile information is set forth in the contract or otherwise provided by the recipient. In all events, the broker may send the notice to the notice address, if any, set forth in the contract. If the contract does not contain a notice address and the broker does not have another address for the recipient of the notice, the broker may send it to the last known address of the recipient. No broker shall be required to make a determination as to the party entitled to receive the earnest money deposit. The broker shall not be deemed to violate any obligation to any client by virtue of making such a determination. A broker who has carried out the above procedure shall be construed to have fulfilled the requirements of this chapter.

A principal broker or supervising broker holding escrow funds for a principal to the transaction may seek to have a court of competent jurisdiction take custody of disputed or unclaimed escrow funds via an interpleader action pursuant to § 16.1-77 of the Code of Virginia.

If a principal broker or supervising broker is holding escrow funds for the owner of real property and such property is foreclosed upon by a lender, the principal broker or supervising broker shall have the right to file an interpleader action pursuant to § 16.1-77 of the Code of Virginia.

If there is in effect at the date of the foreclosure sale a real estate purchase contract to buy the property foreclosed upon and the real estate purchase contract provides that the earnest money deposit held in escrow by a firm or sole proprietorship shall be paid to a principal to the contract in the event of a termination of the real estate purchase contract, the foreclosure shall be deemed a termination of the real estate purchase contract, and the principal broker or supervising broker may, absent any default on the part of the purchaser, disburse the earnest money deposit to the purchaser pursuant to such provisions of the real estate purchase contract without further consent from, or notice to, the principals.

b.   Lease transactions: security deposits. Any security deposit held by a firm or sole proprietorship shall be placed in an escrow account by the end of the fifth business banking day following receipt, unless otherwise agreed to in writing by the principals to the transaction. Each such security deposit shall be treated in accordance with the security deposit provisions of the Virginia Residential Landlord and Tenant Act, Chapter 13.2 (§ 55-248.2 et seq.) of Title 55 of the Code of Virginia, unless exempted therefrom, in which case the terms of the lease or other applicable law shall control. Notwithstanding anything in this section to the contrary, unless the landlord has otherwise become entitled to receive the security deposit or a portion thereof, the security deposit shall not be removed from an escrow account required by the lease without the written consent of the tenant. If there is in effect at the date of the foreclosure sale a tenant in a residential dwelling unit foreclosed upon and the landlord is holding a security deposit of the tenant, the landlord shall handle the security deposit in accordance with applicable law, which requires the holder of the landlord's interest in the dwelling unit at the time of termination of tenancy to return any security deposit and any accrued interest that is duly owed to the tenant, whether or not such security deposit is transferred with the landlord's interest by law or equity, and regardless of any contractual agreements between the original landlord and his successors in interest. Nothing herein shall be construed to prevent the landlord from making lawful deductions from the security deposit in accordance with applicable law.

    c.   Lease transactions: prepaid rent or escrow fund advances. Unless otherwise agreed in writing by all principals to the transaction, all prepaid rent and other money paid to the licensee in connection with the lease shall be placed in an escrow account by the end of the fifth business banking day following receipt be treated in accordance with the prepaid rent provision of the Virginia Residential Landlord and Tenant Act, Chapter 13.2 (§ 55-248.2 et seq.) of Title 55 of the Code of Virginia.

2. a.   Purchase transactions. Unless otherwise agreed in writing by all principals to the transaction, a licensee shall not be entitled to any part of the earnest money deposit or to any other money paid to the licensee in connection with any real estate transaction as part of the licensee's commission until the transaction has been consummated.

    b.   Lease transactions. Unless otherwise agreed in writing by the principals to the lease or property management agreement, as applicable, a licensee shall not be entitled to any part of the security deposit or to any other money paid to the licensee in connection with any real estate lease as part of the licensee's commission except in accordance with the terms of the lease or the property management agreement, as applicable. Notwithstanding anything in this section to the contrary, unless the landlord has otherwise become entitled to receive the security deposit or a portion thereof, the security deposit shall not be removed from an escrow account required by the lease without the written consent of the tenant.

3. On funds placed in an account bearing interest, written disclosure in the contract of sale or lease at the time of contract or lease writing shall be made to the principals to the transaction regarding the disbursement of interest.

4. A licensee shall not disburse or cause to be disbursed moneys from an escrow or property management escrow account unless sufficient money is on deposit in that account to the credit of the individual client or property involved.

5. Unless otherwise agreed in writing by all principals to the transaction, expenses incidental to closing a transaction (e.g., fees for appraisal, insurance, credit report, etc.) shall not be deducted from a deposit or down payment.

C. Actions including improper maintenance of escrow funds include:

1. Accepting any note, nonnegotiable instrument, or anything of value not readily negotiable, as a deposit on a contract, offer to purchase, or lease, without acknowledging its acceptance in the agreement;

2. Commingling the funds of any person by a principal or supervising broker or his employees or associates or any licensee with his own funds, or those of his corporation, firm, or association;

3. Failure to deposit escrow funds in an account or accounts designated to receive only such funds as required by subdivision A 1 of this section;

4. Failure to have sufficient balances in an escrow account or accounts at all times for all funds that are designated to be held by the firm or sole proprietorship as required by this chapter; and

5. Failing, as principal broker, to report to the board within three business days instances where the principal broker reasonably believes the improper conduct of a licensee, independent contractor, or employee has caused noncompliance with this section.

Maintenance and Management Of Financial Records (18 VAC 135-20-185)

A. A complete record of financial transactions conducted under authority of the principal broker's Virginia license shall be maintained in the principal broker's place of business, or in a designated branch office. When the principal broker's office is located outside of Virginia and the firm has a branch office in Virginia, a copy of these records shall be maintained in the Virginia office. These records shall show, in addition to any other requirements of the regulations, the following information: from whom money was received; the date of receipt; the place of deposit; the date of deposit; and, after the transaction has been completed, the final disposition of the funds.

B. The principal broker shall maintain a bookkeeping or recordkeeping system which shall accurately and clearly disclose full compliance with the requirements outlined in this section. Accounting records which are in sufficient detail to provide necessary information to determine such compliance shall be maintained.

C. Actions constituting improper recordkeeping by a principal broker or supervising broker include:

1. Failing to retain for a period of three years from the date of execution, each brokerage agreement, each disclosure and consent to dual agency or dual representation, and each disclosure and consent to designated agency or designated representation. Each disclosure of a brokerage relationship to an unrepresented party shall be retained for three years from the date provided to the party;

2. Failing to retain for a period of three years from the date of closing or from ratification, if the transaction fails to close, a complete and legible copy of each executed contract of sale, any executed release from contract, any executed lease agreement, any executed property management agreement, and each settlement statement related to a real estate transaction, in the broker's control or possession unless prohibited by law;

3. Failing to maintain a complete and accurate record of such receipts and their disbursements for moneys received on behalf of others for a period of three years from the date of the closing or termination of the sales transaction or termination of a lease or conclusion of the licensee's involvement in the lease; and

4. Failing to maintain any records required by this section for three years.

The next section on advertising was rewritten in the new regulations to account for current means of advertising electronically.

Advertising by Licensees (18 VAC 135-20-190)

A. Definitions. The following definitions apply unless a different meaning is plainly required by the context:

"Advertising" means all forms of representation, promotion and solicitation disseminated in any manner and by any means of communication to consumers for any purpose related to licensed real estate activity.

"Contact information" means telephone number or web address.

"Disclosure" in the context of electronic media advertising means (i) advertising by the firm that contains the firm's licensed name and the city and state in which the firm's main office or branch office is located or (ii) advertising by an affiliated licensee that contains the licensee's name, the name of the firm with which the licensee is active, and the city and state in which the licensee's place of business is located, and this disclosure shall be viewable on the main page or no more than one click away from the main page. "Disclosure" in the context of all other advertising means (i) advertising by the firm that contains the firm's licensed name or (ii) advertising by an affiliated licensee that contains the licensee's name and the name of the firm with which the licensee is active.

"Viewable page" means a page that may or may not scroll beyond the borders of the screen and includes the use of framed pages.

B. All advertising must be under the direct supervision of the principal broker or supervising broker, in the name of the firm and, when applicable, comply with the disclosure required by § 54.1-2138.1 of the Code of Virginia. The firm's licensed name must be clearly and legibly displayed on all advertising.

C. Electronic media advertising.

1. Any electronic media advertising undertaken for the purpose of any licensed activity is subject to the provisions of this chapter.

2. All electronic media advertising that can be viewed or experienced as a separate unit (i.e., email messages and web pages) must contain disclosure that shall be viewable on the main page or is no more than one click away from the main page.

3. All electronic media listings advertised must be kept current and consistent as follows:

   a. Electronic media listing information must be consistent with the property description and actual status of the listing. The licensee shall update in a timely manner material changes to the listing status authorized by the seller or property description when the licensee controls the electronic media site.

   b. The licensee shall make timely written requests for updates reflecting material changes to the listing status or property descriptions when a third-party electronic media listing service controls the website displaying the listing information.

D. Other advertising.

1. For sale and for lease signs placed on the property shall include but not be limited to the firm's name and the firm's primary or branch office telephone number.

2. Business cards shall include but not be limited to the licensee's name, the firm name, and contact information.

E. The following activities shall be prohibited:

1. Implying that property listed by a licensee's firm and advertised by the firm or licensee is for sale, exchange, rent or lease by the owner or by an unlicensed person;

2. Failing to include a notice in all advertising that the owner is a real estate licensee if the licensee owns or has any ownership interest in the property advertised (previously, disclosure was not required if the licensee listed the property with a firm);

3. Failing to include the firm's licensed name on any sign displayed outside each place of business;

4. Failing to obtain the written consent of the seller, landlord, optionor or licensor Prior to advertising a specific identifiable property; and

5. Failing to identify the type of services offered when advertising by general description a property not listed by the party making the advertisement.

False Advertising

Legislation passed in 2013 clarified that licensed real estate brokers or salesperson are not liable for false advertising when relying on public records or information from a third party. This includes any civil action or regulatory action brought under the real estate licensing laws.

In response to a growing trend for plaintiffs suing an agent for false advertising in a civil proceeding to claim that the licensee is guilty of criminal false advertising, legislation now requires attorneys in a civil case to provide supporting evidence, as they would with any other court pleading.

Disclosure of Interest (18 VAC 135-20-210)

If a licensee knows or should have known that he, any member of his family, his firm, any member of his firm, or any entity in which he has an ownership interest, is acquiring or attempting to acquire or is selling or leasing real property through purchase, sale, or lease and the licensee is a party to the transaction, the licensee must disclose in writing that he is a licensee and that he, any member of his family, his firm, any member of his firm, or any entity in which he has an ownership interest has or will have an ownership interest to the other parties to the transaction. This disclosure shall be made to the purchaser, seller, lessor, or lessee upon having substantive discussions about specific real property.

Disclosure of Brokerage Relationships (18 VAC 135-20-220)

A. Purchase transactions.

1. Unless disclosure has been previously made by a licensee, a licensee shall disclose to an actual or prospective buyer or seller who is not the client of the licensee and who is not represented by another licensee and with whom the licensee has substantive discussions about a specific property or properties, the person whom the licensee represents pursuant to a brokerage agreement, as that term is defined in § 54.1-2130 of the Code of Virginia.

2. Except as otherwise provided in subdivision 3 of this subsection, such disclosure shall be made in writing at the earliest practical time, but in no event later than the time specific real estate assistance is first provided. Any disclosure complying with the provisions of § 54.1-2138 A of the Code of Virginia shall be deemed in compliance with this disclosure requirement.

3. A licensee acting as a dual or designated agent or as a dual or designated representative shall obtain the written consent of all clients to the transaction at the earliest practical time. Such consent shall be presumed to have been given by a client who signs a disclosure complying with the provisions of §§ 54.1-2139, 54.1-2139.01, and 54.1-2139.1 of the Code of Virginia. Such disclosure shall be given to, and consent obtained from, (i) the buyer not later than the time an offer to purchase is presented to the licensee who will present the offer to the listing agent or seller, and (ii) the seller not later than the time the offer to purchase is presented to the seller.

4. Any disclosure required by this subsection may be given in combination with other disclosures or information, but, if so, the disclosure must be conspicuous, printed in bold lettering, all capitals, underlined, or within a separate box or as otherwise provided by § 54.1-2138 of the Code of Virginia.

B. Lease transactions.

1. Unless disclosure has been previously made by a licensee, a licensee shall disclose to an actual or prospective landlord or tenant who is not the client of the licensee and who is not represented by another licensee, that the licensee has a brokerage relationship with another party or parties to the transaction. Such disclosure shall be in writing and included in the application for lease or the lease itself, whichever occurs first. If the terms of the lease do not provide for such disclosure, the disclosure shall be made in writing not later than the signing of the lease.

2. This disclosure requirement shall not apply to lessors or lessees in single or multi-family residential units for lease terms of less than two months.

The Voluntary Compliance Program has been in place for several years but is now codified and made part of the Real Estate Regulations.

Audits (VAC 135-20-225)

A. Procedures for voluntary compliance, self audit, or third-party audit; broker immunity.

1. A principal broker or supervising broker may conduct, or may have another person conduct, an audit of the practices, policies, and procedures of his firm or sole proprietorship in accordance with § 54.1-2111.1 of the Code of Virginia. The methods and findings of the audit shall be documented as described in this subsection.

2. A principal broker or supervising broker shall notify the board in writing within 30 days following the conclusion of a self audit, or within 30 days from the receipt of the final report of a third-party audit, of any matter he believes to constitute noncompliance with the provisions of Real Estate Board regulations or law. The principal broker or supervising broker shall also submit (i) a statement that such noncompliance has been remediated or (ii) a plan to correct such noncompliance within 90 days. Failure to comply with these requirements may result in loss of immunity from regulatory enforcement action.

3. A principal broker or supervising broker shall sign and date any report made pursuant to subdivision 2 of this subsection. Such report, properly submitted, shall provide immunity from enforcement against the principal broker or supervising broker by the board for the matters reported therein.

4. Immunity from enforcement action provided by this section shall not apply if the noncompliance with provisions of Real Estate Board regulations or law by the principal broker or supervising broker was intentional or was the result of gross negligence by the principal broker or supervising broker.

5. Immunity from enforcement action provided by this section shall apply only to the principal broker and supervising broker who conduct an audit and submit a voluntary compliance plan in accordance with this section and shall not extend to any other broker or salesperson who may not be in compliance with Real Estate Board regulations or law.

6. Failure to complete the voluntary compliance program within 90 days from the date of plan submission shall result in the loss of immunity from regulatory enforcement action. Repeated instances of a violation found as a result of an audit that was subject to the voluntary compliance program may be deemed by the board to constitute a failure to complete the prior voluntary compliance program.

B. Procedures for mandatory audit.

1. A principal broker or supervising broker shall conduct or have a third party conduct an audit at least once during each license term in accordance with § 54.1-2106.2 of the Code of Virginia. Such audit shall be documented on a form developed by the board.

2. In conducting an audit of practices, policies, and procedures of the firm or sole proprietorship, the principal broker or supervising broker or a third party shall examine and document all matters regarding the compliance by the firm or sole proprietorship with law and regulation regarding:

   a. Proper handling of escrow deposits and maintenance of a complete record of financial transactions;

   b. Compliance with federal and state fair housing laws and regulations if the firm or sole proprietorship engages in residential brokerage, residential leasing, or residential property management;

   c. Advertising in all forms and media;

   d. Negotiation and drafting of contracts, leases, and brokerage agreements;

   e. Use of unlicensed individuals;

   f. Agency or independent contractor relationships;

   g. Distribution of information on new or changed statutory or regulatory requirements;

   h. Proper documentation of required disclosures; and

   i. Such other matters as necessary to assure the competence of licensees to comply with this chapter and Chapter 21 (§ 54.1-2100 et seq.) of Title 54.1 of the Code of Virginia.

3. If at the conclusion of a mandatory audit the principal broker or supervising broker or third party believes there is noncompliance with the provisions of the Real Estate Board regulations or law, the principal broker or supervising broker may avail himself of the procedures for voluntary compliance described in subsection A of this section.

Upon request by any investigator, or by another agent of the board, a broker shall cooperate in the provision of records and documents pursuant to 18 VAC 135-20-240 within 10 days of receipt of the request, and for other requests by the board and its agents pursuant to 18 VAC 135-20-250, within 21 days of receipt.

Provision of Records to the Board (18 VAC 135-20-240)

Unless otherwise specified by the board, or as set forth in § 54.1-2108 of the Code of Virginia, a licensee of the Real Estate Board shall produce to the board or any of its agents within 10 days of the request evidence of signature cards or bank records, any document, book, or record concerning any real estate transaction in which the licensee was involved, or for which the licensee is required to maintain records for inspection and copying by the board or its agents. The board may extend such time frame upon a showing of extenuating circumstances prohibiting delivery within such 10-day period.

Response to Any Inquiry of the Board (18 VAC 135-20-250)

A licensee must respond to an inquiry by the board, other than requested under 18 VAC 135-20-240, or its agents within 21 days.

Sections 260 through 320 were originally designated as Standards of Practice and Conduct and were substantially rewritten in the 2015 Real Estate Regulations. The words "Unworthiness and Incompetence" were replaced with "Prohibited Acts."

Prohibited Acts (18 VAC 135-20-260)

The following are prohibited acts:

1. Furnishing substantially inaccurate or incomplete information to the board in obtaining, renewing, reinstating, or maintaining a license;

2. Holding more than one license as a real estate broker or salesperson in Virginia except as provided in this chapter;

3. As a currently licensed real estate salesperson, sitting for the licensing examination for a salesperson's license;

4. As a currently licensed real estate broker, sitting for a real estate licensing examination;

5. Signing an experience verification form without direct supervision or actual knowledge of the applicant's activities as defined in §§ 54.1-2100 and 54.1-2101 of the Code of Virginia or unreasonably refusing to sign an experience verification form;

6. Having been convicted or found guilty regardless of the manner of adjudication in any jurisdiction of the United States of a misdemeanor involving moral turpitude, sexual offense, drug distribution or physical injury, or any felony, there being no appeal pending therefrom or the time for appeal having elapsed. Review of convictions shall be subject to the requirements of § 54.1-204 of the Code of Virginia. Any plea of nolo contendere shall be considered a conviction for the purposes of this subdivision;

7. Failing to inform the board in writing within 30 days of pleading guilty or nolo contendere or being convicted or found guilty regardless of adjudication of any convictions as stated in subdivision 6 of this section;

8. Having had a license as a real estate broker or real estate salesperson that was suspended, revoked, or surrendered in connection with a disciplinary action or that has been the subject of discipline in any jurisdiction;

9. Failing to inform the board in writing within 30 days of a disciplinary action as stated in subdivision 8 of this section;

10. Having been found in a court or an administrative body of competent jurisdiction to have violated the Virginia Fair Housing Act, the Fair Housing Laws of any jurisdiction of the United States, including without limitation Title VIII of the Civil Rights Act of 1968 (82 Stat. 73), or the Civil Rights Act of 1866 (14 Stat. 27), there being no appeal therefrom or the time for appeal having elapsed;

11. Actions constituting failing to act as a real estate broker or salesperson in such a manner as to safeguard the interests of the public, including but not limited to the following:

    a. A principal broker or supervising broker failing to ensure proper supervision and accountability over the firm's day-to-day financial dealings, escrow account or accounts, and daily operations;

    b. A broker failing to disburse funds from an escrow account according to the regulations or failing to properly retain documents relating to the basis for disbursal;

    c. A broker failing to ensure the licensees for whom the broker has oversight responsibility hold **active licenses** while practicing real estate;

    d. A broker failing to provide accurate and timely reports to the board about a licensee's compliance with the board's laws and regulations;

    e. A broker failing to have signatory authority on all accounts;

    f. A broker failing to account for or remit any moneys coming into a licensee's possession that belong to another;

    g. A licensee failing to submit to the broker in a timely manner, all earnest money deposits, contracts, listing agreements, deeds of lease, or any other documents for which the broker has oversight responsibility;

    h. A licensee negotiating leases for a third party through an unlicensed firm or without a principal broker;

    i. A licensee operating an unlicensed firm or acting as a principal broker;

    j. A licensee practicing real estate with an inactive or expired license;

    k. A licensee knowingly providing the broker with an earnest money deposit check from an account with insufficient funds;

    l. A licensee allowing unsupervised access to a home without the owner's authorization;

    m. A licensee failing to inform the broker of a transaction; and

    n. A licensee submitting unauthorized altered copies of a contract or contracts to the broker; and

12. Actions constituting engaging in improper, fraudulent, or dishonest conduct, including but not limited to the following:

    a. A licensee attempting to divert commission from the firm or sole proprietorship and direct payment to a licensee or an unlicensed individual who is not a party to the transaction;

Unit 8

b. A licensee fabricating or altering any document with the intent to mislead;

c. A licensee signing any documents on a client's behalf without first obtaining a client's proper written permission or authorization to sign said documents on his behalf;

d. A licensee making an earnest money deposit payable to himself or negotiating the check without written authority;

e. A licensee misrepresenting ownership of a property;

f. A licensee submitting copies of the same earnest money deposit check for inclusion with multiple offers;

g. A licensee entering into agreements to be compensated for real estate services while his license is inactive;

h. A licensee representing in offers he received the earnest money deposit when he has not or he knows the check is worthless; and

i. A licensee misrepresenting who is holding the earnest money deposit.

Conflict of Interest (18 VAC 135-20-270)

Actions constituting a **conflict of interest** include:

1. Being active with a real estate broker other than the licensee's principal broker, without the written consent of the principal broker;

2. Acting for more than one client in a transaction governed by the provisions of §§ 54.1-2139, 54.1-2139.01, and 54.1-2139.1 of the Code of Virginia without first obtaining the written consent of all clients; and

3. Performing regulated activities as a standard agent, limited service agent, or independent contractor for any client outside the licensee's brokerage firm(s) or sole proprietorship(s).

Improper Brokerage Commission (18 VAC 135-20-280)

Actions resulting in an improper brokerage commission include:

1. Offering to pay or paying a transaction-based fee, fees, or other valuable consideration to any person not licensed in this or any jurisdiction for services that require a real estate license;

2. Accepting a commission, fee, or other valuable consideration, as a real estate salesperson or associate broker, for any real estate services from any person or entity except the licensee's principal broker or supervising broker at the time of the transaction;

3. Receiving financial benefit from the use of any information about the property, the transaction, or the parties to the transaction, when the information is gained as a result of the performance of acts specified in Chapter 21 (§ 54.1-2100 et seq.) of Title 54.1 of the Code of Virginia without the prior written consent of the licensee's principal broker;

4. Receiving financial benefit from any person other than the licensee's principal broker at the time of the transaction, for the performance of any of the acts specified in Chapter 21 (§ 54.1-2100 et seq.) of Title 54.1 of the Code of Virginia without the prior written consent of the licensee's principal broker;

5. Receiving financial benefit or other valuable consideration for any work or service related to a transaction without the prior written acknowledgment of the person paying for such work or service; and

6. Making a listing contract or lease which provides for a "net" return to the seller/lessor, leaving the licensee free to sell or lease the property at any price he can obtain in excess of the "net" price named by the seller/lessor.

Improper Dealing (18 VAC 135-20-290)

Actions constituting improper dealing include:

1. Offering real property for sale or for lease without the knowledge and consent of the owner or the owner's authorized representative, or on any terms other than those authorized by the owner or the owner's authorized representative;

2. Placing a sign on any property without the consent of the owner of the property or the owner's authorized representative; and

3. Causing any advertisement for sale, rent, or lease to appear in any format or medium without including in the advertisement the name of the firm or sole proprietorship.

Misrepresentation/Omission (18 VAC 135-20-300)

Actions constituting misrepresentation or omission, or both, include:

1. Using "bait and switch" tactics by advertising or offering real property for sale or rent with the intent not to sell or rent at the price or terms advertised, unless the advertisement or offer clearly states that the property advertised is limited in specific quantity or for a specified time period and the licensee did in fact have at least that quantity for sale or rent at that price or terms at the time of advertising;

2. Failure by a licensee representing a seller or landlord as a standard agent to disclose in a timely manner to a prospective purchaser or tenant all material adverse facts pertaining to the physical condition of the property which are actually known by the licensee;

3. Failing as a licensee to tender promptly to the buyer and seller every written offer, every written counteroffer, and every written rejection to purchase, option or lease obtained on the property involved;

4. Failure by a licensee acting as an agent to disclose in a timely manner to the licensee's client all material facts related to the property or concerning the transaction when the failure to so disclose would constitute failure by the licensee to exercise ordinary care as defined in the brokerage agreement;

5. Notwithstanding the provisions of subdivision 4 of this section, a licensee acting as a dual representative shall not disclose to one client represented in the dual representation confidential information relating to the transaction obtained during the representation of another client in the same dual representation unless otherwise provided by law;

6. Failing to include the complete terms and conditions of the real estate transaction, including but not limited to any lease, property management agreement or offer to purchase;

7. Failing to include in any application, lease, or offer to purchase identification of all those holding any deposits;

8. Knowingly making any false statement or report, or willfully misstating the value of any land, property, or security for the purpose of influencing in any way the action of any lender upon:

a. Applications, advance discounts, purchase agreements, repurchase agreements, commitments or loans;

b. Changes in terms or extensions of time for any of the items listed in this subdivision 8 whether by renewal, deferment of action, or other means without the prior written consent of the principals to the transaction;

c. Acceptance, release, or substitution of security for any of the items listed in subdivision 8a of this section without the prior written consent of the principals to the transaction;

9. Knowingly making any material misrepresentation; and

10. Making a false promise through agents, salespersons, advertising, or other means.

Improper Delivery of Instruments (18 VAC 135-20-310)

Actions constituting improper delivery of instruments include:

1. Failing to make prompt delivery to each principal to a transaction, complete and legible copies of any written disclosures required by §§ 54.1-2138, 54.1-2139, 54.1-2139.01, and 54.1-2139.1 of the Code of Virginia, listings, lease, offers to purchase, counteroffers, addenda and ratified agreements, and other documentation required by the agreement;

2. Failing to provide in a timely manner to all principals to the transaction written notice of any material changes to the transaction;

3. Failing to deliver to the seller and buyer, at the time a real estate transaction is completed, a complete and accurate statement of receipts and disbursements of moneys received by the licensee, duly signed and certified by the principal or supervising broker or his authorized agent; provided, however, if the transaction is closed by a settlement agent other than the licensee or his broker, and if the disbursement of moneys received by the licensee is disclosed on the applicable settlement statement, the licensee shall not be required to provide the separate statement of receipts and disbursements; and

4. Refusing or failing without just cause to surrender to the rightful owner, upon demand, any document or instrument which the licensee possesses.

Principal and Supervising Broker's Responsibility for Acts Of Licensees And Employees (18 VAC 135-20-330)

Any unlawful act or violation of any of the provisions of Chapter 21 (§ 54.1-2100 et seq.) of Title 54.1 or of Chapter 5.1 (§ 36-96.1 et seq.) of Title 36 of the Code of Virginia or of the regulations of the board by any real estate salesperson, employee, partner or affiliate of a principal broker, supervising broker, or both, may not be cause for disciplinary action against the principal broker, supervising broker, or both, unless it appears to the satisfaction of the board that the principal broker, supervising broker, or both, knew or should have known of the unlawful act or violation and failed to take reasonable action under the circumstances to remedy the situation.

Effect of Disciplinary Action on Subordinate Licensees (18 VAC 135-20-340)

Action by the board resulting in the revocation, suspension, or denial of renewal of the license of any principal broker or sole proprietor shall automatically result in an order that the licenses of any and all individuals active with the affected firm be returned to the board until such time as they are reissued upon the written request of a sole proprietor or principal broker pursuant to 18 VAC 135-20-170 B.

Effect of Disciplinary Action on Concurrent Licenses (18 VAC 135-20-345)

The board shall suspend, revoke or deny renewal of existing concurrent broker licenses when the board suspends, revokes or denies renewal of another broker's license held by the same individual.

Part IV Schools

Sections 350 to 410 are regulations for proprietary schools followed by a section on Forms.

The Licensing Examination

Once a license applicant has successfully completed the educational requirements, the applicant's next step is to take and pass an examination administered by the REB or a designated testing service. In Virginia, real estate licensing examinations are prepared by PSI Examination Services.

Applicants must obtain approval from the REB before taking the exam. The application is sent to PSI. When PSI receives the application and the required application fee and registers the applicant into the system, the applicant may schedule the examination.

All new real estate salesperson and broker license applicants must submit a set of fingerprints to the Virginia Central Criminal Records Exchange (CCRE). PSI Exams, Inc., the board's license examination provider, will electronically fingerprint license applicants at one of the PSI's testing locations.

The examination consists of two portions—the state (45 minutes) and the national (105 minutes). The fee is $60.50. The passing score is 70% for the national portion and 75% for the state portion.

The examination is administered by computer, and applicants will know the results as soon as they have completed the exam. If the applicant passes, successful notification appears on the computer screen. License application forms for submittal to the REB will be available at the test center. If the applicant does not pass, unsuccessful notification appears on the screen. Registration forms for submittal to PSI to retake the examination will be available at the test center. There is no prescribed waiting period. The retake fee is $60.50. If the applicant fails one portion of the exam (state or national) that portion must be retaken and passed. All license applications must be received by the DPOR within one year of passing the exam. Exam results are confidential and are reported only to the applicant and to the DPOR.

More information and test application forms may be found at https://candidate.psiexams .com. The website also includes a tutorial on taking the exam and an online practice test.

Unit 8

Referral Agents and REALTORS®

Referral Agent

A **referral agent** is a real estate licensee who does not engage in real estate activities, such as listing and selling property. As the title implies, a referral agent refers prospective buyers or sellers to the broker with whom the agent is affiliated. If a sale results from the referral, the broker may pay the licensee a fee for the referral. The referral agent's license is displayed either in the referral office or in the main office of the broker with whom the agent is affiliated. The REB considers a person acting in the capacity of a referral agent to be active, not inactive. A referral agent will be required to complete the mandatory 16 hours of continuing education within each two-year licensing cycle.

Active
16hrs CE

REALTORS® licensees may become members of professional real estate organizations, such as the National Association of REALTORS® (NAR) and its state and local affiliates. Membership in NAR requires pledging to abide by the NAR Code of Ethics. Violations of the Code will result in disciplinary action by the state or local association. Only a duly licensed person or entity is authorized to engage in acts of real estate brokerage in Virginia. All licensees are subject to the Real Estate Regulations as reprinted here. Violations of the Real Estate Regulations will result in disciplinary action by the REB.

IN PRACTICE

Membership by licensed brokers in most local real estate associations affiliated with NAR typically requires all licensees affiliated with the broker to maintain active membership in the REALTOR® association. A referral company is typically a firm in which the principal broker and the affiliated licensees are not members of a REALTORS® association.

Complaint Procedure

Department of Professional and Occupational Regulation (DPOR)

The Regulatory Programs and Compliance Section reviews consumer reports against licensees to determine whether the DPOR is authorized to process the complaint. The DPOR only processes complaints against individuals or businesses that are subject to the laws or regulations of its regulatory boards. The DPOR and its regulatory boards cannot require any individual or business to refund money, correct deficiencies, or provide other personal remedies. In some cases, private legal action may be the only recourse to resolve a matter. The DPOR cannot provide legal advice.

Any report against a regulant (licensee) for allegedly violating board statutes or regulations must be in writing and received by the DPOR within three years of the occurrence. In cases where a regulant has materially and willfully misrepresented any information required by statute or regulations to be disclosed to a complainant, the filing may be made at any time within two years after discovery of the misrepresentation.

The report is reviewed to determine whether a violation has occurred. If evidence suggests a probable violation of a law or board regulation, the Regulatory Programs and Compliance Section will attempt to resolve the issue informally or investigate further. In some instances, the DPOR may offer Alternative Dispute Resolution.

If an investigation supports probable cause that a violation occurred, the appropriate regulatory board may take disciplinary action to require remedial education, impose a fine, suspend or revoke the license, or fail to renew a license. If an investigation indicates the individual or business is not properly licensed the DPOR may take criminal action. If the investigation does not show probable cause that a violation occurred, the case will be closed.

The Complaint Form is available from the DPOR website. The interactive form allows you to enter information directly onto the form which is submitted electronically. The static form allows you to print the PDF and complete by hand.

Contact information for the DPOR:
Regulatory Programs and Compliance Section
Department of Professional and Occupational Regulation
Mayland Drive, Suite 400
Richmond, Virginia 23233-1463

Phone: 1-804-367-8504
FAX: 1-866-282-3932
Email: ComplaintAnalysis@dpor.virginia.gov

Real Estate Board (REB)

The Informal Fact-Finding Conference (IFFC)

The IFFC is a hearing conducted at the offices of the DPOR; it is presided over by an REB member and supported by the DPOR staff.

The presiding board member

- listens to the testimony of participants,
- asks questions,
- reviews additional information presented,
- leaves the record open for additional evidence to be presented or collected,
- maintains control of the conference by avoiding an adversarial proceeding, and
- remains neutral.

After considering the testimony and evidence, the presiding board member offers a **consent order** or prepares a summary and recommendation.

It is important to note that all disciplinary decisions come before the full REB for review and approval. REB scheduled meetings (there are approximately eight per year) are open to the public. IFFC participants are afforded an opportunity to address the full board at these meetings and may speak for five minutes, but no new evidence may be presented. The board carefully considers the IFFC Summary and Recommendation, which outlines thoughts, analysis, and credibility issues and makes its final decision.

The possible outcomes are the following:

- IFFC Summary and Recommendation: accept, reject, or modify violations or sanctions
- Consent Order: accept, make counteroffer, ask for exhibits, or request an IFFC (if one has not been held)

If the REB finds the licensee guilty, it may impose a monetary penalty of up to $2,500 for each violation. The REB may also suspend, revoke, or deny renewal of the respondent's license. The REB's decision is final although the licensee may appeal the decision through the Court of Appeals. In all of these proceedings, the accused has the right to be represented by legal counsel.

There are two instances in which disciplinary action may be taken against a licensee, and a license may be suspended or revoked without review or a hearing:

- If a licensee does not pay the assessment to the Transaction Recovery Fund, her license will be automatically suspended.

- If a payment is made from the Transaction Recovery Fund, the license of the respondent will be automatically revoked.

The REB has the authority to defer findings or dismiss actions to keep violations from appearing on a licensee's permanent record.

SUMMARY

The Code of Virginia 54.1, Chapter 21, is the section of the statute that governs the practice of real estate professionals. The purpose of the law is to protect the public interest against fraud, misrepresentation, dishonesty, and incompetence in real estate transactions. The law designates the REB as the authority to enforce, amend, and promulgate rules and regulations for implementing the law.

The REB's authority includes

- issuing and renewing real estate licenses;

- enforcing the license law;

- taking disciplinary action for violations of license law or rules and regulations by

  - suspending or revoking a license,

  - levying fines, or

  - denying license renewal;

- establishing requirements for real estate licensing and renewal;

- approving schools for teaching authorized courses for real estate brokers and salespersons;

- determining license fees; and

- waiving all or part of the prelicensing requirements if an applicant for licensure is currently licensed in another state or the District of Columbia.

Individuals or businesses that are exempt from license law are

- owners, lessors, and their employees dealing with their own property;

- persons acting as attorneys-in-fact under a power of attorney;

- attorneys-at-law in the performance of duties as an attorney-at-law;

- receivers, trustees, administrators, executors, and others acting under court order;

- trustees under trust agreements, deeds of trust, or wills or their employees;

- corporations managing rental housing when officers, directors, and members in the ownership corporation and the management corporation are the same persons;

- any existing tenant of a residential dwelling who refers a prospective tenant to the owner;

- auctioneers selling real estate at public auction; and

- any person licensed and in good standing as a real estate broker or salesperson in another state who assists a prospective purchaser, tenant, optionee, or licensee located in another state to purchase, lease, option, or license an interest in commercial real estate in the Commonwealth.

The latest revision of the Real Estate Regulations went into effect November 1, 2015 and is found in the VAC Agency 135. Part I General of the regulations covers important definitions. Part II Entry includes necessity for license, qualifications for licensure, additional qualifications for brokers and for salesperson's or broker's license as a business entity, concurrent licenses, licensure by reciprocity, activation or transfer of license, and application fees. Part III Renewal of License includes renewal requirements, qualifications, continuing education requirements, procedures and fees for renewal, board discretion to deny renewal or reinstatement, grounds for disciplinary action, place of business, duties of supervising broker, maintenance of licenses, death or disability of broker, maintenance and management of escrow accounts and financial records, advertising by licensees, disclosure of interest, audits, provision of records to the board, response to inquiry of the board, prohibited acts, conflict of interest, improper brokerage commission, improper dealing, misrepresentation/omission, improper delivery of instruments, principal and supervising broker's responsibility for acts of licensees and employees, and effect of disciplinary action on subordinate and concurrent licensees. Part IV Schools contains regulations for proprietary schools followed by Forms and is not included in this unit. The final section of the unit deals with the licensing examination.

UNIT 8 QUIZ

1. Which of the following is an accurate description of the Real Estate Board (REB)?
   A. Seven members: six licensees and one consumer
   B. Seven members: five licensees and two consumers
   C. Nine members: either licensed brokers or salespersons
   D. Nine members: seven licensees and two consumers

2. The REB's authority includes all of the following *EXCEPT*
   A. issuing and renewing real estate licenses.
   B. enforcing license law.
   C. administering the Virginia Real Estate Transaction Fund.
   D. administering the Virginia Property Owners Association Act.

3. All of the following may be entitled to exemption from the requirement of licensure under the REB *EXCEPT*
   A. persons acting under a power of attorney.
   B. attorneys-at-law in the performance of their regular duties.
   C. a real estate license selling her own property.
   D. auctioneers selling real estate at public auction.

4. A licensee who acts for a client pursuant to a brokerage agreement that specifies what duties of a standard agent will *NOT* be done is
   A. a dual standard agent.
   B. a designated standard agent.
   C. a limited service agent.
   D. an independent contractor.

5. Every applicant for an individual salesperson's or broker's license must fulfill all of the following qualifications *EXCEPT*
   A. have a college degree.
   B. be at least 18 years old.
   C. meet the current educational requirements.
   D. have a good reputation for honesty, truthfulness, and fair dealing.

6. A licensee was out of town on a business assignment. When she returned on October 10, she found her license renewal notice and realized that her license had expired on July 1. If she wants to remain licensed, she must
   A. reapply for a new license as a new applicant.
   B. meet the current educational requirements.
   C. apply for reinstatement of her license and pay the current reinstatement fee.
   D. apply to have her license placed on inactive status.

7. Real estate licenses are renewed in Virginia
   A. annually, in the month issued.
   B. every two years, in the month of the licensee's birthday.
   C. on June 30 of each even-numbered year.
   D. biennially, on the last day of the month in which issued.

8. Eight of the required 16 hours of continuing education for salespersons must be in the subjects of all of the following *EXCEPT*
   A. fair housing law.
   B. marketing.
   C. ethics.
   D. legal updates.

9. The latest required topic in the legal update part of the mandated 8 of the 16 hours required for salesperson's renewal is
   A. the American Disabilities Act.
   B. flood zone areas and the National Flood Insurance Program.
   C. transfer of licenses.
   D. the Virginia Utility Damage Prevention Act.

10. The real estate regulations include a long list of the duties of a supervising broker. The *MOST* recent duty to be added to the list is
    A. availability to review and approve all documents.
    B. availability of training and written procedures and policies.
    C. ensuring that all affiliated licensees have an active, current license.
    D. ensuring that all brokerage services are carried out competently.

11. Upon the death or disability of a licensed real estate broker who was engaged in a proprietorship or was the only licensed broker in a corporation or partnership, the first choice of the REB for a person to carry on the business of the deceased or disabled broker for 180 days is
    A. a personal representative qualified by the court to administer the deceased broker's estate.
    B. an agent designated under a power of attorney of the deceased or disabled broker.
    C. the executor nominated in the deceased broker's will.
    D. an adult family member of the disabled or deceased broker.

12. If a broker establishes an account to hold money belonging to others, all of the following statements are true *EXCEPT*
    A. All accounts, checks, and bank statements must be labeled "escrow."
    B. Funds in the escrow account may never include moneys which will ultimately belong to the licensee.
    C. Lease application fees must be placed in escrow by the end of the fifth business day.
    D. The balance in the escrow account will be sufficient to account for all designated funds.

13. EMDs may be distributed from the broker's escrow account in any of the following situations *EXCEPT*
    A. at settlement on the property.
    B. when all parties to the transaction agree to disbursement.
    C. when requested by one party's attorney.
    D. when the broker determines distribution according to the terms of the contract.

14. A broker created a web page to advertise the firm's listings for sale. Electronic media disclosure requirements require that the broker include on each page
    A. the firm's licensed name and broker's address.
    B. the firm's licensed name and city and state in which the main office is located.
    C. the broker's name, address, and phone number.
    D. the broker's name, firm's name and address, and the jurisdiction in which the firm is licensed.

15. Several weeks after a closing, an associate broker received a thank-you letter and a nice bonus check from the seller of the house. The associate broker cashed the check because he felt it was appropriate in his situation. Which of the following statements regarding his decision is *TRUE*?
    A. The associate broker may accept the bonus because he is licensed as an associate broker.
    B. Accepting the money is allowed if more than 30 days have elapsed since the closing.
    C. The associate broker may accept the money if his broker permits him to do so.
    D. Accepting the money is a violation of REB regulations.

16. A principal or supervising broker must conduct an audit of the practices, policies, and procedures of his firm at least once during each license term. The audit should document compliance with the law and regulations in all of the following areas *EXCEPT*
    A. handling of escrow deposits.
    B. advertising in all forms of media.
    C. immunity from enforcement action.
    D. agency or independent contractor relationships.

17. When a principal broker has her license suspended for two years, the effect on the affiliated associate brokers and salespeople is that
    A. the affiliates' licenses will be revoked, subject to reinstatement after one year.
    B. the affiliates' licenses will be also be suspended for a two-year period.
    C. the suspension has no effect on the affiliates.
    D. the affiliates' licenses must be returned to the REB.

18. When a salesperson is alleged to have violated the license law, which of the following statements is *TRUE*?
    A. An investigation will be conducted by the DPOR.
    B. The salesperson is entitled to a jury trial before any action can be taken.
    C. The salesperson's license will be temporarily suspended until the REB can schedule a formal hearing.
    D. The employing broker also is charged with the same violation.

19. If the REB finds a licensee guilty of violating license law, it may impose any of the following *EXCEPT*
    A. monetary penalty up to $5,000.
    B. suspend the license.
    C. revoke the license.
    D. deny renewal of the license.

20. One instance in which a licensee's license can be suspended or revoked without review or a hearing is if the licensee
    A. allowed unsupervised access to a home without the owner's authorization.
    B. failed to submit an EMD to the broker in a timely manner.
    C. does not pay a required assessment to the Transaction Recovery Fund.
    D. failed to inform the board in writing within 30 days of pleading guilty to a misdemeanor.

UNIT
9

Leasing Real Estate in Virginia

LEARNING OBJECTIVES

When you have completed this unit, you will be able to

> **review** the general principles of leasing real estate in Virginia;
> **describe** the obligations and remedies that apply to a landlord under the Virginia Residential Landlord and Tenant Act;
> **describe** the obligations and remedies that apply to a tenant under the Virginia Residential Landlord and Tenant Act; and
> **define** the following key terms:

distress warrant	prepaid rent	reasonable modification
eviction	retaliation	security deposit
pay or quit notice	reasonable accommodation	unlawful detainer action

OVERVIEW

Leases and landlord-tenant relationships are governed by Title 55—Property and Conveyances in Chapter 13—Landlord and Tenant of the Code of Virginia. Chapter 13 (§ § 55-217–55-248) covers general leasing principles under the Virginia Landlord Tenant Act (VLTA). Chapter 13.2 deals specifically with the Virginia Residential Landlord and Tenant Act (VRLTA) (§ § 248.2–248.40). Chapter 13.3 covers manufactured home rentals.

This first part of this unit on leasing covers general leasing principles that are covered under the VLTA. The rest of the unit covers the six articles of VRLTA.

For more information on leasing in Virginia, refer to Virginia General Assembly Legislative Information System, Code of Virginia, Title 55, Chapter 13 at http://leg1.state.va.us.

GENERAL LEASING PRINCIPLES

Fair Housing

One of the most important aspects of the landlord-tenant relationship is to uphold all provisions of both federal and state fair housing acts. The majority of fair housing complaints come from rental situations. Fair housing will be covered in detail in Unit 10, but the following brief checklist may be helpful for all new landlords.

Landlords may

- ask qualifying questions, as long the same questions are asked of all applicants;
- check references of prospective tenants;
- verify the prospective tenant's ability to pay the stated rent;
- develop rules to be followed by all tenants, taking care that none are discriminatory; and
- require that any modifications made for a tenant with a disability be restored to the original condition if the modification would affect the value of the property.

Landlords may not

- refuse to rent to anyone based on discrimination against any of the protected classes (race, color, religion, national origin, sex, elderliness, familial status, or handicap);
- apply different rules, deposits, or amount of rent to different tenants;
- make false statements about the availability of any unit;
- refuse to make **reasonable modifications** or accommodations for a tenant with a disability;
- intimidate or retaliate against a tenant who makes a complaint; or
- advertise in any way that shows potential discrimination.

The handicap provision of fair housing law is more often referred to today as a person with a disability. The law requires the landlord to provide reasonable modifications and **reasonable accommodations** that may be required in order for the person with a disability to be able to enjoy the full use of the housing.

Reasonable Modifications

Reasonable modifications are those that affect the physical features of a property. Depending on the type of disability, the tenant might require a ramp at the entrance, widening of doorways, grab bars in kitchen and bathroom, lowered electrical outlets, or removal of carpet. The tenant is responsible for paying for the modifications and can be required to restore the property to its original condition when the lease is terminated if it actually affects the value of the property. The landlord is not required to make unreasonable modifications, such as installing an elevator or completely redoing a kitchen. If the modifications are substantial, the landlord can require the tenant to pay into an interest-bearing escrow account in an amount sufficient to restore the property. No additional **security deposit** may be charged.

Reasonable Accommodations

Reasonable accommodations are changes to existing rules and procedures that may be needed in order for the tenant to enjoy full use of the dwelling place, such as a requirement that all tenants come to the second floor rental office to personally sign the lease. To meet the needs of a person with a disability, it may be necessary to agree to meet on the first floor or hand-deliver the lease to a place of the tenant's choosing.

Other examples of reasonable accommodations include

- allowing service animals in a no pets policy building,
- providing accessible parking near the unit for the person with a disability, and
- having lease documents available in braille or audio format.

Sale of Rental Property

When property that is currently being rented is sold, the new owner stands in the same legal relationship to the lessee as did the previous owner. Likewise, the lessee may have the same benefits of the lease as were enjoyed with the previous owner "except the benefit of any warranty in deed or law." (§ 55-218)

Unless specifically stated otherwise in the lease, the tenant retains the same rights and privileges when the rental property is sold. If the new owner is another investor, an existing lease is generally a plus. However, if the new owners want to move in, they will either have to wait until the lease terminates or make special arrangements with the existing tenants.

Nonresident Agents

A nonresident of Virginia who owns real property consisting of four or more rental units (whether residential or commercial) must appoint a Virginia resident as agent for the purpose of receiving any notices, service of process, or other legal paper that would otherwise have been served on the owner. If an agent is not appointed, or if the one appointed cannot be found, the secretary of the Commonwealth serves as agent. The secretary forward any papers to be served on the owner to the owner's home address. (§ 55-218.1)

Termination of Lease

Virginia law requires different notice periods, depending on the length of the lease being terminated. The notice periods are

- a three-month notice to terminate a year-to-year lease,
- a 30-day notice to terminate a month-to-month lease, or
- a 120-day written notice to terminate a month-to-month lease, where the termination is due to rehabilitation of the property or a change in the property's use (such as conversion to a condominium).

If a definite termination date has been established, no notice is required. (§ 55-222)

Unit 9

Tenant Holdover

A tenant who, through no fault of his own, is unable to vacate the premises at the end of the lease term is not legally held to another full term of the lease. Rather, the tenant is liable to the lessor only for use and occupation of the premises and for any loss or damage suffered by the lessor. There may, however, be further legal issues. (§ 55-223)

Additions to Article 13—§ 55-225

In 2011, the general assembly passed legislation expanding Sections 55-225.9 and 55-225.10 and also added four new sections: 55-225.11, 55-225.12, 55-225.13, and 55-225-14, as follows. These changes are also reflected in the Virginia Residential Landlord and Tenant Act.

§ 55-225.9

Where a mold condition exists, the landlord may require the tenant to temporarily vacate the dwelling to a comparable dwelling unit or hotel room at the landlord's expense. (The tenant is still responsible for payment of rent.)

In 2016, this section was further clarified that unless a tenant is at fault for creating a situation resulting in the need for mold remediation, the landlord is obligated to pay all costs associated with the tenant's temporary relocation as well as the costs of the remediation.

§ 55-225.10

The landlord must give written notice to the tenant of any mortgage default, acceleration, or notice of foreclosure on the dwelling unit within five business days after such notice is received by the landlord. If such notice is not provided, the tenant will have the right to terminate the rental agreement with written notice at least five days before the date of termination. This requirement for disclosure also applies for any dwelling units being offered for rent.

§ 55-225.11

If the landlord has actual knowledge of the existence of defective drywall within the unit, written disclosure must be given to any prospective tenant. A tenant may terminate the lease agreement within 60 days of discovery of defective drywall with written notice to be effective 15 days from the mailing of the notice or the date through which rent has been paid, whichever is later. In no event may the termination exceed one month from the date of mailing.

§ 55-225.12

This rather lengthy section deals with a tenant's assertion that conditions exist on the leased premises that constitute a fire hazard or serious threat to the life, health, or safety of occupants. The assertion is filed in a general district court and the forms of relief are listed in subsection C. The tenant must show the court that written notice has been served to the landlord who has not remedied the situation, that rent has been paid to the court, and that the condition was not caused by the tenant.

§ 55-225.13

If there is a material noncompliance by the landlord with the rental agreement or any condition materially affecting health and safety, the tenant may serve written notice to the landlord specifying the breach and setting a termination date not less than 30 days after receipt of the notice if the breach is not remedied within 21 days.

§ 55-225.14

This section stipulates the requirements for a tenant to pay rent into a court escrow account when a continuance of the tenant's case is requested.

§ 55-225.16

This section was added to clarify that early termination of a lease can be required in cases of family abuse, sexual abuse, or criminal sexual assault.

§ 55-225.17

This section was added in 2016 and conforms with the general requirement that disclosure must be made if a property has been previously used for the manufacture of methamphetamine and has not been cleaned according to state guidelines. If such disclosure is not made, the tenant may terminate the lease up to 60 days from discovery.

§ 55-225.18

Added in 2016 to clarify that a landlord is prohibited from any retaliatory conduct such as increasing rent, or decreasing services to a tenant making a complaint against the landlord.

Destruction of Premises

In some states, if the improvements on leased land are destroyed, the lessee is still bound by the terms of the lease and must continue paying full rent. Virginia has repealed this common law doctrine. Tenants who are not at fault in the destruction of the improvements are entitled to a reduction in the amount of rent until the improvements are rebuilt and the tenants' previous use of the property can be restored (§ 55-226).

Seizure of Tenant Property

Goods belonging to a tenant may be seized for nonpayment of rent for up to five years after the rent is due, whether or not the lease has ended. The seizure is made by a sheriff or other officer, based on a warrant issued by a judge or magistrate. The warrant is based on a petition from the lessor. The lessor's petition must show (1) the grounds for believing that the rent is due and (2) the exact amount owed. The lessor must post a bond.

A copy of the **distress warrant** (the order of seizure) is given to each defendant, along with a copy of the bond. The goods subject to seizure may include anything on the premises belonging to the tenant (including any assignees' or subtenants' goods) or goods that have been removed within the 30 days before seizure. If any of the goods seized are subject to a prior lien, the lessor's proceeds may be based only on the interest the tenant actually had in the personal property. Any sublessee is liable only to the extent that money is owed to the original tenant.

The seizure of a tenant's property arises from enforcing a landlord's lien, which is a statutory right. The landlord's lien relates back to the beginning of the tenancy, not merely to the time the rent became delinquent.

If seizure of the tenant's property is made for rent due and any irregularity or unlawful act is performed during the proceeding by or for the landlord, the tenant may sue to recover damages from the landlord. However, the distress warrant itself is still lawful, and the tenant still owes the rent, despite any improper enforcement actions. (§ § 55-230–55-236)

Section 55-237.1 covers the authority of the sheriff to store and sell any personal property left on the premises by a tenant. The rights of the tenant to redeem the property are also covered in this section.

Prevention of Forfeiture

If a tenant who has been served with a **pay or quit notice** pays the arrears before her case comes to trial, the tenant will hold the tenancy just as she did before the proceedings began, without a new lease or conveyance. This could be looked upon as a type of right of redemption, similar to a debtor's right to recover property before a foreclosure sale. However, a tenant may exercise this right only once in any 12-month period. (§ 55-243)

Landlord Right of Reentry

If a tenant's rent is in arrears or the tenant has breached the lease, the landlord may post a written **eviction** notice in a conspicuous location on the premises. The notice must be in lieu of a demand and reentry; on proof to the court that the rent claimed was due and no sufficient distress was put upon the premises or that the terms of the lease were broken before the service of the eviction notice and that the landlord had power to reenter, the landlord will be due all rent in arrears and regain possession of the unit. (§ 55-244)

Publication and recordation and certification of eviction proceedings must be made by the sheriff to the appropriate court jurisdiction. (§ 55-245)

VIRGINIA RESIDENTIAL LANDLORD AND TENANT ACT (VRLTA)

Title Section 55, Chapter 13.2 of the Code of Virginia, the VRLTA, became law in 1974. As stated in Article 1, the purposes of the act are to

- simplify, clarify, modernize and revise the law governing the rental of dwelling units and the rights and obligations of landlords and tenants;

- encourage landlords and tenants to maintain and improve the quality of housing; and

- establish a single body of law relating to landlord and tenant relations throughout the Commonwealth.

The VRLTA supersedes all local, county, or municipal ordinances or regulations concerning landlord and tenant relations and the leasing of residential property.

A full copy of VRLTA, effective July 1, 2011, is available at www.dhcd.virginia.gov, with a search entry of "Landlord Tenant Handbook."

The 2014 general assembly enacted legislation that changed the applicability of VRLTA to owners of more than two rental properties plus their principal residence. The trigger number was formerly four rental properties in urban areas and a total of 10 statewide. This legislation also eliminated the payment of interest on security deposits, effective in 2015. Originally, the interest rate allowed was subject to the Federal Reserve discount rate and had remained at zero since 2009.

In 2016, legislation clarified that in order to determine whether an owner of single-family residences is subject to the VRLTA, the owner only needs to count the number of properties owned in Virginia. For example, one residence plus two rental properties is subject to VRLTA.

Article 1—General Provisions

Exemptions

As the title implies, the act concerns itself with residential property. However, not everyone or every residential property is subject to the act. The act does not apply to the following:

- Residence at a public or private institution if incidental to detention or the provision of medical, geriatric, educational, counseling, religious, or similar services

- Occupancy under a contract of sale of a dwelling unit by the purchaser of a property

- Occupancy by a member of a fraternal or social organization in a portion of a structure operated for the benefit of the organization

- Occupancy in a hotel, motel, or similar location for not more than a 90-day period if occupied continuously (changed from 30 days in 2013)

- Occupancy by an employee of a landlord whose right to occupancy is a requirement or benefit of employment (such as a property manager)

- Occupancy by an owner of a condominium unit or holder of a proprietary lease in a cooperative

- Occupancy under a rental agreement covering premises used primarily in connection with business, commercial, or agricultural purposes

- Occupancy in HUD-regulated housing, where regulation is inconsistent with the statute

- Occupancy by a tenant who pays no rent

- Property owners who do not rent more than two single-family residences or condominium units (§ 55-248.5)

Note that Virginia Fair Housing Law applies to owners of three or more properties.

In Virginia, a Community Land Trust (CLT) is not considered to be a landlord as long as the CLT is nonprofit, conveys property under long-term ground leases, transfers ownership of structural improvements to the lessee, and retains an option to purchase such improvements at a price determined to ensure that the improvement remains affordable to low- and moderate-income families. (§ 55-221.1)

Application Fees

The landlord may require an application fee and a separate application deposit at the time the tenant applies to lease a dwelling. If the tenant does not rent the property, the landlord will refund all fees in excess of the landlord's expenses and damages (costs incurred for preparing the dwelling for occupancy, holding an unoccupied unit, etc.) within 20 days. If the application fees were made by cash, certified check, cashier's check, or money order, the refund will be made within 10 days of the applicant's failure to rent if such failure was due to the landlord's rejection of the application. (§ 55-248.6:1)

An application deposit must be placed in an escrow account within five business days from approval of the tenant's application.

Terms and Conditions

Terms and conditions in a rental agreement may include rent, charges for late payment of rent, term of the agreement, automatic renewal of the agreement, requirements for notice of intent to vacate or terminate the agreement, and other provisions governing the rights and obligations of the parties. In the absence of a rental agreement, the tenant must pay fair rental value. Legislation enacted in 2013 allows a landlord to include provisions for an early termination in the lease. Legislation in 2014 allows the landlord to use a mathematical formula to allocate energy service for tenants in a building as long as this provision is clearly stated in the rental agreement or lease. Legislation in 2015 provided that nothing in this law prohibits an owner of a commercial or residential building from including water, sewer, electrical, natural gas, or other utilities in the amount of rent as specified in the rental agreement or lease.

Rent will be payable without demand or notice at the place designated by the landlord. Periodic rent is payable at the beginning of any term of one month or less and otherwise in equal installments at the beginning of each month. A copy of the written agreement signed by both landlord and tenant must be provided to the tenant within one month of the effective date of the agreement. (§ 55-248.7)

A tenant may offer and a landlord may accept **prepaid rent**. A landlord who accepts prepaid rent must deposit the total amount in an escrow account and withdraw the monthly installments as they come due. Prepaid rent means rent paid more than one month in advance of the rent due date. (§ 55-248.7:1)

Required Insurance

The landlord can require that the tenant pay the cost of premiums for both renter's insurance and damage insurance. In the case of damage insurance, the cost of premiums is not considered as a security deposit but rather as rent. The landlord cannot require that the tenant pay both security deposit and premiums if the amount exceeds two months' rent. Similarly, in the case of renter's insurance, the cost of premiums is considered rent, not a security deposit. If premiums are paid before the tenancy, the total of all payments for security deposits and renter's insurance as well as damage insurance must not exceed two months' rent. Otherwise, the landlord may charge additional monthly rent to cover the costs. For both types of insurance, the tenant may elect to obtain separate policies. (§ 55-248.7:2)

Unsigned or Undelivered Leases

If a written lease is not signed by either the lessor or the lessee but the agreed rent is paid and accepted, the rental agreement is binding on both parties. Similarly, even if a lease is never delivered but the rent payments are accepted, the lease remains binding. In such cases, if the term of the lease provides for a term longer than one year, it is only effective for one year. (§ 55-248.8)

Prohibited Provisions

A rental agreement must not contain provisions that the tenant will agree to waive or forego any rights or remedies covered in this chapter, will agree to pay landlord's attorney fees, or to any limitation of the landlord's liability. There must be no provision that the tenant will agree to a limitation on lawful possession of a firearm or will pay more than two months for a combined security deposit and insurance premium. If a landlord brings a court action to enforce any of the prohibited provisions, the tenant may recover actual damages plus attorney fees. (§ 55-248.9)

Confidentiality Exemptions

Section 55-248.9:1 covers the specific situations where a landlord or managing agent may release information about a tenant or prospective tenant to a third party, for example, where tenant has given prior consent, information is a matter of public record, is requested by a law enforcement official or information is requested by a lender for financing of the rental property or by the landlord's attorney. The landlord is allowed to enter into an agreement with a third-party service provider to maintain tenant records in electronic format with no liability in the event of a breach of the electronic data by the third-party provider. (§ 55-248.9:1)

Article 2— Landlord Obligations

Under VRLTA, landlords have specific obligations and responsibilities.

§ 55-248.11:1 Inspection of Premises

Within five days of occupancy, a written report itemizing damages to the unit existing at the time of occupancy will be prepared by either the landlord, the tenant, or done jointly. Both the landlord and the tenant must sign the written report and receive a copy. The landlord is not obligated to make repairs of such damages unless otherwise required to under VRLTA such as for mold.

§ 55-248.11:2 Disclosure of Mold in Dwelling Units

The written report of the move-in inspection should disclose any evidence of mold. If there is visible mold evidence, the tenant has the option to terminate the tenancy. If the tenant agrees to take possession, the landlord must promptly remediate the mold condition within five days.

§ 55-248.12 Disclosure of Ownership

The landlord must disclose to the tenant the name and address of the property owner or anyone authorized to manage the property or otherwise act on behalf of the owner. The disclosure must be in writing and be provided to the tenant before the beginning of the tenancy. If the property is sold, the tenant must be supplied with the name, address, and telephone number of the purchaser. If the property is being converted to a condominium or cooperative, or if the tenant will be displaced due to the demolition or rehabilitation of the property within the next six months, the tenant is entitled to written notice of the situation.

§ 55-248.12:1 Required Disclosures for Properties Located Adjacent to a Military Air Installation; Remedy for Nondisclosure

The landlord of property in any locality in which a military air installation is located, or any person authorized to enter into a rental agreement on the landlord's behalf, must provide to a prospective tenant a written disclosure that the property is located in a noise zone or accident potential zone, or both, as designated by the locality on its official zoning map.

Disclosure must be provided before the execution by the tenant of a written lease agreement, or in the case of an oral lease agreement, before occupancy by the tenant. The disclosure must specify the noise zone or accident potential zone in which the property is located according to the official zoning map of the locality.

An inaccurate disclosure made regarding the location of the noise zone or accident potential zone will be deemed as nondisclosure unless the inaccurate information is provided by an officer or employee of the locality in which the property is located.

Failure to disclose gives the tenant rights of termination in the first 30 days of occupancy.

§ 55-248.12:2 Required Disclosures for Properties With Defective Drywall; Remedy for Nondisclosure

If the landlord has actual knowledge of the existence of defective drywall that has not been remediated, the landlord must provide the tenant with a written disclosure before occupancy.

A tenant who is not provided the disclosure may terminate the lease agreement within 60 days of notice of discovery of the existence of defective drywall with written notice to the landlord.

§ 55-248.12:3 Required Disclosures for Property Previously Used to Manufacture Methamphetamine; Remedy for Nondisclosure

As of July 1, 2014, any landlord who has actual knowledge that the property has been used for the manufacture of methamphetamine and has not been cleaned in accordance with Virginia Department of Health guidelines must provide a written disclosure when renting the property. A tenant may terminate the tenancy if the disclosure is not provided.

§ 55-248.13 Landlord to Maintain Fit Premises

The landlord must

- comply with the requirements of applicable building and housing codes materially affecting health and safety;

- make all repairs and do whatever is necessary to put and keep the premises in a fit and habitable condition;

- keep all common areas shared by two or more dwelling units of the premises in a clean and structurally safe condition;

- maintain in good and safe working order and condition all electrical, plumbing, sanitary, heating, ventilating, air-conditioning, and other facilities and appliances, including elevators, supplied or required to be supplied by the landlord;

- maintain the premises in such a condition as to prevent the accumulation of moisture and the growth of mold and promptly respond to any written notices from a tenant;

- provide and maintain appropriate receptacles and conveniences, in common areas, for the collection, storage, and removal of ashes, garbage, rubbish, and other waste incidental to the occupancy of two or more dwelling units and arrange for the removal of same;

- supply running water and reasonable amounts of hot water at all times, reasonable air-conditioning if provided, and heat in season, except where the dwelling unit is so constructed that heat, air-conditioning, or hot water is generated by an installation within the exclusive control of the tenant or supplied by a direct public utility connection; and

- upon request in writing, install carbon monoxide alarms within 90 days of request. The tenant can be charged a reasonable fee for installation. As of 2016, it is the tenant's responsibility to maintain the alarm once installed to the standards established in the Uniform Statewide Building Code.

The landlord must perform foregoing duties imposed in accordance with law; however, the landlord will only be liable for the tenant's actual damages caused by the landlord's failure to exercise ordinary care.

Note that the landlord and tenant may agree in writing that the tenant will perform the landlord's duties specified previously and also specified repairs, maintenance tasks, alterations and remodeling, but only if the transaction is entered into in good faith and not for the purpose of evading the obligations of the landlord and if the agreement does not diminish or affect the obligation of the landlord to other tenants in the premises.

§ 55-248.13:1 Landlord to Provide Locks and Peepholes

The governing body of any county, city, or town may require by ordinance that any landlord who rents five or more dwelling units in any one building must install the following to meet the requirements of the Uniform Statewide Building Code:

- Dead-bolt locks and peepholes in any exterior entrance door unless the door has a glass panel

- Manufacturer's locks and removable metal pins or Charlie bars on exterior sliding glass doors at any level

- Locking devices on all exterior windows

Any ordinance adopted pursuant to this law must provide a reasonable time for the landlord to comply.

§ 55-248.13:2 Access of Tenant to Cable, Satellite, and Other Television Facilities

The landlord may not demand or accept payment of any fee or charge from providers of television or modem service in exchange for granting the provider access to the landlord's tenants with the exception of a service agreement to provide marketing and other delivery services.

The landlord may not demand or accept payment from tenants for such service or discriminate in rental charges. Nothing prohibits a landlord from requiring the provider of the service and the tenant bear the entire cost of the installation, operation, or removal of the facilities.

§ 55-248.13:3 Notice to Tenants for Pesticide Use

The landlord must give written notice to a tenant no less than 48 hours before an application of an insecticide or pesticide. If the tenant requests the application, the 48-hour notice is not required. The tenant must prepare the dwelling unit for the application and follow any written instructions to eliminate the insects or pest.

The landlord must post notice of all insecticide or pesticide applications in areas other than dwelling units at least 48 hours before application.

§ 55-248.14 Limitation of Liability

A landlord who conveys premises that include a dwelling unit to a bona fide purchaser is relieved of liability under the rental agreement. Unless otherwise agreed, a managing agent is relieved of liability under the rental agreement as to events occurring after written notice of termination of management.

§ 55-248.15 Tenancy at Will

A notice of change of any terms or provisions of a tenancy at will constitute a notice to vacate the premises.

§ 55-248.15:1 Notice to Tenant in Event of Foreclosure

The landlord must notify the tenant, by certified mail, of a mortgage default, notice of mortgage acceleration, or notice of foreclosure sale within 10 business days after the landlord receives written notice. Failure to provide this notice will immediately terminate the rental agreement at the option of the tenant, with return of the security deposit with no deductions, within 10 days after termination of the tenancy. With a vacant unit, disclosure must be made to any prospective tenant.

§ 55-248.15:1 Security Deposits

The landlord may require that the tenant provide a security deposit at the time the property is leased. The security deposit is to protect the landlord against unpaid rents or damage—other than normal wear and tear—caused by tenants or pets during the lease period.

 The security deposit may not exceed an amount equal to two months' rent. The deposit must be returned to the tenant within 45 days after the tenant vacates the property. If the landlord intends to withhold a portion of the security deposit to cover damages or losses, the tenant must be provided a written itemized list of such deductions. In certain circumstances, the landlord may withhold a reasonable amount of the security deposit to cover outstanding utility bills that were an obligation of the tenant as long as proper notice is given. The landlord must make a final inspection of the dwelling within 72 hours of the termination of the lease. The landlord must notify the tenant of the date and time of the inspection and the inspection must be at a reasonable time. The tenant has the right to be present during the landlord's inspection but must advise the landlord in writing of the intent to be present.

As of 2014, a landlord may charge an administrative fee for expedited return of the security deposit at the tenant's written request. If no forwarding address is given, the deposit is paid to the Virginia Department of Housing and Community Developed earmarked for the Virginia Housing Trust Fund one year and 45 days following lease termination. (This changed in 2016 from paid to state treasury.)

Article 3—Tenant Obligations

Article 3 of the VRLTA specifies obligations of the tenant as follows.

§ 55-248.16 Tenant to Maintain Dwelling Unit

In addition to provisions of the rental agreement, the tenant agrees to the following:

- Comply with all applicable building and housing codes that materially affect health and safety
- Keep the leased premises as clean and safe as conditions permit
- Keep the premises free from insects and pests and promptly notify landlord of the existence of any insects or pests
- Remove all ashes, garbage, rubbish, and other waste in the appropriate receptacles provided by the landlord
- Keep all plumbing fixtures as clean as their condition permits
- Use in a reasonable manner all electrical, plumbing, sanitary, heating, ventilating, and air-conditioning systems and equipment, including any elevators on the premises
- Not deliberately destroy, deface, damage, impair, or remove any part of the premises or permit anyone else to do so
- Not remove or tamper with smoke detectors or carbon monoxide detectors
- Use reasonable efforts to prevent accumulation of moisture and the growth of mold and promptly notify landlord if such conditions occur
- Not paint or disturb painted surfaces or make alterations in the unit without prior written approval of landlord in any unit built before 1978 that is subject to lead-based paint disclosure and regulations
- Be responsible for tenant's own conduct and conduct of other persons on the premises to insure that neighbors' peaceful enjoyment of the premises is not disturbed
- Abide by all reasonable rules and regulations imposed by the landlord

§ 55-248.17 Rules and Regulations

A landlord, from time to time, may adopt rules or regulations concerning the tenants' use and occupancy of the premises. Such rules or regulations are only enforceable if the purpose is to promote the convenience, safety, or welfare of the tenants, to preserve the property from abusive use, or to make a fair distribution of services and facilities. The rules must apply to all tenants who must be provided with a written copy of the rules and regulations before entering into the rental agreement. Changes made after the tenant enters into the rental agreement must be given reasonable notice and not work a substantial modification of the original bargain.

Note that a change in swimming pool hours or a requirement that parking decals be shown on cars are appropriate house rule changes. A change in the number of persons allowed to reside in each unit is an alteration of the rental agreement.

§ 55-248.18 Access; Consent

The tenant may not unreasonably withhold consent to the landlord to enter the unit in order to inspect the premises, make necessary repairs, decorations, alterations, or improvements, or to exhibit the unit to prospective or actual purchasers, mortgagees, tenants, or workmen. The landlord may only enter the unit without consent in the case of emergency. The landlord must give the tenant at least 24 hours' notice of routine maintenance. The law continues in § 55-248.18 to outline procedures for any required temporary vacation of the property.

If, following an inspection of the unit, the landlord determines there has been a violation of the lease or of the law which materially affects health and safety and can be remedied by repairs, the landlord may make such repairs and send the tenant an invoice for payment.

As of 2016, the landlord may recover damages, costs and reasonable attorney fees against a tenant if the tenant, without reasonable justification, declines to permit the landlord or managing agent to exhibit the dwelling unit for sale or lease.

§ 55-248.18:1 Access Following Entry of Certain Court Orders

A tenant who has obtained a court order excluding any co-tenants from occupancy may request that the landlord install new locks or security devices on exterior doors of the unit, or permit the tenant to do so as long as no permanent damage occurs, and the tenant is responsible for removing such devices upon termination of the lease.

§ 55-248.18:2 Relocation of Tenant Where Mold Remediation Required

Where a mold condition in the unit materially affects the health or safety of any tenant, the landlord may require the tenant to temporarily vacate the unit in order for mold remediation to be performed for a period not to exceed 30 days. The landlord must provide a comparable dwelling unit or hotel room at no cost to the tenant. The tenant remains responsible for rent.

§ 55-248.19 Use and Occupancy by Tenant

Unless otherwise agreed, the tenant may occupy the unit only as a residence.

§ 55-248.20 Tenant to Surrender Possession of Dwelling Unit

At the termination of the tenancy, whether by expiration of the rental agreement or by reason of default by the tenant, the tenant must promptly vacate the premises, removing all items of personal property and leaving the premises in good and clean order, reasonable wear and tear accepted. If the tenant fails to vacate, the landlord may bring an action for possession and damages, including reasonable attorney's fees.

§ 55-248.24 Fire or Casualty Damage

In a case of fire or casualty damage, the landlord may terminate the rental agreement by giving 14 days note. (This changed from 30 days in 2015.)

Article 4—Tenant Remedies

Article 4 and Article 5 of the VRLTA specify tenant and landlord remedies. These paragraphs are lengthy and cover legal issues that may require the assistance of legal counsel. The paragraphs, along with a brief summary, are listed here to be used as a reference tool.

§ 55-248.21 Noncompliance by Landlord

If the landlord violates the lease agreement or is in violation of any provision affecting health and safety, the tenant may notify the landlord in writing of the violations and state that the lease agreement will terminate on a date not less than 30 days after the notice if the violations are not corrected in 21 days. If the landlord adequately corrects the violations, the lease agreement will not terminate. In certain situations, the tenant may be able to recover damages, reasonable attorney fees, injunctive relief, and security deposits.

§ 55-248.21:1 Early Termination of Rental Agreement by Military Personnel

Any member of the Armed Forces of the United States and any member of the National Guard serving on full-time duty or as a civil service technician with the National Guard may, through the procedure detailed in the following list, terminate his rental agreement if the member

- has received permanent change of station orders to depart 35 miles or more (radius) from the location of the dwelling unit;
- has received temporary duty orders in excess of three months' duration to depart 35 miles or more (radius) from the location of the dwelling unit;
- is discharged or released from active duty with the Armed Forces of the United States or from his full-time duty or technician status with the National Guard; or
- is ordered to report to government-supplied quarters resulting in the forfeiture of basic allowance for quarters.

Tenants who qualify to terminate a rental agreement under these circumstances must do so by giving the landlord a written notice of termination to be effective on a date stated in the notice. This date cannot be less than 30 days after the date on which the next rental payment (after the date on which the written notice is given) is due and payable. The termination date must be no more than 60 days before the date of departure required by the official orders or any supplemental instructions for interim training or duty before the transfer. Before the termination date, the tenant must furnish the landlord with a copy of the official notification of the orders or a signed letter, confirming the orders, from the tenant's commanding officer.

The landlord may not charge any liquidated damages.

§ 55-248.221:2 Early Termination of Rental Agreements by Victims of Family Abuse, Sexual Abuse, or Criminal Sexual Assault

Legislation in 2013 allows victims of domestic abuse or sexual assault to terminate a lease with 30 days' notice. The landlord should be provided with a copy of the court-ordered conviction. Other cotenants remain responsible for their lease obligations. A landlord may terminate the lease and recover damages if the sole remaining tenant is the perpetrator of the crime.

§ 55-248.22 Failure to Deliver Possession

If the landlord fails to deliver possession of the unit, rent is abated, and the tenant can terminate the agreement or demand performance. If the failure to deliver possession is willful and not in good faith, the tenant may recover actual damages and reasonable attorney's fees.

§ 55-248.23 Wrongful Failure to Supply Heat, Water, Hot Water, or Essential Services

If the landlord willfully or negligently fails to supply heat, running water, hot water, electricity, gas, or other essential services, the tenant must serve notice specifying the breach and may recover damages based on the diminution in the fair rental value, or procure reasonable substitute housing, and is excused from paying rent for the period of the landlord's noncompliance.

§ 55-248.24 Fire or Casualty Damage

If the dwelling unit is damaged or destroyed by fire or casualty to an extent that the tenant's enjoyment of the unit is substantially impaired or if required repairs can only be accomplished if the tenant vacates the dwelling, either the tenant or the landlord may terminate the rental agreement. The tenant may vacate the premises and serve notice within 14 days to the landlord of the intent to terminate the agreement. The landlord may terminate the agreement by giving the tenant 30 days' notice with return of security deposit and any prepaid rent.

§ 55-248.25 Landlord's Noncompliance as Defense to Action for Possession for Nonpayment of Rent

In an action for possession based on nonpayment of rent, the tenant may assert as a defense that there exists a condition which constitutes a fire hazard or serious threat to the life, health, or safety of occupants. This defense will be conditioned on whether, before the commencement of the action for rent or possession, the landlord was served written notice of the aforesaid conditions and has refused to remedy them. The rent due is to be held by the court that is making a ruling.

§ 55-248.25:1 Rent Escrow Required for Continuance of Tenant's Case

Where a landlord has filed an **unlawful detainer action** seeking possession of the premises, and the tenant seeks a continuance of the action, the court will order the tenant to pay the rent into the court escrow account.

§ 55-248.26 Tenant's Remedies for Landlord's Unlawful Ouster, Exclusion, or Diminution of Service

If the landlord unlawfully removes or excludes the tenant from the premises or willfully diminishes services, the tenant may recover possession or terminate the rental agreement and recover actual damages and reasonable attorney's fees.

§ 55-248.27 Tenant's Assertion; Rent Escrow

The tenant may assert that there exists a condition which constitutes a material noncompliance by the landlord that, if not corrected, will constitute a fire hazard or threat to life, health, or safety of occupants. Before granting of any relief, the tenant must show that written notice was served to the landlord and that the landlord refused to remedy the condition. The rent has to have been paid into the court (many legal issues are covered in this paragraph, and legal counsel is recommended). (§ 55-226.12, 2011)

Article 5— Landlord Remedies

§ 55-248.31 Noncompliance With Rental Agreement

If the tenant violates the terms of the lease or is in violation of the tenant's responsibility to maintain the dwelling so that it materially affects health and safety, the landlord may notify the tenant of the violation in writing and state that the rental agreement will terminate on a date not less than 30 days after notice is given, unless the tenant corrects the violation within 21 days. If the violation can be satisfied by repairs or by payment for damages and the tenant takes action to correct the violation, the leased agreement may not be terminated. If the tenant fails to take action within 14 days, the landlord may enter the property, correct the problem, and charge the tenant for any costs incurred. In an emergency, the landlord may enter and correct the violation as promptly as necessary.

For tenant violations that cannot be corrected, the landlord will notify the tenant in writing of the violation and state that the rental agreement will terminate on a date not less than 30 days after notification. For violations that involve a criminal or willful act, cannot be corrected, and pose a threat to health and safety, the landlord may terminate the rental agreement immediately and proceed with actions to obtain possession. The court hearing for possession will be held within 15 calendar days from the date the tenant was notified. Any illegal drug activity will constitute an immediate non-remediable violation, and the landlord may proceed to terminate the agreement without waiting for a court conviction. This section of the law also provides direction for procedures to be followed if the tenant is a victim of family abuse.

Nonpayment of Rent

If rent payments are not received when due, the landlord may take the following actions:

- *Five-day pay or quit notice*—The landlord may issue a written notice giving the tenant five days to pay the rent or vacate the property.

- *Unlawful detainer warrant*—The landlord may begin eviction proceedings immediately after issuing this warrant. The tenant remains obligated to pay the rent.

- *Eviction*—If full payment of rent is not received within five days, the landlord may file suit to have the tenant evicted. The landlord may not remove or exclude the tenant from the property or deny essential services until such time as the court takes eviction action. As of 2013, during an eviction, the landlord may remove the tenant's personal property from the dwelling, the premises, or any on-site storage area.

The unlawful detainer process now requires an initial hearing within 21 days, and the execution of the writ of possession by the sheriff should occur within 15 calendar days from the date received. Legislation in 2014 now allows for additional rent that is due from the time of the filing and the date of the hearing to be added to the amount due.

As of 2013, failed electronic rent payments are subject to the same civil action as a bad check. This legislation also allows the landlord's attorney or agent to present affidavits in court proceedings listing outstanding rent, fees, and damages owed and receive a judgment if the defendant does not appear. The unlawful detainer tenant redemption remedy may only be used once in any 12-month period.

§ 55-248.31:01 Barring Guest or Invitee of Tenants

A guest or invitee of a tenant may be barred from the premises upon written notice served personally on the guest or invitee for conduct that violates the terms and conditions of the rental agreement, a local ordinance, or a state or federal law.

§ 55-248.31:1 Sheriffs Authorized to Serve Certain Notices; Fees Therefore

The sheriff of any county or city, upon request, may deliver any notice to a tenant on behalf of a landlord for a fee not to exceed $12.

§ 55-248.32 Remedy by Repair, etc.; Emergencies

If there is a violation affecting health and safety that can be remedied by repair, replacement of a damaged item, or cleaning, the landlord must send written notice to the tenant specifying the breach and stating that the landlord will enter the unit and perform the work necessary and then submit an itemized bill to the tenant due with the next rent payment.

§ 55-248.33 Remedies for Absence, Nonuse, and Abandonment

During any absence of the tenant in excess of seven days, the landlord may enter the property for the purpose of protecting it. If the terms of the lease require tenant notification of extended absences and if the tenant fails to advise the landlord, the tenant may be responsible for any damage that occurs during the absence.

§ 55-248.34:1 Landlord's Acceptance of Rent With Reservation

Provided the landlord has given written notice to the tenant that the rent will be accepted with reservation, the landlord may accept full payment of all rent and receive an order of possession from a court of competent jurisdiction pursuant to an unlawful detainer action. The landlord must include this written notice in the termination notice given to the tenant or in a separate written notice given to the tenant within five business days of receiving the rent. The landlord must continue to accept the rent with reservation until the alleged violation has been remedied or the matter has been adjudicated in a court of competent jurisdiction.

§ 55-248.35 Remedy After Termination

If the rental agreement is terminated, the landlord may have a claim for possession and rent, plus a separate claim for actual damages for breach of the rental agreement. Actual damages may include a claim for rent that would have accrued until the expiration of the term.

§ 55-248.36 Recovery of Possession Limited

A landlord may not recover or take possession of the dwelling unit by willful diminution of services or by refusal to permit the tenant access unless pursuant to a court order.

§ 55-248.37 Periodic Tenancy; Holdover Remedies

The landlord or tenant may terminate a week-to-week tenancy by serving written notice at least seven days before the next rent due date. A month-to-month tenancy requires 30 days' notice.

§ 55-248.38:1 Disposal of Property Abandoned by Tenants

If any items of personal property are left in the premises or any storage area after the rental agreement has terminated and delivery of possession has occurred, the landlord may consider such property to be abandoned. The landlord may dispose of the property provided a termination notice has been given to the tenant that includes a statement that any items of personal property left in the premises is disposed of within a 24-hour period after termination. The tenant has the right to remove the property within that 24-hour period.

Any funds received from the sale of the abandoned property may be used to offset debts owed by the tenant, including the cost of moving and storing the property.

§ 55-248.38:2 Authority of Sheriffs to Store and Sell Personal Property Removed From Residential Premises; Recovery of Possession by Owner; Disposition or Sale

When personal property is removed from a dwelling unit pursuant to an action of unlawful detainer or ejectment, the sheriff will oversee the removal of such personal property to be placed into the public way. The tenant will have the right to remove personal property during the 24-period after eviction. After expiration of the 24-hour period, the landlord may remove or dispose of any such personal property remaining in the public way.

Unit 9

§ 55-248.38:3 Disposal of Property of Deceased Tenants

If a tenant, who is the sole occupant of the dwelling unit, dies and there is no person authorized by order of the circuit court to handle probate matters for the deceased tenant, the landlord may dispose of the personal property left in the premises, or in a storage area provided by the landlord, provided the landlord has given at least 10 days' written notice to

1. the person identified in the rental application, lease agreement, or other landlord document as the authorized person to contact in the event of the death of the tenant; or

2. the tenant if no such person is identified in the rental application, lease agreement, or other landlord document as the authorized contact person.

The notice given under clause (1) or (2) must include a statement that any items of personal property left in the premises will be treated as abandoned property and disposed of, if not claimed within 30 days.

Note that while the second option in the previous list might appear nonsensical, the possibility exists that a person unknown to the landlord has been duly authorized by the tenant and could act on behalf of the tenant's estate upon receiving the notice among the pieces of mail sent to the tenant's address.

Article 6— Retaliatory Action

§ 55-248.39 Retaliatory Conduct Prohibited

A landlord may not retaliate against a tenant who sues or otherwise seeks to enforce her legal rights or rights under the lease. Rent increases, a decrease in service, or termination of the lease are all barred retaliatory actions. The tenant is protected from **retaliation** if the landlord has notice of any of the following:

- The tenant has complained to the government about building code violations or conditions dangerous to health or safety
- The tenant has made a complaint to or filed suit against the landlord for violation of any provision of the VRLTA
- The tenant has organized or has become a member of a tenants' organization
- The tenant has testified against the landlord in court
- The tenant has complained about possible fair housing law violations

If the landlord acts in violation of this section, the tenant is entitled to recovery of actual damages and may assert such retaliation as a defense in any action for possession. The burden of proving retaliatory intent will be on the tenant.

§ 55-248.40 Actions to Enforce Chapter

Any person adversely affected by an act or omission prohibited under this chapter may institute an action for injunction and damages against the person responsible.

MANAGEMENT RESPONSIBILITY

A property manager shares the owner's responsibility for ensuring that landlord-tenant relations comply with the VRLTA. As the owner's agent, a property manager could be liable for any violations, especially fair housing and tenants' rights issues.

Property managers often take on the responsibility for making or contracting for repairs on behalf of the landlord. Care should especially be taken when dealing with issues like mold or remediating a meth lab. The owner must remain liable and the rental agent is under no obligation to lease the property until such repairs are complete.

The specific duties of a licensee engaged to manage real estate are listed under the law of agency covered in Unit 2.

SUMMARY

Leases and landlord-tenant relationships are governed by Title 55—Property and Conveyances of the Code of Virginia in Chapter 13—Landlord and Tenant. Chapter 13.2 deals specifically with the VRLTA. Chapter 13.3 covers manufactured home rentals.

One of the most important aspects of the landlord-tenant relationship is to uphold all provisions of both federal and state fair housing law. The law requires the landlord to provide reasonable modifications and reasonable accommodations necessary for a person with a disability to enjoy full use of the housing.

General leasing principles include the following:

- When a rental property is sold, the tenant retains the same rights and privileges as held under the previous landlord.

- A nonresident owning four or more rentals must appoint a Virginia resident as agent.

- Termination notice periods are a three-month notice to terminate a year-to-year lease, a 30-day notice to terminate a month-to-month lease, or a 120-day written notice to terminate a month-to-month lease, where the termination is due to rehabilitation of the property or a change in the property's use (such as conversion to a condominium).

- The landlord may require the tenant to temporarily vacate the dwelling for repairs.

- The landlord must give written notice of any mortgage default, acceleration, or foreclosure pending.

- The landlord must disclose existence of defective drywall.

- The landlord must report conditions constituting a fire hazard or threat to life.

- Rent must be paid into a court escrow account when a case is continued.

- Early termination is allowed in cases of family or sexual abuse, or criminal assault.

- The landlord must disclose property used to manufacture methamphetamine and not properly cleaned.

- Landlords are prohibited from retaliatory conduct such as increasing rent or decreasing services.

- Contrary to common-law doctrine, in Virginia tenants not at fault in the destruction of the property are entitled to a reduction in rent until previous use of the property can be restored.

- Goods belonging to a tenant may be seized for nonpayment of rent for up to five years.
- If a tenant is served with a pay-or-quit notice, it must be paid in arrears before trial, then tenancy resumes.
- If rent is in arrears, the landlord may post a written eviction notice in a conspicuous location.

The VRLTA became law in 1974 to simplify, clarify, modernize, and revise the law governing rental of dwelling units and rights and obligations of landlords and tenants. In 2014, the general assembly enacted legislation that changed the applicability of VRLTA to owners of more than two rental properties plus their principal residence. The law also eliminated the payment of interest on security deposits.

Article 1—General Provisions includes exemptions from the law, application fee restrictions, terms and conditions of rental agreement, required insurance, unsigned leases, prohibited provisions, and confidentiality exemptions.

Article 2—Landlord Obligations covers the many obligations and responsibilities of a landlord with regard to inspections, disclosures of mold, ownership, military air installation, defective drywall, and manufacture of methamphetamine along with remedies for nondisclosure. A landlord must maintain fit premises, provide locks and peepholes, allow access to cable, satellite, and other television facilities, provide notice for pesticide use, and give notice in event of foreclosure. The landlord may require that a tenant provide a security deposit to protect against unpaid rent or damage that may not exceed two month's rent and is to be returned within 45 days less any amount claimed for damages. The landlord must make a final inspection within 72 hours of termination of the lease.

Article 3—Tenant Obligations covers the obligations of the tenant to maintain the dwelling unit, abide by all rules and regulations, allow access when necessary for repairs or improvements, and to permit exhibiting the unit for sale or lease. A tenant who obtains a court order excluding cotenants from occupancy may request landlord install new locks, or permit the tenant to do so. Where a mold condition exists, the landlord may require the tenant to vacate the unit for a period not to exceed 30 days. The tenant must occupy the unit only as a residence and must surrender possession at termination of tenancy. In case of fire or casualty damage, the landlord may terminate the agreement with 14 days' notice.

Article 4—Tenant Remedies and Article 5—Landlord Remedies are lengthy and cover issues that may require legal counsel. They are included in an abbreviated form for reference only.

Article 6—Retaliatory Action prohibits a landlord from taking any retaliatory action against a tenant who sues or seeks to enforce legal rights under the lease.

A property manager shares the owner's responsibility for ensuring that landlord-tenant relations comply with the VRLTA. As the owner's agent, a property manager could be liable for any violations, especially fair housing and tenants' rights issues.

UNIT 9 QUIZ

1. An important aspect of the landlord-tenant relationship is to uphold all provisions of fair housing law. A landlord may do all of the following *EXCEPT*
   A. ask qualifying questions, as long as same questions are asked of all applicants.
   B. verify the prospective tenant's ability to pay the stated rent.
   C. develop special rules for tenants with small children.
   D. require any modifications made by a tenant with a disability be restored to original condition.

2. The owner of an apartment complex that has fallen into disrepair decides to repair and renovate the buildings and convert them to condominiums. The number of days' notice required to terminate the tenants' month-to-month leases is
   A. 30 days.
   B. 60 days.
   C. 90 days.
   D. 120 days.

3. A tenant rents farmland, a barn, and a house. The buildings are destroyed by a fire caused by lightning. Must the tenant still pay the same rent and abide by all the terms of the lease?
   A. Yes, based on common law principles governing ground leases, the tenant must still pay rent.
   B. Yes, any damage to or destruction of the leased premises is the tenant's responsibility.
   C. No, destruction of the improvements terminates a ground lease.
   D. No, if the tenant is not at fault, she is entitled to a reduction in rent until her use of the land is restored.

4. A prospective tenant applies for a lease in an apartment building and pays the mandatory $125 application fee. If the tenant decides *NOT* to sign a lease, the application fee
   A. may be kept by the landlord.
   B. must be returned to the prospective tenant within 20 days.
   C. must be returned to the prospective tenant, less a 10% charge to cover paperwork.
   D. must be returned minus any actual expenses incurred by the landlord.

5. Which of the following is *NOT* subject to the requirements of the Virginia Residential Landlord Tenant Act (VRLTA)?
   A. Someone who owns two rental properties
   B. Someone who owns 10 rental properties in rural counties
   C. Someone who owns three rental properties
   D. Someone who owns four rental properties in an urban area

6. A landlord must disclose in writing the existence of any visible evidence of mold in the dwelling
   A. within three days of occupancy.
   B. within 48 hours of occupancy.
   C. when the lease is signed.
   D. within five days of occupancy.

7. A landlord, who is subject to the VRLTA, charges $750 per month for an apartment. The maximum amount the landlord can require as a security deposit is
   A. $750.
   B. $1,000.
   C. $1,500.
   D. $2,250.

8. The landlord can require a tenant to pay the premium for
   A. only renter's insurance.
   B. only damage insurance.
   C. neither renter's nor damage insurance.
   D. both renter's and damage insurance.

9. Which of the following lease provisions is prohibited under Virginia law?
   A. Two months' rent security deposit required
   B. Prohibition against pets
   C. Restriction against lawful possession of a firearm
   D. Tenant's responsibility for the conduct of guests

10. All of the following statements with regard to security deposits are true *EXCEPT*
    A. The security deposit may not exceed an amount equal to two months' rent.
    B. The security deposit may be used to pay the last month's rent.
    C. The security deposit must be returned to the tenant within 45 days after the tenant vacates the property.
    D. The security deposit is to protect the landlord against unpaid rents or damage.

11. A tenant decides to install a burglar alarm in a rented house. Does the tenant need to inform the landlord?
    A. No, the tenant has full right of possession during the lease.
    B. No, only tenants in multiunit apartment buildings must inform a landlord about a security system.
    C. Yes, the tenant must also give the landlord instructions and passwords.
    D. Yes, the tenant must inform the landlord, but the cost of the system may be deducted from the rent.

12. An Air Force sergeant rented an apartment four months ago. He has now been reassigned to a different airbase with orders to move in 30 days. His landlord may charge him for damages of
    A. one month's rent.
    B. seven months' rent.
    C. one-half of one month's rent.
    D. Nothing, because he is military.

13. The first action that a landlord must take if the rent payment is not received when due, is
    A. the five-day pay or quit notice.
    B. the unlawful detainer warrant.
    C. eviction.
    D. the non-compliant notice.

14. Any items of personal property left on the premises after termination of the rental agreement are considered abandoned. As long as the landlord has given proper notice, the property may be disposed of. The tenant has
    A. no further rights.
    B. the right to remove the property within 24 hours.
    C. the right to remove the property anytime.
    D. the right to sue the landlord for taking the property.

15. Article 6 of the Virginia Residential Landlord Tenant Act (VRLTA) deals with
    A. general leasing principles.
    B. obligations of the landlord.
    C. obligations of the tenant.
    D. retaliatory action.

UNIT
10

Virginia Fair Housing Law

LEARNING OBJECTIVES

When you have completed this unit, you will be able to

› **describe** the makeup and responsibilities of the Virginia Fair Housing Office and Virginia Fair Housing Board (FHB);
› **list** and define exemptions under Virginia Fair Housing Law;
› **identify** unlawful discriminatory housing practices;
› **explain** the procedure for enforcement of the Virginia Fair Housing Law; and
› **define** the following key terms:

civil action	elderliness	hoarding
complainant	familial status	respondent
conciliation	handicap	service animal
dwelling		

OVERVIEW

The Virginia Fair Housing Law falls under Title 36, Chapter 5.1 (§ § 36-96.1–36.96.23) of the Code of Virginia. The law states that it is the policy of the Commonwealth of Virginia to provide for fair housing throughout the Commonwealth for all its citizens, regardless of race, color, religion, national origin, sex, **elderliness**, **familial status**, or **handicap** and that all discriminatory practices in residential housing transactions are prohibited. The law applies to property managers, owners, landlords, real estate agents, banks, savings institutions, credit unions, insurance companies, mortgage lenders, and appraisers.

Fair housing in Virginia is also covered by the Virginia Administrative Code, 18 VAC 135-50-10 through 135.50-550, as published in the Real Estate Board Fair Housing Regulations, effective September 22, 2007.

Title 54.1 Chapter 23.2, Sections 54.1-2343 and 54.1-2344, relates to the DPOR and the creation of the Fair Housing Board (FHB). The Virginia Fair Housing Office also falls under the auspices of the DPOR and serves as the investigative arm of both the FHB and the REB.

VIRGINIA FAIR HOUSING OFFICE

The Virginia Fair Housing Office (VFHO) is the investigative arm for both the FHB and the REB. It consists of an administrator, who has overall responsibility for the office; an investigative supervisor, who oversees all investigations; a program conciliator, who attempts to resolve complaints through informal negotiation; and four field investigators and two administrative investigators. The VFHO has two mandates: investigation and training.

Investigation Mandate

After the investigator has completed interviews with the **complainant**, **respondent**, and witnesses and reviewed pertinent documents and records, a final report is prepared and submitted to the appropriate board. During the investigative process, the program conciliator attempts to resolve the complaint through **conciliation**—a voluntary process where the parties attempt to resolve the complaint by agreeing to mutually acceptable terms. If conciliation is not successful, the investigation continues.

Training Mandate

Each year, staff from the VFHO travel throughout Virginia providing training to housing providers, consumers, and local and state officials. Presentations range from handouts to PowerPoint presentations, are interactive, and are offered at no cost to participants.

The VFHO can be reached by phone at 1-804-367-8530 or 1-888-551-3247 or by email at fairhousing@dpor.virginia.gov.

VIRGINIA FAIR HOUSING BOARD

The FHB was created at the DPOR in 2003 to administer and enforce the provisions of both state and federal fair housing law. The FHB also oversees an education-based certification program for individuals involved in selling or renting **dwellings**. Both the REB and the FHB have the power to initiate and receive complaints, conduct investigations, attempt resolution of complaints by conference or conciliation, and issue a charge to be referred to the attorney general for action. The REB is responsible for the administration and enforcement of the fair housing law with respect to real estate licensees or their employees. The FHB is responsible for all others who violate the fair housing law. A case that involves both licensees and a member of the general public will be heard by the REB.

The FHB is composed of 12 members, appointed by the governor for four-year terms, as follows:

- One representative of local government
- One architect licensed in accordance with Chapter 4 (§ 54.1-400 et seq.) of this title
- One representative of the mortgage lending industry
- One representative of the property and casualty insurance industry
- Two representatives of the residential property management industry not licensed in accordance with Chapter 21 (§ 54.1-2100 et seq.) of this title
- One contractor licensed in accordance with Chapter 11 (§ 54.1-1100 et seq.) of this title
- One representative of the disability community

- One representative of the residential land lease industry subject to Chapter 13.3 (§ 55-248.41 et seq.) of Title 55

- Three citizen members selected in accordance with Section 54.1-107

The FHB can be reached by phone at 1-804-367-0115 or by email at fhcertification@dpor .virginia.gov.

VIRGINIA FAIR HOUSING LAW

Protected Classes In Virginia

The Virginia Fair Housing Law prohibits discrimination in housing and real estate activities on the basis of

- race,
- color,
- religion,
- national origin,
- sex,
- elderliness,
- familial status, or
- handicap.

Virginia added the additional protected class of elderliness to the seven federal protected classes.

Important Definitions

Certain terms in the fair housing law have specific legal definitions. A few of the most relevant ones are:

Aggrieved person—An aggrieved person is any person who (i) claims to have been injured by a discriminatory housing practice or (ii) believes that such person will be injured by a discriminatory housing practice that is about to occur.

Complainant—A complainant is a person who files a fair housing complaint.

Conciliation—Conciliation is the attempted resolution of issues raised by a complainant through informal negotiations involving the aggrieved person, the respondent, their respective authorized representatives, and the FHB.

Dwelling—A dwelling is all or part of any building or structure designated or intended for use as a residence by one or more families. The term also includes vacant land offered for sale or lease for the construction or location of any residential building or structure.

Elderliness—For purposes of the fair housing law, elderliness refers to individuals who have attained their 55th birthday.

Familial Status—The familial status class protects individuals under the age of 18 who live with either

- a parent or other person having legal custody, or
- the designee of a parent or other person having custody with the written permission of the parent or other person.

The definition also includes pregnant women and people who are in the process of securing legal custody of a minor.

IN PRACTICE

Three related adults, including one 19-year-old, have applied to rent a one-bedroom apartment and have been turned down by the landlord based on a reasonable occupancy standard. Regardless of the reasonable occupancy standard, they then claim that they are a family under familial status and are entitled to rent the unit as a family regardless of the occupancy standard.

The fair housing law protects individuals, not families, and does not apply in this situation. However, if one party was a minor, the law could apply under familial status.

Family—A family includes a single individual, whether male or female.

Handicap—A person is considered handicapped if that person suffers from a physical or mental impairment that substantially limits one or more major life activities. Having a record of such impairment, or being regarded as having such an impairment, also constitutes a handicap under the fair housing law. The law does apply to individuals in a recognized drug treatment program. The term does not apply to current, illegal use of or addiction to a controlled substance as defined by law. *Transvestites* are specifically excluded from the definition of handicap. The term *disabled* is used more often today than *handicapped*.

Hoarding—Hoarding is now classified by the Diagnostic Manual of Mental Disabilities as a disability. A reasonable accommodation must be allowed to enable remedying any adverse effects created by the hoarding.

Respondent—A respondent is the person or entity alleged to have violated the provisions of the fair housing law.

Exemptions

As with the federal law, there are some exemptions in Virginia, as follows:

- A single-family residence sold or rented by the owner is exempt from the statute, as long as the owner owns no more than three such homes at the time. In the case of a sale where the owner was not residing in the home at the time of the sale or was not the resident of the home before the sale, the exemption applies to only one sale within any one 24-month period. The sale or rental of any such single-family dwelling will be exempt only if the property is sold or rented without the use of any real estate broker or broker facilities and without the use of any advertisement that is in violation of fair housing law.

- Rooms or units in one- to four-family structures are exempt if the owner occupies one of the units and does not use discriminatory advertising.

- Religious organizations, institutions, associations, or societies may limit the sale or rental of property they own or operate for other than commercial purposes to persons of the same religion. Such organizations may give preference to their members, as long as membership in the organization is not restricted on the basis of race, color, national origin, sex, elderliness, familial status, or handicap.

- Private, state-owned, or state-supported educational institutions, hospitals, nursing homes, religious organizations, and correctional institutions may, for personal privacy reasons, require single-sex occupancy of its owned and operated single-family residences, rooms, and units. Single-sex restrooms in such dwellings or buildings are not illegal.

- Private membership clubs not open to the public that provide lodging that they own or operate for other than commercial purposes may give preference to their members.

- An individual who intends to share living quarters with another may advertise on the basis of sex, but only on the basis of sex. For example, an ad could say, "Females only need apply," but it could not say, "Christian females" or "white females."

- Certain restrictive covenants and zoning laws exist that restrict housing in an area to single-family housing. According to the Virginia Fair Housing Law, a family care home, foster home, or group home in which persons reside who are physically handicapped, mentally ill, mentally retarded, or developmentally disabled, together with resident counselors or staff, is considered single-family occupancy for zoning purposes. For purposes of restrictive covenants, there is no maximum number of residents.

- Condominium unit owners' association may, if permitted by the bylaws, restrict the number of occupants in any unit, as long as the limitation is reasonable and not more restrictive than the local zoning ordinance.

- It is legal to discriminate on the basis of age to permit housing for elderly persons. Housing is exempt from the familial status protection if it is provided under a state or federal program designed to assist the elderly, or if it is intended for and solely occupied by persons at least 62 years of age, or if it has at least one person 55 years of age or older in 80% of the occupied units. Qualified housing in this second category must adhere to published policies and procedures that demonstrate the intent to provide such housing.

Criminal Background

People who have been convicted of the illegal manufacture or distribution of controlled substances are not protected by the fair housing law.

Rental applications may require the disclosure of any criminal convictions, and applicants may be required to consent to and to pay for a criminal background check. A building manager or property owner may refuse to rent a dwelling to an individual who has a record of prior criminal convictions involving harm to persons or property, and whose presence would pose a threat to the health or safety of others. Consistently applying a criminal background check means that the policy must be in writing, must have the applicant's permission, and must be applied to all applicants.

Similarly, the law's protections do not make it unlawful for an owner to deny or limit residential rentals to persons who pose a clear and present threat of substantial harm to others or the premises.

IN PRACTICE

Local counties, cities, and towns may enforce legislation adopted before 1991 that is *more restrictive* (protective of more classes) than either the state or the federal law. Any amendments to the local legislation, however, must conform to the state's law. Because licensees often practice in more than one jurisdiction within the state, they must be aware of all local legislation that differs from federal and state laws.

Liability for Licensees

It is illegal for real estate licensees to be involved in discriminatory housing practices in any way. While licensees should be aware of the exemptions in order to fully comply with the law when acting in the best interests of client, it is of more vital importance that they personally comply with the law's nondiscriminatory intent. The law (§ 36.96.2A) states, "this exemption shall not apply to or inure to the benefit of any licensee of the Real Estate Board or regulant of the Fair Housing Board, regardless of whether the licensee is acting in his personal or professional capacity."

In other words, there are no exemptions from fair housing law for real estate licensees in Virginia.

UNLAWFUL DISCRIMINATORY HOUSING PRACTICES

In Virginia, it is illegal for anyone to commit any of the following discriminatory acts on the basis of a person's race, color, religion, national origin, sex, elderliness, familial status, or handicap:

- Refusing to sell or rent a dwelling to any person who has made a bona fide offer to do so or refusing to negotiate the sale or rental of a dwelling

- Discriminating against any person in the terms, condition, or privileges of the sale or rental of a dwelling or in providing services or facilities

- Making, printing, or publishing any notice, statement, or advertisement with respect to the sale or rental of a dwelling that indicates an actual or intended preference, limitation, or discrimination

- Falsely representing that a dwelling is not available for inspection, sale, or rental

- Denying membership or participation in a multiple listing service (MLS), real estate brokers' organization, or any other service, organization, or facility related to the business of selling or renting dwellings

- Including any discriminatory restrictive covenant in the transfer, sale, rental, or lease of housing or honoring any discriminatory restriction

- Inducing or attempting to induce the sale or rental of a dwelling by representations regarding the entry or prospective entry into the neighborhood of protected persons

- Refusing to sell, rent, or negotiate with anyone on the basis of their own handicap, that of anyone who will be residing in the dwelling, or that of anyone associated with them

- Discriminating in the terms, conditions, or privileges of the sale or rental of a dwelling or in its services or facilities on the basis of an individual's handicap or that of anyone associated with the individual

Additional Prohibited Actions

Virginia Fair Housing Regulations list the following additional actions that are prohibited:

- Failing or delaying maintenance or repairs of sales or rental dwellings

- Limiting the use of privileges, services, or facilities associated with a dwelling

- Discouraging the purchase or rental of a dwelling by exaggerating drawbacks or failing to inform of desirable features

- Communicating to a prospective purchaser or renter that they would not be comfortable or compatible with existing residents of a community

- Assigning any one to a particular section of a community or particular floor or section of a building

- Denying or limiting services or facilities because a person failed or refused to provide sexual favors

Discriminatory Advertising

The law applies to all written or oral notices or statements, including applications, flyers, brochures, deeds, signs, banners, posters, billboards, or documents.

The use of words or symbols associated with a particular religion, national origin, sex, or race is considered prima facie evidence of an illegal preference. The use of such words or symbols may not be overcome by a general disclaimer that no discrimination is intended.

An ad with directions to a rental property that included "turn left at St. Matthew's Cathedral" or "three blocks past the new mosque" might be considered to be steering people of a certain religion to a property.

The selective use of language, geography, or human models should always reflect the true demographic makeup of a community.

The HUD-approved fair housing poster should be displayed at all places of business that sell or rent dwellings. All advertising of residential real estate for sale, rent, or financing should contain an equal housing opportunity logotype, statement, or slogan.

Special Rules for Handicapped Persons

Persons with disabilities must be permitted to make reasonable modifications, at their own expense, of existing premises to make the premises fully accessible to the individual. A landlord may make modification of rented premises conditional on the tenant's agreement to restore the premises to their original condition (reasonable wear and tear accepted) if it affects the value of the property.

It is unlawful to refuse to make reasonable accommodations in rules, practices, policies, or services in order to afford handicapped individuals equal opportunities to use and enjoy a dwelling. For example, a no pets policy should be flexible enough to accommodate **service animals**, such as a guide dog or an assistance monkey.

On October 26, 2016, the REB published a guidance document on Reasonable Accommodation Requests for Assistance Animals. The rather lengthy document can be viewed on the DPOR website at www.dpor.virginia.gov.

Hoarding is now classified as a mental disability. A reasonable accommodation is allowing time for the tenant or someone assisting the tenant to correct lease violations, such as odor, pest infestation, blocked exits, or fire hazards. Any imminent threats should be addressed immediately.

New multifamily dwellings, that is, those with four or more units, must be designed and constructed in such a way that the public use and common areas are readily accessible to handicapped persons. All ground-floor units must have doors that allow passage by persons in wheelchairs plus light switches, electrical outlets, thermostats, and environmental controls that are accessible by persons in wheelchairs. Kitchens and bathrooms must be designed for full maneuverability with reinforced bathroom walls to allow later installation of grab bars. In four or more unit buildings with elevators, all units must meet the accessibility requirements.

The Americans with Disabilities Act (ADA) prohibits discrimination against people with disabilities in employment, transportation, public accommodations, communications, and governmental activities. The Architectural and Transportation Barriers Compliance Board (also called the Access Board) issues guidelines to ensure that buildings, facilities, and transit vehicles are accessible and usable by people with disabilities. Although ADA standards do not apply to all residential dwellings, they do apply to any area that has public access, such as common use areas or any real estate or rental management office.

Fair Housing Application for Lending Institutions

The fair housing law also applies to lending institutions and other businesses involved in residential real estate transactions. It is unlawful to discriminate in the availability, terms, or conditions of real estate financing on the basis of race, color, religion, national origin, sex, elderliness, familial status, or handicap. It is not unlawful for any person or business engaging in residential real estate transactions to require any applicant to qualify financially. If any lending institution is found to be engaging in unlawful discriminatory practices, the fair housing law forbids state, county, city, or municipal treasurers or other government officials to deposit public funds in the institution. Existing deposits of public funds must be withdrawn from offending lenders although the action may be deferred for one year to avoid financial loss to the state, county, city, or agency. If the lender corrects its practices, there is no prohibition against the deposit of public funds.

The Virginia Fair Housing Law also applies to those who are involved indirectly in the sale or rental of real property, such as newspapers and other publications. Appraisers cannot include any discriminatory information in appraisal reports.

ENFORCEMENT OF THE FAIR HOUSING LAW

Persons who feel that their rights under the fair housing law have been violated may take action against the party alleged to have discriminated. Complaints involving persons licensed by the REB must be filed with the REB, which is empowered to initiate and receive complaints against licensees, investigate alleged violations, and resolve conflicts either by conference and conciliation or by issuing a charge and referring the matter to the attorney general for action. Complaints against non-licensees may be made to the Fair Housing Board (FHB) at fairhousing@dpor.virginia.gov. The procedures to be followed are the same for both the FHB and the REB. Effective July 1, 2013, the REB has the authority to hear fair housing violations with multiple respondents, at least one of whom is a licensee.

A complaint must be filed in writing with the board within one year of the occurrence or termination of the alleged discriminatory practice.

In any action brought under the Virginia Fair Housing Law, the burden of proof is upon the complainant. The board must acknowledge receipt of the complaint and advise the claimant of time limits and choices of forums for hearing the complaint.

Accused persons must be notified of the allegation and of their legal rights within 10 days. Proceedings must commence within 30 days after receiving the complaint. The investigation should be completed within 100 days. If the board is unable to complete the investigation within 100 days, both the complainant and the respondent will be notified in writing of the reasons for not doing so.

The REB may issue subpoenas, interview witnesses, and request the production of documents in the course of its investigation. During the investigative period, it is possible for the complainant and respondent to enter into a conciliation agreement, subject to REB approval. A conciliation agreement may provide for binding arbitration and may award appropriate relief, including monetary relief.

If reasonable cause exists to believe that a discriminatory housing practice has occurred or is about to occur, the REB must seek resolution by conciliation or forward the charge to the attorney general for **civil action**. If no reasonable cause exists, the case will be dismissed. If the board determines that a discriminatory housing practice involving the legality of any local zoning or land use ordinance has occurred, the complaint will be immediately referred to the attorney general for civil action.

Penalties

If the case results in civil action by the attorney general, the court may

- award preventive relief by temporary or permanent injunction, restraining order, or other necessary order;
- assess a civil penalty of up to $50,000 for a first violation and up to $100,000 for any subsequent violation; and
- award the prevailing party reasonable attorney's fees and costs.

Whether or not a complaint has been filed with the REB, a civil action may also be initiated by an injured person in a U.S. district court or state court within two years after the occurrence or termination of an alleged discriminatory housing practice. If a civil action is filed at the same time a complaint is filed with the REB, the REB will delay action until the court rules. If a conciliation agreement is breached, a civil action may be filed within two years of the breach.

If any real estate licensee is found guilty of violating the fair housing law, the REB will take appropriate steps to consider suspension or revocation of the license or to take other disciplinary action.

Additional information about the Virginia Fair Housing Law is available at http://law.lis .virginia.gov/vacode/title36/chapter5.1/.

SUMMARY

The Virginia Fair Housing Law falls under Title 36, Chapter 5.1 of the Code of Virginia. The law applies to property managers, owners, landlords, real estate agents, banks, savings institutions, credit unions, insurance companies, mortgage lenders, and appraisers.

The VFHO is the investigative arm for both the FHB and the REB. After the investigator has completed interviews with the complainant, respondent, and witnesses and reviewed pertinent documents and records, a final report is prepared and submitted to the appropriate board. The FHB was created at the DPOR in 2003 to administer and enforce the provisions of both state and federal fair housing law.

The Virginia Fair Housing Law is included in the VAC, 18 VAC 135-50-10. The law prohibits discrimination in housing and real estate activities on the basis of

- race,
- color,
- religion,
- national origin,
- sex,
- elderliness,
- familial status, or
- handicap.

Virginia added the additional protected class of elderliness to the seven federal protected classes. Other specific legal definitions are included in the law such as aggrieved person, complainant, familial status, and handicap (disability). Two new additions are family—which includes a single individual, and hoarding—now classed as a mental disability.

Exemptions to the Virginia law are:

- A single-family residence sold or rented by the owner as long as the owner owns no more than three homes at the time and the sale or rental is done without the use of a real estate broker and without any discriminatory advertising.

- Rooms or units in one- to four-family structures are exempt if the owner occupies one of the units and does not use discriminatory advertising.

- Religious organizations, institutions, associations, or societies may limit the sale or rental of property they own or operate for other than commercial purposes to persons of the same religion as long as membership in the organization is not restricted on the basis of race, color, national origin, sex, elderliness, familial status, or handicap.

- Private, state-owned, or state-supported educational institutions, hospitals, nursing homes, religious organizations, and correctional institutions may, for personal privacy reasons, require single-sex occupancy of its owned and operated single-family residences, rooms, and units.

- Private membership clubs not open to the public that provide lodging that they own or operate for other than commercial purposes may give preference to their members.

- An individual who intends to share living quarters with another may advertise on the basis of sex, but only on the basis of sex. For example, an ad could say, "Females only need apply," but it could not say, "Christian females" or "white females."

- Certain restrictive covenants and zoning laws exist that restrict housing in an area to single-family housing. According to the Virginia Fair Housing Law, a family care home, foster home, or group home in which persons reside who are physically handicapped, mentally ill, mentally retarded, or developmentally disabled, together with resident counselors or staff, is considered single-family occupancy for zoning purposes. For purposes of restrictive covenants, there is no maximum number of residents.

- Condominium unit owners' association may, if permitted by the bylaws, restrict the number of occupants in any unit, as long as the limitation is reasonable and not more restrictive than the local zoning ordinance.

- It is legal to discriminate on the basis of age to permit housing for elderly persons. Housing is exempt from the familial status protection if it is provided under a state or federal program designed to assist the elderly, or if it is intended for and solely occupied by persons at least 62 years of age, or if it has at least one person 55 years of age or older in 80% of the occupied units. Qualified housing in this second category must adhere to published policies and procedures that demonstrate the intent to provide such housing.

It is illegal for real estate licensees to be involved in discriminatory housing practices in any way. No exemptions apply to licensees. The law lists specific discriminatory housing practices:

- Refusing to sell or rent a dwelling to any person who has made a bona fide offer

- Discriminating against any person in the terms, condition, or privileges of the sale or rental of a dwelling or in providing services or facilities

- Making, printing, or publishing any notice, statement, or advertisement that indicates an actual or intended preference, limitation, or discrimination

- Falsely representing that a dwelling is not available for inspection, sale, or rental

- Denying membership or participation in a MLS, real estate brokers' organization, or any other service, organization, or facility related to the business of selling or renting dwellings

- Including any discriminatory restrictive covenant in the transfer, sale, rental, or lease of housing or honoring any discriminatory restriction

- Inducing or attempting to induce the sale or rental of a dwelling by representations regarding the entry or prospective entry into the neighborhood of protected persons

- Refusing to sell, rent, or negotiate with anyone on the basis of their own handicap, that of anyone who will be residing in the dwelling, or that of anyone associated with them.

- Discriminating in the terms, conditions, or privileges of the sale or rental of a dwelling on the basis of an individual's handicap or that of anyone associated with the individual.

Virginia Fair Housing Regulations list the following additional actions that are prohibited:

- Failing or delaying maintenance or repairs of sales or rental dwellings

- Limiting the use of privileges, services, or facilities associated with a dwelling

- Discouraging the purchase or rental of a dwelling by exaggerating drawbacks or failing to inform of desirable features

- Communicating to a prospective purchaser or renter that they would not be comfortable or compatible with existing residents of a community

- Assigning any one to a particular section of a community or particular floor or section of a building

- Denying or limiting services or facilities because a person failed or refused to provide sexual favors

The law regarding advertising applies to all written or oral notices or statements, including applications, flyers, brochures, deeds, signs, banners, posters, billboards, or documents. The use of words or symbols associated with a particular religion, national origin, sex, or race is prohibited. The selective use of language, geography, or human models should always reflect the true demographic makeup of a community. Inclusion of the HUD-approved fair housing poster and logo is recommended.

Persons with disabilities must be permitted to make reasonable modifications at their own expense of existing premises. A landlord may require restoration to original condition (reasonable wear and tear accepted) if it affects the value of the property.

It is unlawful to refuse to make reasonable accommodations in rules, practices, policies, or services in order to afford handicapped individuals equal opportunities to use and enjoy a dwelling. For example, a no pets policy should be flexible enough to accommodate service animals. Hoarding is now classified as a mental disability and reasonable accommodation must be made.

New multifamily dwellings with four or more units, must be designed and constructed so that public use and common areas are readily accessible to handicapped persons. Specific standards apply to all ground-floor units. All units must meet the accessibility requirements in buildings with elevators.

Persons who feel that their rights under the fair housing law have been violated may take action against the party alleged to have discriminated. Complaints involving persons licensed by the REB must be filed with the REB. Complaints against non-licensees may be made to the FHB at fairhousing@dpor.virginia.gov. A complaint must be filed in writing with the appropriate board within one year of the occurrence or termination of the alleged discriminatory practice.

If the case results in civil action by the attorney general, the court may

- award preventive relief by temporary or permanent injunction, restraining order, or other necessary order;

- assess a civil penalty of up to $50,000 for a first violation and up to $100,000 for any subsequent violation; and

- award the prevailing party reasonable attorney's fees and costs.

Whether or not a complaint has been filed with the REB, a civil action may also be initiated by an injured person in a U.S. district court or state court within two years after the occurrence. If any real estate licensee is found guilty of violating the fair housing law, the REB will take appropriate steps to consider suspension or revocation of the license or to take other disciplinary action.

UNIT 10 QUIZ

1. The Fair Housing Board (FHB) consists of 12 members. How many citizen members are appointed to the board?
   A. One
   B. Two
   C. Three
   D. Five

2. Which of the following is a protected class under the Virginia Fair Housing Law?
   A. Marital status
   B. Familial status
   C. Source of income
   D. Age

3. All of the following are protected by the Virginia Fair Housing Law's provisions for the handicapped or elderly *EXCEPT*
   A. a 55-year-old recovered heroin addict.
   B. a 62-year-old currently using cocaine.
   C. a paralyzed veteran.
   D. a person who is a hoarder.

4. A landlord (who is not a real estate licensee) refuses to rent an apartment to an elderly man who has a guide dog, stating that his advertisement clearly states "no pets." If the man wishes to file a fair housing complaint, he should contact the Virginia
   A. REB.
   B. Fair Housing Board.
   C. Housing Development Authority.
   D. Attorney General's Office.

5. Which of the following is *NOT* exempt under Virginia Fair Housing Law?
   A. Single-family residence rented by an owner who owns no more than three homes
   B. Presbyterian Home for the Aged
   C. Single-sex occupancy of a state-supported nursing home
   D. Owner-occupied four-unit building advertising as "singles only"

6. Housing projects for the elderly are exempt from the familial status category of fair housing law as long as
   A. all occupants are at least 60 years old.
   B. 75% of occupants are at least 60 years old.
   C. all occupants of 80% of the units are at least 55 years old.
   D. at least one of the occupants in 80% of the units is 55 years old.

7. A single woman placed the following advertisement in the local paper: "Share lovely town house. Large wooded lot, near transportation, shops, and recreation. $650 per mo. Female only." Which of the following is *TRUE*?
   A. The ad is a violation of the fair housing law because it discriminates against males.
   B. The ad violates the fair housing law's prohibition against sexual discrimination.
   C. The ad is legal because she is sharing her own home.
   D. The newspaper is now subject to a civil action for publishing a discriminatory ad.

8. A building manager receives a lease application from a prospective tenant. The application disclosed that he served time in prison for income tax evasion but now has regular income from a manufacturing job. Can the building manager lawfully refuse to rent an apartment to him?
   A. No, the fair housing law prohibits discrimination on the basis of prior criminal record.
   B. No, his criminal conviction did not involve harm to persons or property.
   C. Yes, the fair housing law permits a building manager to refuse to rent to any convicted criminal.
   D. Yes, the fair housing law does not apply to actions by building managers—property owner or building manager can refuse to rent to an individual whose presence would pose a threat to the health and safety of others.

9. When a young couple recently emigrating from El Salvador attempted to rent an apartment, they were told that no units were available, when in fact there were at least four available at that time. The rental company was guilty of
   A. nothing; it has the right to say what it pleases.
   B. nothing; it has the right to limit rentals to U.S. citizens.
   C. unlawful discriminatory housing practice of false representation.
   D. discrimination based on age.

10. Two people apply for a mortgage loan. One is a 65-year-old blind male with no income or savings, and the other is a 35-year-old black female with no debts and a six-figure income from her law practice. Based on these facts alone, if both applicants are turned down, the lender has *MOST* likely committed unlawful discrimination against
    A. the 65-year old blind male.
    B. the 35-year old black female.
    C. both applicants.
    D. neither applicant.

11. All of the following are discriminatory acts according to Virginia Fair Housing Law *EXCEPT*
    A. falsely representing that a dwelling is not available for sale or rental.
    B. denying membership in an MLS.
    C. inducing the sale or rental of a dwelling by representation regarding the prospective entry into the neighborhood of protected persons.
    D. requiring a handicapped tenant to pay for installation of an access ramp.

12. Under the fair housing law, what symbol or logo is deemed discriminatory if printed on a flyer advertising new houses?
    A. HUD's Equal Housing symbol
    B. The REALTOR® logo/symbol
    C. A local MLS's logo/symbol
    D. A religious cross or symbol

13. Special rules for persons with disabilities include all of the following *EXCEPT*
    A. all multifamily dwelling units must be wheelchair accessible.
    B. permission to make reasonable modifications to the property.
    C. landlord cannot refuse to make reasonable accommodations in rules or services.
    D. accommodation must be made for any type of service animal.

14. Investigations of fair housing complaints should be completed within
    A. 30 days.
    B. 60 days.
    C. 100 days.
    D. 1 year.

15. A civil action brought by the attorney general for a first violation of the Virginia Fair Housing Law could subject a guilty party to a monetary civil penalty of
    A. up to $10,000 for a first offense.
    B. up to $25,000 for a first offense.
    C. up to $50,000 for a first offense.
    D. actual damages and legal fees only.

APPENDIX

INFORMATION SOURCES

Common Interest Community (CIC) Board
9960 Mayland Drive, Suite 400
Richmond, VA 23233-1485
1-804-367-0362
www.dpor.virginia.gov/Boards/CIC-Board

Department of Professional and Occupational Regulation (DPOR)
9960 Mayland Drive, Suite 400
Richmond, VA 23233-1485
1-804-367-8500
www.dpor.virginia.gov

PSI Exams—Virginia Real Estate Candidate Information Bulletin
https://candidate.psiexams.com

Virginia Association of REALTORS (VAR)
10231 Telegraph Road
Glen Allen, VA 23059
1-804-264-5033
www.virginiarealtors.org

Virginia Department of Taxation
Office of Consumer Service
P.O. Box 1115
Richmond, VA 23218-1115
1-804-367-8031
www.tax.virginia.gov

Virginia Fair Housing Office
9960 Mayland Drive, Suite 400
Richmond, VA 23233-1463
1-804-367-8530 or 1-888-551-3247
fairhousing@dpor.virginia.gov
www.dpor.virginia.gov/FairHousing/

Virginia Housing Development Authority (VHDA)
601 S. Belvidere Street
Richmond, VA 23220
1-804-782-1986 or 1-877-834-2123
www.vhda.com

Virginia Real Estate Board (REB)
9960 Mayland Drive, Suite 400
Richmond, VA 23233-1485
1-804-367-8552
www.dpor.virginia.gov/Boards/Real-Estate/

Virginia State Bar
1111 East Main Street, Suite 700
Richmond, VA 23219-3565
1-804-775-0500
http://www.vsb.org

Virginia State Police—Sex Offender and Crimes Against Minors Registry
http://sex-offender.vsp.virginia.gov/sor/
U.S. Department of Housing and Urban Development (HUD)
451 7th St. SW
Washington, D.C. 20410
1-202-708-1112
https://portal.hud.gov

U.S. Environmental Protection Agency—Lead
www.epa.gov/lead

PRACTICE EXAM

1. The Virginia Real Estate Board (REB) is authorized to do all of the following *EXCEPT*
   A. license real estate salespersons and brokers.
   B. regulate schools offering real estate courses.
   C. develop criteria for approving continuing education courses.
   D. administer the Residential Property Disclosure Act.

2. The residential property disclosure statement that contains notice to purchasers disclosing seller's representations regarding the property is now found in
   A. the Code of Virginia.
   B. the REB rules and regulations.
   C. the REB website.
   D. the Virginia Administrative Code (VAC).

3. If the buyer receives the required residential property disclosure statement three days after the contract is signed, the buyer can terminate the contract
   A. within 15 days of date sent, if emailed.
   B. within 10 days, if hand-delivered.
   C. within 5 days of postmark, if mailed.
   D. never; under the doctrine of caveat emptor, cannot terminate the contract.

4. If the Real Estate Transaction Recovery Fund falls below $400,000, how much money may the REB assess each licensee?
   A. $20 from each salesperson; $40 from each broker
   B. $20 from each inactive licensee; $40 from each active licensee
   C. $20 from each salesperson and broker, inactive or active
   D. $40 from each salesperson and broker, inactive or active

5. The Common Interest Community (CIC) Board is a separate agency under
   A. the Code of Virginia.
   B. the VAC.
   C. the REB.
   D. the Department of Professional and Occupational Registration.

6. The additional written disclosure requirements on the residential property disclosure statement include all of the following *EXCEPT*
   A. Megan's Law.
   B. military air installation.
   C. manufacture of methamphetamine.
   D. septic system permits.

7. The term *broker* refers to
   A. a firm.
   B. a principal broker.
   C. a managing broker.
   D. all of these.

8. All of the following transfers of property are exempt from the Virginia Residential Property Disclosure Act *EXCEPT*
   A. a transfer made pursuant to a court order.
   B. a transfer made between two co-owners.
   C. a transfer made without the assistance of a real estate broker.
   D. a transfer made to or from a government entity.

9. All of the following statements with regard to stigmatized property are true *EXCEPT*
   A. stigmatized property is any property that is made undesirable.
   B. houses in which a homicide or suicide have occurred may be called stigmatized.
   C. stigmatized property must be disclosed to potential buyers.
   D. any discussion of HIV or AIDS is specifically prohibited.

10. Other provisions of Virginia law that affect real estate practice but are not regulated under the REB regulations include all of the following *EXCEPT*
    A. mandatory licensing for home inspectors.
    B. first-time homebuyer's savings account.
    C. Virginia Utility Damage Prevention Act.
    D. American Taxpayer Relief Act.

11. Two salespersons work for the same broker. One represents the seller and the other represents the buyer in the same transaction. In this situation, the broker has assigned the salespersons as
    A. associate brokers.
    B. subagents.
    C. single agents.
    D. designated agents.

12. The duties that an agent owes to his client are established by
    A. statute.
    B. common law.
    C. the agent's broker.
    D. the agent's client.

13. All of the following are ways to terminate a brokerage relationship *EXCEPT*
    A. default by either party.
    B. death of the salesperson.
    C. expiration of the agreement.
    D. mutual agreement by the parties to terminate.

14. Under Virginia Real Estate License Law, an independent contractor is
    A. anyone practicing real estate in Virginia.
    B. a salesperson that must pay federal taxes on an estimated quarterly basis.
    C. a licensee representing a client according to a written brokerage agreement and not as a standard agent.
    D. a person contracted with to add a deck to the property.

15. As of July 1, 2012, all brokerage agreements must include all of the following *EXCEPT*
    A. a definite termination date.
    B. be in writing.
    C. a list of duties to be performed.
    D. prohibition of dual representation.

16. An agent is holding an open house on her new listing and is approached by a potential buyer who wants to write an offer to purchase. She is able to proceed with the transaction under all of the following circumstances *EXCEPT*
    A. disclose her brokerage relationship to the seller and treat the buyer as a customer.
    B. explain disclosed dual agency to both the potential buyer and the seller and proceed if written permission is received.
    C. request her broker to designate another agent to represent the buyer.
    D. proceed with the sale working in the best interests of both parties.

17. The statutory duty that may be different according to the type of client and for limited service agents is to
    A. perform according to the terms of the brokerage relationship.
    B. promote the best interests of the client.
    C. maintain confidentiality of all personal and financial information.
    D. account for all money and property received.

18. A seller can be represented by any of the following types of listing agreements *EXCEPT*
    A. open listing.
    B. exclusive agency listing.
    C. exclusive right-to-sell listing.
    D. net listing.

19. A limited service agent must do all of the following *EXCEPT*
    A. have a brokerage agreement in writing.
    B. provide a list of services to be provided.
    C. provide a list of services of a standard agent that will not be provided.
    D. have a signed independent contractor agreement.

20. Property management agreements must be in writing and include all of the following *EXCEPT*
    A. a definite termination date.
    B. the amount of management fees and how they will be paid.
    C. the services to be rendered.
    D. a proposed operational budget.

21. All of the following statements regarding eminent domain are true *EXCEPT*
    A. the process by which the state takes property is called condemnation.
    B. any taking of private property must be for public use.
    C. just compensation must be paid to the owner.
    D. the state is under no obligation to attempt to purchase the property.

22. If a married woman with three children dies intestate, her property will be distributed
    A. to her spouse under laws of dower and curtesy.
    B. one-third to her spouse, the remaining two-thirds to her children equally.
    C. one-half to her spouse, the other half to her children equally.
    D. two-thirds to her spouse, the remaining third to her children equally.

23. What is the total maximum homestead exemption if the person filing has property totaling $475,000?
    A. $4,750
    B. $5,000   *set amt.*
    C. $237,500
    D. $475,000

24. A man died, leaving his spouse $10,000 and all of the rest of his property to his two children. The surviving spouse renounced the will in order to claim her elective share of the deceased's augmented estate. She will now be entitled to
    A. all of his estate.
    B. one-half of his estate.
    C. one-third of his estate.
    D. none of his estate, but she may continue to live there.

25. Doctors A, B, and C purchased an office building as joint tenants. Doctor A sells his tenancy to doctor D. Which of the following is *TRUE* of this situation?
    A. Doctors B, C, and D are now joint tenants.
    B. Doctors B, C, and D are now tenants in common.
    C. Doctors B and C are tenants in common with joint tenancy with doctor D.
    D. Doctors B and C are joint tenants with tenancy in common with doctor D.

26. Two individuals own property as tenants in common. When one dies intestate, her interest passes to
    A. her heirs.
    B. the other party as a sole owner.
    C. her heirs with the other party as a joint tenant.
    D. her heirs if the property is sold.

27. The owner of an individual unit in a condominium building wants to sell it. All of the following documents must be included in the disclosure packet *EXCEPT*
    A. a statement of all assets and fees currently imposed.
    B. a copy of the current budget.
    C. a copy of the current bylaws and rules and regulations.
    D. a plat map indicating the location of the condominium building.

28. A couple recently signed a contract to purchase a town house in a development governed by a property owner's association. They will be able to cancel this contract if they
    A. change their minds.
    B. cancel any time before closing.
    C. cancel within three days of receiving the POA disclosure packet.
    D. cancel within 14 days of receiving the POA disclosure packet.

29. The biggest difference between purchasing a condominium unit and purchasing a cooperative unit is that
    A. the buyer is purchasing shares in the corporation (personal property).
    B. condominium units are larger.
    C. cooperative projects are always much smaller.
    D. there is no significant difference.

30. All of the following would be exempt from real estate taxation *EXCEPT*
    A. a nonprofit public library.
    B. a home of a veteran with a 100% service-connected disability.
    C. a for-profit preschool operated by a church.
    D. a historic residence.

31. If a contractor records a mechanic's memorandum of lien on September 15, 2016, he must file a suit to enforce it by
    A. October 15, 2016.
    B. December 31, 2016.
    C. March 15, 2017.
    D. September 15, 2017.

    6 months

32. If all of the following liens are recorded against a property and the bank forecloses, the first to be paid will be the
    A. real estate tax lien.
    B. mechanic's lien.
    C. deed of trust lien.
    D. vendor's lien.

33. What method of legal description is the following statement?

    All those certain lots, pieces or parcels of land, situated in the city of Roanoke, Virginia, known, numbered and designated on the Plat of Hampton Square and recorded in the clerk's office of the Circuit Court of the City of Roanoke, Virginia, in Map Book 26, page 7, as Lots No. 9 and 10.
    A. Metes and bounds
    B. Rectangular survey
    C. Government survey
    D. Lot and block

34. The *MOST* common description of real estate in Virginia is a combination of
    A. metes and bounds and government survey.
    B. metes and bounds and lot and block.
    C. lot and block and government survey.
    D. rectangular survey and government survey.

35. Statutory disclosures to be included in every sales contract written in Virginia include all of the following *EXCEPT*
    A. disclosure of brokerage relationship.
    B. disclosure of dual or designated representation if applicable.
    C. residential property disclosure.
    D. lead-based paint disclosure.

36. An implied warranty against structural defects on new construction continues for
    A. six months after the date of transfer of title or the buyer's taking possession.
    B. one year after the date of transfer of title or the buyer's taking possession.
    C. two years after the date of transfer of title or the buyer's taking possession.
    D. five years after the date of transfer of title or the buyer's taking possession.

37. A deed of trust is the instrument used in Virginia to establish collateral for a mortgage loan. All of the following statements regarding a deed of trust are true *EXCEPT*
    A. the parties involved in a deed of trust are the borrower, the lender, and a trustee.
    B. the borrower waives the right to a court hearing in case of foreclosure.
    C. the power of sale clause in the deed of trust gives the right to sell to the lender.
    D. the power of sale clause in the deed of trust gives the right to sell to the trustee.

38. When foreclosing on a deed of trust, the trustee is responsible to do all of the following *EXCEPT*
    A. purchase the property if it does not sell.
    B. obtain the best price possible.
    C. advertise within the stated time frame.
    D. pay any real estate tax liens from the proceeds.

39. One of the primary functions of the Virginia Housing Development Authority (VHDA) is to
    A. build housing for low/moderate-income people.
    B. research new methods of housing development.
    C. provide housing financing for low- and moderate-income residents of Virginia.
    D. enforce Fair Housing and RESPA regulations.

40. The Consumer Financial Protection Bureau (CFPB) was created in 2010 to issue regulations that protect consumers and promote fair, transparent, and competitive markets. The CFPB new rules for mortgage servicers that went into effect in 2014 include all of the following *EXCEPT*
    - A. the servicer must provide at least two months' warning of any change in adjustable-rate mortgage interest.
    - B. the servicer must promptly credit mortgage payments.
    - C. the servicer must declare a moratorium on payments if borrower is having difficulty making payment.
    - D. the servicer must work with the borrower having difficulties before starting foreclosure.

41. The CFPB created the TILA-RESPA Integrated Disclosures (TRID) that became mandatory on October 3, 2015. Under the TRID regulations, a new Loan Estimate (LE) form was created that replaced
    - A. the GFE.
    - B. the initial Truth in Lending statement.
    - C. both the GFE and the initial Truth in Lending statement.
    - D. the HUD-1 Settlement Statement.

42. The goal of the VHDA is to make housing more affordable for low- and moderate-income households. VHDA funding comes from
    - A. Fannie Mae.
    - B. the U.S. government.
    - C. the Virginia General Fund.
    - D. bonds sold through the private sector.

43. All of the following are requirements for a valid deed *EXCEPT*
    - A. the signature of the grantee.
    - B. consideration.
    - C. accurate legal description of the property.
    - D. delivery and acceptance of the deed.

44. Establishing title to a property through adverse possession requires
    - A. use of the property with the knowledge of the owner.
    - B. 20 years of possession.
    - C. tacking over a 15-year period.
    - D. hostile and continuous use of the property.

45. An elderly lady was very careful to execute a will leaving her beachfront condominium to her favorite niece. The niece will receive title to the property
    - A. after the will has gone through probate court.
    - B. anytime she wants to file with the clerk's office.
    - C. immediately after the will is read.
    - D. as soon as she pays the next month's condo fee.

46. Under the Real Estate Settlement Act (RESA), the choice of settlement agent is left to
    - A. the seller.
    - B. the buyer.
    - C. the broker.
    - D. either the seller or the buyer.

47. A gap in the chain of title could be caused by any of the following *EXCEPT*
    - A. the deed for one transfer of the property was never recorded.
    - B. the seller was divorced in a foreign country.
    - C. the name of the party on the deed was changed but never recorded.
    - D. the property was sold to a relative for $1 with a recorded deed.

48. The members of the REB are
    - A. elected by the public.
    - B. selected by the Virginia Association of REALTORS®.
    - C. appointed by the governor.
    - D. volunteers from real estate community.

49. A young man completes his real estate salesperson course on June 20, 2016. He then takes and passes the Virginia licensing exam on July 15, 2016. To avoid having to retake the exam, he must apply for his license by
    - A. December 20, 2016.
    - B. January 15, 2017.
    - C. June 20, 2017.
    - D. July 14, 2017.

50. If a licensee is found in violation of the license law or rules and regulations, the REB may take any of the following disciplinary actions *EXCEPT*
    A. impose a prison sentence of no more than one year.
    B. levy fines.
    C. deny license renewal.
    D. suspend or revoke a license.

51. One of the necessary activities of the REB is to
    A. arbitrate disputes between salespersons and brokers.
    B. establish requirements for licensure and renewal.
    C. recommend commission rates and commission splits.
    D. approve standardized listing agreements and sales contracts.

52. A licensee's salesperson license is about to expire, so she signs up for some continuing education classes. She takes two hours of Virginia Real Estate Laws and Regulations, three hours of Ethics and Standards of Conduct, two hours of Real Estate Taxes, and two hours of Escrow Requirements. Assuming she successfully completes these courses, will she have met her renewal education requirements?
    A. Yes, because she has completed at least eight hours of continuing education.
    B. No, because she has failed to take a course on federal real estate laws.
    C. No, because she has failed to take a course on the ADA.
    D. No, because she has failed to take the mandatory two hours of Fair Housing, and has not completed a total of 16 hours of continuing education.

53. A licensee accidentally let his salesperson's license expire, but two months later is ready to renew it. He will need to send the REB the current annual fee for
    A. a salesperson renewal.
    B. reinstatement.
    C. renewal plus the current fee for reinstatement.
    D. renewal plus reinstatement plus $100 fine.

54. As of July 2009, an additional requirement for licensure is that all applicants must
    A. have a college degree.
    B. submit to fingerprinting.
    C. be at least 21 years old.
    D. achieve a grade of 90% or better on the required education course.

55. A salesperson decides to leave one brokerage firm and work at another firm. She will need to
    A. file a Change of Brokerage form with the REB.
    B. give her license to her new broker.
    C. fill out the application for the change, obtain the new broker's signature, and send with appropriate fee to the REB.
    D. file a Termination of Brokerage form with the REB.

56. A licensee is currently holding her salesperson's license in inactive status. She decides to sell her home with the help of a local brokerage firm. Should she disclose her license status to potential buyers?
    A. Yes, because disclosure is required regardless of an inactive license status.
    B. No, because the local brokerage firm will be earning the commission from the sale.
    C. No, because disclosure is not required when a licensee sells her own home.
    D. No, because disclosure is not required when a license is inactive.

57. A salesperson finds a buyer for a home he has listed. The buyer gives him an earnest money cashier's check for $2,000. When a sales contract is ratified, the salesperson should
    A. keep the check until closing.
    B. deposit the check in his escrow account within three business banking days.
    C. deposit the check in his escrow account within five business banking days.
    D. immediately give it to his broker.

58. A salesperson has recently completed the education requirements and passed the state broker's exam. In her first year of licensure she must complete
    A. 30 hours post-license training.
    B. 16 hours (8 required, 8 elective).
    C. 24 hours (8 required, 8 elective, 8 related to broker supervision and management).
    D. 30 hours (24 required, 8 broker supervision and management).

59. A young college graduate is thinking about getting a real estate license. His plan is to affiliate with a broker and use the marketing skills of his unlicensed spouse to expand his practice. The unlicensed spouse will be able to
    A. show properties when the agent is available.
    B. show properties when the agent is not available.
    C. assist one of the agent's buyers in filling out a contract.
    D. design and mail brochures for the agent.

60. The duties of a supervising broker are spelled out in 18 VAC 135-20-165 and include all of the following *EXCEPT*
    A. be available to review and approve all documents.
    B. have available training and written procedures and policies.
    C. maintain regular office hours in the brokerage office.
    D. ensure that all affiliated licensees have an active, current license.

61. All of the following are requirements for a broker's escrow account *EXCEPT*
    A. must be held in a federally insured Virginia bank.
    B. balance must be sufficient to account for all funds designated as escrow.
    C. principal broker will have signatory authority on the account.
    D. account, checks, and bank statements will be labeled *escrow*.

62. If a sales transaction does not go to settlement, the funds held in an escrow account will be held until
    A. one of the parties agrees to the disposition.
    B. a court orders disbursement.
    C. the broker returns the funds to the party providing them.
    D. 120 days have passed.

63. The section on advertising was rewritten in the 2015 real estate regulations to account for current means of advertising electronically. The regulations now include all of the following *EXCEPT*
    A. electronic media advertising that can be experienced on a web page (not email) must contain disclosure viewable on the main page or no more than a click away.
    B. disclosure in advertising by an affiliated licensee must contain licensee's name, name of firm, and city and state where licensee's place of business is located.
    C. all electronic media listings advertised must be kept current and consistent with the property description and actual status of the listing.
    D. licensee must make timely written requests for updates reflecting material changes when a third-party electronic media listing service controls the website.

64. A landlord has just purchased a rental property that has four months to go on the current lease. The present tenants now have the right to
    A. continue their lease under current terms.
    B. move out immediately.
    C. sue the former owner for breaking the terms of their lease.
    D. demand repainting and new carpet by the new owner.

65. If a tenant leaves one couch and two chairs in his apartment or storage unit after the lease has ended, the landlord is allowed to sell them within 24 hours after termination
    A. provided the tenant is given adequate written termination notice.
    B. within one week of the lease's termination date.
    C. because Virginia includes an abandoned property clause in all leases.
    D. never, because the furniture remains the property of the tenant.

66. A landlord must make disclosure of all of the following *EXCEPT*
    A. defective drywall.
    B. mold.
    C. military air installation noise or accident zone.
    D. name and phone number of the owner.

67. The Virginia Residential Landlord Tenant Act (VRLTA) now applies to any landlord who has
    A. two rental properties.
    B. more than two rental properties.
    C. four rental properties.
    D. ten rental properties.

68. A landlord asks for two months' security deposit on all rentals and requires all tenants to pay the cost of renters and damage insurance (premiums) available from the landlord. If the premiums total $100 per year per unit and all units rent for $995 per month, what is the maximum the landlord can receive as a security deposit?
    A. $1,790
    B. $1,890
    C. $1,990
    D. $2,090

69. A landlord could safely decline renting to
    A. a wheelchair-bound person wishing to live on the top floor of a three-story walkup.
    B. a handicapped person requiring major modifications at the landlord's expense.
    C. an ex-drug user currently in a rehab program.
    D. a blind veteran with no guide dog.

70. A landlord will be in violation of the Virginia Fair Housing Law if he refuses to rent his two-bedroom apartment for any of the following reasons *EXCEPT*
    A. the couple applying are from Nigeria.
    B. the couple has two small children.
    C. the applicant is 65 years old.
    D. the applicants do not have adequate income.

71. If an alleged fair housing discriminatory act has taken place, the injured party must file a complaint with the REB within
    A. three months.
    B. six months.
    C. nine months.
    D. one year.

72. A landlord has a house for rent and placed the following ad on the supermarket bulletin board: "SF house for rent, $2,200 per month, no children, no smokers, no old folks." If the landlord is found guilty of discrimination, he could be fined
    A. $25,000.
    B. $50,000.
    C. $75,000.
    D. $100,000.

73. A landlord is also a licensee and has had a fair housing complaint filed against her. Her hearing will be held before
    A. the nine-member REB.
    B. the 11-member FHB.
    C. the VRLTA Board.
    D. a combined session of both the FHB and REB.

74. ADA standards must be met in all of the following *EXCEPT*
    A. the entry lobby to a condominium.
    B. the common area swimming pool.
    C. the second floor residence in a building without an elevator.
    D. the real estate sales office.

75. A young handicapped woman needs the skills of her service spider monkey. With rent of $1,550, her landlord can charge a pet deposit of
    A. $55.
    B. $310.
    C. $1,550.
    D. none of these.

ANSWER KEY

Unit 1 Quiz Answers

1. **c** The answer is Virginia Administrative Code. The REB rules and regulations are found in the Virginia Administrative Code (VAC), Title 18 – Professional and Occupational Licensing, Agency 135. L.O. 1.1

2. **c** The answer is regulate the Property Owners' Association Act. Regulation of the Property Owners' Association Act falls under the authority of the Common Interest Community Board (CIC). L.O. 1.1

3. **b** The answer is REB. The Virginia Real Estate Board administers the Virginia Real Estate Transaction Recovery Fund. L.O. 1.1

4. **d** The answer is November 1, 2015. The most current real estate regulations provided by the Virginia Real Estate Board went into effect November 1, 2015. L.O. 1.1

5. **d** The answer is Residential Property Disclosure Act. The regulation of the Residential Property Disclosure Act falls under the authority of the Real Estate Board. L.O. 1.1

6. **b** The answer is licensure. Permanent regulations for CIC managers became effective on April 1, 2010. Specific guidelines were established for licensure of individual CIC managers. L.O. 1.1

7. **c** The answer is officiate in making adverse decisions. The CIC Board ombudsman receives notices of final adverse decisions but does not participate in making them. L.O. 1.1

8. **d** The answer is principal in a brokerage relationship. The principal is either the seller or the buyer. L.O. 1.2

9. **c** The answer is serve as managing broker. A managing broker must have a broker license. L.O. 1.2

10. **c** The answer is a written agreement between licensee and client. The independent contractor does not act as an agent but has a separate written brokerage agreement with the client. L.O. 1.2

11. **a** The answer is she does not need a real estate license to sell her own property. Any individual or firm can sell their own property without having a real estate license. L.O. 1.2

12. **c** The answer is an officer of a firm who actively participates in brokerage business. All officers of a firm who actively participate in brokerage must have a broker license. L.O. 1.2

13. **c** The answer is reimburse consumers who suffer monetary loss due to a licensee's misconduct. The fund was created to provide relief to consumers who suffer financial loss to a licensee's misconduct after all other means of collecting damages have been exhausted. L.O. 1.2

14. **b** The answer is $400,000. If the fund falls below a balance of $400,000, each licensee may be assessed. L.O. 1.2

15. **b** The answer is transfers made without the assistance of a licensed real estate broker. The Virginia Residential Property Disclosure Act applies to the sale of property even though no licensed real estate broker is involved. Most of the general public does not know this. L.O. 1.3

16. **c** The answer is REB website. To avoid the use of an incorrect disclosure form, the buyer is now directed to the REB website for a list of seller representations. The licensee's duty is to inform the client of this. L.O. 1.3

17. **c** The answer is any time before settlement. The timely receipt of the property disclosure form is essential. Lack of provision of the statement could lead to a termination of the contract any time prior to settlement. L.O. 1.3

18. **a** The answer is Federal Emergency Management Agency (FEMA). FEMA is responsible for determining designated flood hazard areas. Based on this information, a lender may require flood insurance. L.O. 1.4

19. **b** The answer is within 18 months of a consumer inquiry. The law is actually for a response made within three months of the inquiry. L.O. 1.4

20. **d** The answer is purchase of flood insurance (NFIP). The purchase of flood insurance is related to obtaining a mortgage loan. It does affect daily procedures in a real estate brokerage firm. L.O. 1.4

Unit 2 Quiz Answers

1. **d** The answer is all of these. Changes were made to Agency law (Title 54.1 §§ 2130 to 2142.5) to clarify the difference in residential and commercial transactions. L.O. 2.1

2. **c** The answer is an independent contractor. An independent contractor is not an agent, but a representative of the client, subject to the obligations set forth in the brokerage agreement. L.O. 2.1

3. **c** The answer is ministerial acts. Ministerial acts are routine activities that require no discretion nor judgment on the part of the agent that can be carried out by an agent on behalf of someone who is not the client. L.O. 2.1

4. **a** The answer is one party unilaterally firing the other. Ideally, the relationship terminates when the transaction is successfully accomplished, but can be done with mutual agreement. L.O. 2.1

5. **d** The answer is no one because the sellers have their own agent. The disclosure of brokerage relationship is only required for the person who is not represented by the licensee, and who is not represented by another agent. L.O. 2.2

6. **b** The answer is licensee may also serve as an independent contractor. An independent contractor is not an accepted form of agency. The independent contractor serves as a representative, not an agent, but is still subject to certain provisions required under agency law. L.O. 2.2

7. **d** The answer is the broker may assign the two salespersons as designated agents and provide a disclosure form to be signed by both the sellers and the prospective buyers. Designated agents are the best option for the broker to avoid any potential conflict of interest with dual agency. L.O. 2.2

8. **d** The answer is never; none will be needed. Since the prospective buyer already has a signed agency agreement with another licensee, no signed disclosure is required. The listing agent should, however, while still on the phone, make it clear to the prospective buyer that he solely represents the seller. L.O. 2.2

9. **d** The answer is never, no written disclosure is required yet because no specific assistance was given. It would be a good idea, however, for the agent to discuss agency with the prospect while they are driving around. L.O. 2.2

10. **b** The answer is to always be obedient to the client's demands. The agent is obligated to promote the best interests of the client but that does not mean strict obedience to any demands. The client might actually demand some action that would be contrary to the law. L.O. 2.3

11. **a** The answer is conduct marketing activities. The only variation in the duties required of an agent is in the area of promoting the best interests of the seller. Only the agent of a seller or landlord is required to conduct marketing activities. L.O. 2.3

12. **c** The answer is defective drywall in the house. The law makes it clear that physical condition of the property does not refer to matters outside the boundaries, adjacent properties, or matters relating to governmental land use regulations or highways and public streets. L.O. 2.3

13. **b** The answer is have a suggested termination date of one year. The law actually requires that a definite termination date be given. If not, the agreement will terminate in 90 days. L.O. 2.3

14. **a** The answer is must decline this listing agreement because the clause violates REB regulations. This agreement would constitute a net listing, which is prohibited by REB regulations and law. Hopefully, the broker could explain how an exclusive right-to-sell would be more favorable for the potential client. L.O. 2.4

15. **c** The answer is marketing plan. No marketing plan is required as a duty for an agent representing a buyer but a presentation of how the agent goes about locating properties would be a good idea. L.O. 2.4

Unit 3 Quiz Answers

1. **c** The answer is a county zoning ordinance change. A change in a county ordinance does not constitute the exercise of eminent domain by the process of condemnation. L.O. 3.1

2. **d** The answer is a 52-foot sailboat purchased during the marriage. Properties purchased during the marriage cannot be excluded from an augmented estate. L.O. 3.1

3. **d** The answer is the family bible, wedding rings, and burial plots are in addition to the $5,000

exemption. The law specifically lists those items that are exempt from the bankruptcy. L.O. 3.1

4. **c** The answer is inconvenience is a basis for the easement. Inconvenience on the part of either party is not a basis for an easement by necessity. L.O. 3.1

5. **d** The answer is and the creditors cannot make any claim to the property. Under tenants by the entirety, when one spouse dies, the property automatically is now held by the surviving spouse. L.O. 3.2

6. **d** The answer is Virginia is not a community property state. There are no specific laws regarding community property in Virginia. L.O. 3.2

7. **a** The answer is tenants by the entirety. Tenants by the entirety is reserved for married couples. They could make arrangements to take title as joint tenants with rights of survivorship. L.O. 3.2

8. **b** The answer is 10 days. Contracts for the initial purchase of a cooperative unit may be rescinded without penalty 10 days after contract ratification or the receipt of the Public Offering Statement (POS). Contracts for initial purchase of a condominium may be rescinded without penalty five days after ratification or receipt of POS. L.O. 3.3

9. **a** The answer is place a lien against the unit. If a condominium unit owner fails to pay the owners' association assessment, the association can place a lien against the unit. L.O. 3.3

10. **a** The answer is 3 days. After hand-delivery of the documents, buyer B will have three days to cancel the contract, six days after the post-mark date if mailed. L.O. 3.3

11. **b** The answer is time-share estate. The time-share estate means a right to occupy a unit during five or more time periods over a period of at least five years, with renewal options. The time-share use is similar except that there is no freehold estate or estate for years. L.O. 3.3

12. **c** The answer is 7 calendar days after ratification of contract. The developer is required to deliver the Public Offering Statement (POS) prior to ratification. L.O. 3.3

13. **c** The answer is within 3 days after receiving the POA disclosure packet. The purchaser has the right to cancel the contract within 3 days after

receiving the disclosure packet or notification that the packet is not available if hand-delivered, six days after a post-mark date if mailed. L.O. 3.4

14. **a** The answer is $163.97 for two hard copies. The original amount allowed was $150 but the law allowed for a cost of living increase every five years. In 2013, the amount was raised to $163.97. L.O. 3.4

15. **c** The answer is prohibits associations from requiring the name of tenants. The new law prohibits associations from demanding a copy of a lease for a rented unit. They can still require that the name of the tenants, authorized occupants, authorized agents and vehicle information be provided. L.O. 3.4

Unit 4 Quiz Answers

1. **a** The answer is tax rates and assessments must be uniformly applied to similar properties. Article X of the Virginia Constitution specifies that all property shall be levied at fair market value and shall be uniform upon the same class of subjects. L.O. 4.1

2. **b** The answer is they will be classified differently, according to use. The house would be classified as residential use, the bakery as commercial use. L.O. 4.1

3. **a** The answer is a for-profit cemetery. Either a private or public nonprofit burial ground would be exempt, but not a for-profit cemetery. L.O. 4.1

4. **d** The answer is taxes are estimated based on comparable values for the area. In the case of new construction, taxes are prorated based on taxes for the past year. This may result in an artificially low tax because it may be based only on the value of the land and not the improvement. L.O. 4.1

5. **a** The answer is the buyer. In Virginia, the buyer owns a property (for real estate tax purposes) on the date of sale (not true in all states). Taxes will be prorated between the seller and buyer as of the day of settlement. L.O. 4.1

6. **c** The answer is property tax lien. Property tax liens have first priority over all other liens. L.O. 4.2

7. **c** The answer is no more than 90 days. A mechanic may wait no more than 90 days after the work was done before filing a mechanic's lien. L.O. 4.2

8. **b** The answer is within six months. A mechanic has six months to enforce a lien by filing suit. L.O. 4.2

9. **a** The answer is as part of the sales contract exactly as written in the act. Specific language is provided in the act that must be part of a sales contract. L.O. 4.2

10. **d** The answer is twenty years. A creditor on a judgment must enforce the judgment within 20 years once it is rendered. L.O. 4.3

11. **d** The answer is 10 years. A lien against the property of a resident decedent remains enforceable for 10 years. L.O. 4.3

12. **c** The answer is the name of prospective purchaser. The name of a prospective purchaser is not necessary for a lis pendens. If the lis pendens is not docketed, a purchaser without notice takes good title, with no lien on the land. L.O. 4.3

Unit 5 Quiz Answers

1. **d** The answer is "proceeding 120 feet due west of the intersection of the east line of J Street and the north line of 11th Street to a point; thence north 10 degrees 31 minutes west 100 feet." This description does not enclose a parcel of land. L.O. 5.1

2. **d** The answer is yes, enough correct information remains to permit identification. The fact that block F has only six lots and the street address is lot 5 is still enough correct information to permit identification. The deed is valid. L.O. 5.1

3. **a** The answer is yes, a lender may require the services of either licensed or exempt surveyors, but the lender cannot require that a particular surveyor conduct the survey. To engage in the practice of land surveying in Virginia, a person must hold a valid surveyor's license, unless exempted by the statute. L.O. 5.1

4. **d** The answer is as-build survey. An as-build survey (also called a physical survey) is a house location survey showing all other physical features of the subject property. A recently recorded survey of a property may reveal matters not shown in the record. L.O. 5.1

5. **d** The answer is the sale is unenforceable under the statute of frauds, but the parties are free to comply with its terms. The statute of frauds requires a written contract to be enforceable, but the parties are free to comply with its terms done on an oral basis. L.O. 5.2

6. **c** The answer is may take any form. There is no set standard form for a sales contract. Most brokerage firms and larger local associations provide a printed form. L.O. 5.2

7. **c** The answer is age of the parties to the contract. As long as the parties are of legal age to sign a contract, there is no requirement for their age to be made part of the contract. L.O. 5.2

8. **c** The answer is well and septic system inspection. This requirement for an inspection would depend on the subject property and is generated by the wish of the purchaser or requirement of the lender. It is not addressed by statute. L.O. 5.2 d

9. **d** The answer is residential contracts for the sale to purchasers with small children. Any property built before 1978 may have lead-based paint and requires disclosure of the hazards, especially to small children. L.O. 5.2

10. **c** The answer is home inspection disclosure. Having a home inspection is always a good idea, but it is not required by Virginia law. L.O. 5.2

11. **a** The answer is only the buyer is liable according to Virginia law. However, most contracts written in Virginia provide that the seller remains responsible until the day of settlement. L.O. 5.3

12. **c** The answer is yes, due to the implied warranty against foundation defects. Most new homes include either a 5-year or 10-year warranty against foundation defects. L.O. 5.3

13. **c** The answer is no, insurable title list exceptions for which it will not insure. An insurable title is not necessarily marketable. The present buyer might accept the fact that certain items are insurable, and others are not, but a buyer in the future might not accept this. L.O. 5.3

14. **c** The answer is builder warranty. The difference is that the builder warranty covers the foundation and other structural features of the home. The Homeowner Warranty covers the systems and appliances in the house. L.O. 5.3

15. **d** The answer is the seller's brother who is an attorney. Virginia prefers a specific power of attorney for the transaction and the parties involved. To avoid any potential conflict of interest, the agents should not be used, but a licensed attorney instead. L.O. 5.3

Unit 6 Quiz Answers

1. **c** The answer is initiate a nonjudicial foreclosure. The deed of trust gives the power of sale to the trustee, who acts on behalf of the beneficiary (lender). No court action is required. L.O. 6.1

2. **b** The answer is 5%. In Virginia, late charges may not exceed 5% of the installment due and cannot be collected unless the payment is not made within seven calendar days after the due date. Most lenders permit 15 days. L.O. 6.1

3. **b** The answer is the lender. The note and deed of trust are generally prepared by the lender. L.O. 6.1

4. **c** The answer is government loans. FHA loans are insured by the government; VA loans are guaranteed by the government. L.O. 6.1

5. **b** The answer is FHFA. The FHFA continues to regulate Fannie and Freddie and has the authority to establish conforming mortgage loan limits. L.O. 6.1

6. **d** The answer is the annual Mortgage Insurance Premium (MIP) is amortized over the life of the loan. The annual fee is divided by 12 and added to the monthly payment, which can make a significant difference in the amount due each month. The upfront MIP is amortized over the life of the loan. L.O. 6.1

7. **a** The answer is protect the financial interests of the consumer. The goal of the CFPB is to issue regulations that protect consumers and promote fair, transparent, and competitive markets. L.O. 6.2

8. **d** The answer is allow a six month's moratorium for delinquent loans. The lender must work the borrower to resolve the financial problem, but there is no obligation for a moratorium on payments. L.O. 6.2

9. **b** The answer is the QRM requires a down payment of 20% of the sales price. This was one of the biggest problems with gaining acceptance

of the QRM. After much deliberation, this requirement was dropped. L.O. 6.2

10. **d** The answer is both the GFE and the initial Truth in Lending statement. The other new form under TRID is the Closing Disclosure, which replaces the HUD-1 Settlement Statement and the final Truth in Lending statement. L.O. 6.2

11. **b** The answer is make housing more affordable for low-income and moderate-income buyers. VHDA is self-supporting and provides both single-family and multifamily loan products. L.O. 6.3

12. **c** The answer is sale of bonds in the private sector. Federal and state tax dollars are not used to fund VHDA lending programs. L.O. 6.3

13. **a** The answer is schools. VHDA builds and operates residential housing, nursing care facilities, and nursing homes providing medical and related facilities for the residence and care of the elderly, but no schools. L.O. 6.3

14. **b** The answer is administration of the Virginia Residential Landlord and Tenant Act. The VRLTA falls under Chapter 13 of Title 55 of the Code of Virginia. L.O. 6.3

15. **a** The answer is the expenses of executing the trust, including 5% commission to the trustee. The trustee must apply the proceeds of the sale in the order listed. The trustee must then file a report and accounting with the commissioner of accounts within four months of the sale. L.O. 6.4

16. **d** The answer is bankruptcy. It is important for licensees to be aware that bankruptcy of the mortgagor is an automatic stay of foreclosure. L.O. 6.4

17. **a** The answer is purchase the property. Due to a potential conflict of interest, a trustee may not purchase the property without written permission from the trustor. The trustee is bound by law to secure the highest possible price for the property. L.O. 6.4

18. **b** The answer is a short sale is one where the lender agrees to accept than the full amount due. Lenders may be reluctant to accept a short sale, but eventually may realize that their less can be less with the short sale than if they proceed with foreclosure. L.O. 6.4

Unit 7 Quiz Answers

1. **d** The answer is no, a person is presumed competent unless a court has ruled otherwise. A will may be changed any time before a person dies. L.O. 7.1

2. **a** The answer is seller. Any affidavits or sworn statements the seller is required to deliver at the closing must be signed by the seller; they cannot be signed by an attorney-in-fact. L.O. 7.1

3. **c** The answer is grantor tax of $0.50 per $500 of purchase price. The grantor's tax is paid by the seller and is collected at closing and paid to the clerk of the county where the deed is recorded. L.O. 7.1

4. **c** The answer is a person who has been entering an orchard and taking apples every October for 15 years. Entering an orchard and taking apples every October would not constitute possession of the property. L.O. 7.2

5. **b** The answer is the will is valid. The witnesses watched the woman approve her friend signing for her and signed the will; therefore, the will is valid. L.O. 7.2

6. **c** The answer is handwritten wills are never valid. A handwritten will is valid if it is in the testator's handwriting, signed by the testator, and signed by at least two witnesses. L.O. 7.2

7. **b** The answer is the buyer. The law includes specific language to be included in all sales contracts. L.O. 7.3

8. **a** The answer is prepare the HUD-1 Statement. Under the new TRID regulations, the HUD-1 Statement was replaced by the Closing Disclosure form, which is prepared by the lender. L.O. 7.3

9. **d** The answer is provide legal advice to the parties to the transaction. Only practicing lawyers are authorized to give legal advice. A settlement agent who is also an attorney must still remain neutral to all parties to the transaction. L.O. 7.3

10. **c** The answer is 60 years. A full search goes back for at least 60 years. Anything less than 60 years is called a limited search and is appropriate for loan assumptions and second mortgage closings. L.O. 7.4

11. **a** The answer is a change from a fee simple to a life estate. Minor errors can be corrected with a correction deed from the same grantor to the same grantee but changing a greater estate to a lesser estate cannot be done. L.O. 7.4

12. **b** The answer is the seller. It is the responsibility of the seller to locate the parties, then to correct the deed. L.O. 7.4

13. **d** The answer is at settlement. The seller is required to have marketable title at the time of settlement and must be given a reasonable time to correct any title defects. L.O. 7.4

14. **c** The answer is list of names in the chain of title. The chain of title consists of consecutive terms of ownership and any gap could postpone or terminate the closing but the list of names is not made part of the report. L.O. 7.4

15. **b** The answer is the lender neglected to have a deed of release signed and recorded. The problem is usually easily resolved unless the lender was an individual or private lender, or has gone out of business. L.O. 7.4

Unit 8 Quiz Answers

1. **d** The answer is nine members: seven licensees and two consumers. Appointments are made by the governor for a four-year term. Members of the board select the chairperson. L.O. 8.1

2. **d** The answer is administering the Virginia Property Owners Association Act. That act is administered by the Common Interest Community board. L.O. 8.1

3. **c** The answer is a real estate licensee selling her own property. Real estate licensees are also subject to the real estate law and regulations. L.O. 8.1

4. **c** The answer is a limited service agent. A limited service agent acts according to a brokerage agreement that lists which of the standard agent duties will not be performed and which other obligations will be performed. L.O. 8.1

5. **a** The answer is have a college degree. The requirement is to have a high school diploma or equivalent. L.O. 8.2

6. **c** The answer is apply for reinstatement of her license and pay the reinstatement fee. Applicants for reinstatement of an active license must have met the continuing education requirement; no

continuing education is required to reinstate an inactive license. L.O. 8.2

7. **d** The answer is biennially, on the last day of the month in which issued. The only exception is a concurrent broker license that expires on the same date as the original broker license. L.O. 8.2

8. **b** The answer is marketing. There are many marketing courses available in the market but this is not a subject required for continuing education for license renewal. L.O. 8.2

9. **b** The answer is flood zone areas and the National Flood Insurance Program. A property located in a FEMA designated flood zone may require flood insurance, which could result in termination of a contract. L.O. 8.2

10. **c** The answer is ensuring that all affiliated licensees have an active, current license. The other recent revision was that the supervising broker shall provide adequate supervision over the unlicensed assistants. L.O. 8.3

11. **a** The answer is a personal representative qualified by the court to administer the deceased broker's estate. In the past, it was usually a family member who was designated to take over the business. L.O. 8.3

12. **b** The answer is funds in the escrow account may never include moneys which will ultimately belong to the licensee. Such moneys can be in the escrow account as long as separately identified and paid to the firm by a check drawn on the escrow account. L.O. 8.3

13. **c** The answer is when requested by one party's attorney. A court of competent jurisdiction can order disbursement of the funds, but not an individual's attorney. L.O. 8.3

14. **b** The answer is the firm's licensed name and city and state in which the main office is located. Providing the jurisdiction is no longer required. L.O. 8.3

15. **d** The answer is accepting the money is a violation of REB regulations. All incoming funds must be paid to the broker. The broker may have a separate financial arrangement with the associate broker. L.O. 8.3

16. **c** The answer is immunity from enforcement action. The immunity from enforcement action is granted by the REB to a broker who has

submitted the audit showing full compliance, or in the case of any area of non-compliance, either that the noncompliance has been remediated or a plan to make the correction within 90 days. L.O. 8.3

17. **d** The answer is affiliates' licenses must be returned to the REB. The licenses remain with the REB until reissued upon request of a sole proprietor or principal broker. L.O. 8.3

18. **a** The answer is an investigation will be conducted by the DPOR. A complaint is reviewed by the DPOR with an informal fact-finding conference, presided over by an REB member. L.O. 8.4

19. **a** The answer is monetary penalty up to $5,000. The maximum penalty that can be imposed by the REB is $2,500. L.O. 8.4

20. **c** The answer is does not pay a required assessment to the Transaction Recovery Fund. All of the other actions could result in a complaint, followed by an investigation by the DPOR. L.O. 8.4

Unit 9 Quiz Answers

1. **c** The answer is develop special rules for tenants with small children. Any rules or regulations developed by the landlord must apply to all tenants, taking care that none are discriminatory. L.O. 9.1

2. **d** The answer is 120 days. A 120-day written notice is required to terminate a month-to-month lease, where the termination is due to rehabilitation of the property or a change in the property's use (such as conversion to a condominium). Normally, only a 30-day notice is required. L.O. 9.1

3. **d** The answer is no, if the tenant is not at fault, she is entitled to a reduction in rent until her use of the land is restored. L.O. 9.1

4. **d** The answer is must be returned minus any actual expenses incurred by the landlord. If the tenant decides not to sign a lease, all sums in excess of the landlord's actual expenses must be returned to the prospective tenant. L.O. 9.1

5. **a** The answer is someone who owns two rental properties. Legislation in 2014 made the "trigger" for application of VRLTA two rental properties in addition to a personal residence,

effective throughout Virginia. Formerly, the number was four rental properties in an urban area and 10 statewide. L.O. 9.1

6. **d** The answer is within five days of occupancy. The written report of the move-in inspection should disclose any evidence of mold. If there is visible mold evidence, the tenant has the option to terminate the tenancy; if the tenant agrees to take possession, the landlord shall remediate the mold condition within five days. L.O. 9.2

7. **c** The answer is $1,500. The maximum amount the landlord can require as a security deposit is $1,500 (two months' security). L.O. 9.2

8. **d** The answer is both renter's and damage insurance. The landlord can require that a tenant pay the cost of damage and renter's insurance premiums but the total of the security deposit and the premiums cannot exceed two months' rent. L.O. 9.2

9. **c** The answer is restriction against lawful possession of a firearm. A landlord may not prohibit the lawful possession of a firearm. L.O. 9.2

10. **b** The answer is the security deposit may be used to pay the last month's rent. Unfortunately, many tenants assume this is true. The tenant is responsible for the rent every month of the lease period; the security deposit is to cover any damages or unpaid rent. L.O. 9.2

11. **c** The answer is yes, the tenant must also give the landlord instructions and passwords. The tenant needs to inform the landlord, and the tenant must also give the landlord instructions and passwords. L.O. 9.3

12. **d** The answer is nothing, because he is military. A member of the armed forces can terminate his rental agreement if he has received a permanent change of station 35 miles away, temporary duty orders in excess of three months' duration, discharged or released from active duty, or ordered to report to government-supplied quarters. L.O. 9.3

13. **a** The answer is five-day pay or quit notice. The landlord issues a written notice giving the tenant five days to pay the rent or vacate the property. The second step is the unlawful detainer warrant which can then be followed by filing suit for eviction. L.O. 9.3

14. **b** The answer is the right to remove the property within 24 hours. The landlord must have given the tenant a termination notice that includes a statement that any items of personal property left in the premises will be disposed of within a 24-hour period after termination. L.O. 9.3

15. **d** The answer is retaliatory action. Section §55-225-18 was added in 2016 to clarify that a landlord is prohibited from any retaliatory conduct such as increasing rent, or decreasing service to a tenant making a complaint against the landlord. L.O. 9.3

Unit 10 Quiz Answers

1. **c** The answer is three. The Fair Housing Board consists of 12 members with 3 citizen members. L.O. 10.1

2. **b** The answer is familial status. Familial status is protected by the Virginia Fair Housing Law. Age is not a protected category but elderliness is. Marital status and source of income are provisions of the Equal Credit Opportunity Act. L.O. 10.1

3. **b** The answer is 62-year-old currently using cocaine. Persons currently using drugs are not protected. Those in the recovery process are protected. L.O. 10.1

4. **b** The answer is Fair Housing Board. The FHB is the recipient for fair housing complaints for non-licensees. The REB receives complaints for Virginia licensees. L.O. 10.1

5. **d** The answer is owner-occupied four-unit building advertising as "singles only". Even though it is an owner-occupied four-unit building, the owner may not discriminate in advertising against any protected class. L.O.10.2

6. **d** The answer is at least one of the occupants in 80% of the units is 55 years old. Senior housing where at least one occupant of 80% of the dwellings is 55 years old is exempt from the familial status category. Qualified housing in this category must adhere to published policies and procedures that demonstrate the intent to provide such housing. L.O. 10.2

7. **c** The answer is the ad is legal because she is sharing her own home. An individual who intends to share living quarters with another may advertise on the basis of sex, but only on the basis of sex. L.O. 10.3

8. **b** The answer is no, his criminal conviction did not involve harm to persons or property. L.O. 10.3

9. **c** The answer is unlawful discriminatory housing practice of false representation. Falsely representing that a dwelling is not available for inspection, sale, or rental is an illegal practice. L.O. 10.3

10. **b** The answer is the 35-year-old black female. Based on these facts alone, if both applicants are turned down, the lender has most likely committed unlawful discrimination against the 35-year-old black female only. The 65-year old blind male could be turned down on the basis of lack of income. L.O. 10.3

11. **d** The answer is requiring a handicapped tenant to pay for installation of an access ramp. A landlord is required to allow a handicapped tenant to make alterations to the property, but the tenant must pay for the changes and restore them at the end of the lease. L.O. 10.3

12. **d** The answer is a religious cross or symbol. Under the fair housing law, a religious cross or symbol is deemed discriminatory if printed on any application, flyer, brochure, deed, sign, banner, poster, billboard, or documents. L.O. 10.3

13. **a** The answer is all multifamily dwelling units must be wheelchair accessible. Multifamily dwellings of four or more units must make all ground-floor units readily accessible to handicapped persons. In buildings with elevators, all units must meet the accessibility requirements. L.O. 10.3

14. **c** The answer is 100 days. Investigations of fair housing complaints must be completed within 100 days after a complaint is filed. L.O. 10.4

15. **d** The answer is up to $50,000 for a first offense. A first violation of the Virginia Fair Housing Law could subject a guilty party to a monetary civil penalty of up to $50,000 for a first offense. L.O. 10.4

Practice Examination Answers

1. **d** The answer is administer the Residential Property Disclosure Act. The REB administers the Virginia Real Estate Transaction Recovery Fund. The REB is charged with developing a residential property disclosure statement, not to administer the Act. L.O. 1.1

2. **c** The answer is REB website. As of July 2011, the Residential Property Disclosure Statement is provided on the REB website in order to be sure that the most current form is used. The most recent Disclosure Statement is dated July 2016. L.O. 1.3

3. **c** The answer is within 5 days of postmark, if mailed. Notice to terminate must be given within three days if hand-carried or may be given any time prior to settlement or occupancy. L.O. 1.3

4. **c** The answer is $20 from each salesperson and broker, inactive or active. Each new licensee pays $20 into the fund. Later assessments are based on a proportionate amount but may not be more than $20 during any two-year licensing period. L.O. 1.2

5. **d** The answer is Department of Professional and Occupational Registration. The CIC is Agency 48 within the DPOR, established to regulate common interest community managers. L.O. 1.1

6. **a** The answer is Megan's Law. Megan's Law is not actually a codified regulation but refers to the law that requires disclosure to the public of known sex offenders living within a community. L.O. 1.3

7. **d** The answer is all of the above. In common practice, the term "broker" is used to refer to a firm, a sole proprietor, a principal broker of a firm, associate brokers who work under the supervision of a principal broker, and even of a salesperson affiliated with the firm. L.O. 1.1

8. **c** The answer is a transfer made without the assistance of a real estate broker. Most property owners attempting to sell a property on their own are not aware that they are also subject to the Property Disclosure Act. L.O. 1.3

9. **c** The answer is stigmatized property must be disclosed to potential buyers. Disclosure of stigmatizing type of information is considered immaterial in Virginia and is not required. L.O. 1.3

10. **d** The answer is American Taxpayer Relief Act. ATRA is actually part of federal, not state, law. Mandatory licensing for home inspectors becomes effective July 1, 2017. The first-time homebuyers savings accounts was passed by the General Assembly in 2014. The Virginia Utility

Damage Protection Act is related to digging near utility lines, such as for placing for sale or rent signs. L.O. 1.4

11. **d** The answer is designated agents. In this way, two licensees from the same brokerage firm can take part in the same transaction while retaining standard agent duties to their clients L.O. 2.1

12. **a** The answer is statute. The Virginia agency statute (§ § 54.1-2131 through 54.1-2135) establishes specific duties for a licensee who is in an agency relationship as a standard agent with a seller, buyer, landlord, or tenant or to manage real estate. L.O. 2.3

13. **b** The answer is death of the salesperson. The brokerage relationship is established between the client and the brokers, not the salesperson. L.O. 2.1

14. **c** The answer is a licensee representing a client according to a written brokerage agreement and not as a standard agent. The independent contractor has the obligations agreed to in the brokerage agreement, and is still subject to certain provisions of agency law with regard to confidentiality, ordinary care, accounting, and disclosures. L.O. 2.1

15. **d** The answer is prohibition of dual representation. Dual representation is not prohibited but will require additional disclosures and written consent of the client. L.O. 2.1

16. **d** The answer is proceed with the sale working in the best interests of both parties. Proceeding with the sale as if working in the best interests of both parties would be undisclosed dual agency, which is prohibited without full written disclosure and consent. The dual agency disclosure form points out that the client may be disadvantaged by dual representation. L.O.2.2

17. **b** The answer is promote the best interests of the client. The duties for sellers and buyers, and landlords and tenants, differ in this category. This is also the category that a limited service agent may choose to not perform. L.O. 2.3.

18. **d** The answer is net listing. A net listing in which a broker keeps any amount over whatever return is requested by the seller is prohibited in Virginia. L.O. 2.4

19. **d** The answer is have a signed independent contractor agreement. An independent contractor is a form of representation, not agency. A limited service agent has all of the same responsibilities as a standard agent except in the category of promoting the best interests of the client. L.O. 2.1

20. **d** The answer is a proposed operational budget. There is no requirement by law for a property management agreement to include any type of budget. L.O. 2.1

21. **d** The answer is the state is under no obligation to attempt to purchase the property. The Commonwealth must have made a genuine but ineffectual effort to purchase the property before beginning condemnation proceedings. L.O. 3.1

22. **b** The answer is one-third to her spouse, the remaining two-thirds to her children equally. If there is no surviving spouse or children, the estate is distributed in accordance with the Virginia Code rules of descent and distribution (§ 64.2-200). L.O. 3.1

23. **b** The answer is $5,000. The Virginia homestead exemption is $5,000, regardless of the value of any property owned. L.O. 3.1

24. **c** The answer is one-third of his estate. If a claim for an elective-share is made, the surviving spouse receives one-third of the estate if there are children. If there are no children, the spouse is entitled to one-half the estate (§ 64.2-305). L.O. 3.1

25. **d** The answer is doctors B and C are joint tenants with tenancy in common with doctor D. When one joint tenant sells his interest, the remaining owners continue to be joint tenants but are tenants in common with the new purchaser. L.O. 3.2

26. **a** The answer is her heirs. Any interest as a tenant in common passes to the heirs whether by will or the law of descent and distribution. L.O. 3.2

27. **d** The answer is plat map indicating the location of the condominium building. A plat showing building location is not required in the condominium disclosure packet. L.O. 3.3

28. **c** The answer is cancel within three days of receiving the POA disclosure packet. They have the right to cancel within three days of receiving

the packet by hand or electronic delivery, or five days from postmark if mailed. L.O. 3.4

29. **a** The answer is the buyer is purchasing shares in the corporation (personal property). The purchaser of a unit in a cooperative buys shares in the corporation that owns the property rather than a fee simple interest. The cooperative unit owner has a proprietary lease that allows for use of a particular unit. L.O. 3.3

30. **c** The answer is for-profit preschool operated by a church. Only a non-profit school would be exempt, even if owed by a church. Church property used for worship or residence is also exempt. L.O. 4.1

31. **c** The answer is March 15, 2017. If the contractor records a mechanic's memorandum of lien on September 15, 2016, he has six months to file a suit to enforce. L.O. 4.2

32. **a** The answer is real estate tax lien. A real estate lien is paid first, after deducting for all court costs, even if other liens have been filed first. L.O. 4.3

33. **d** The answer is Lot and block. The description refers to a recorded plat. L.O. 5.1

34. **b** The answer is metes and bounds and lot and block. A combination of the metes and bounds and lot and block methods is most common in Virginia. A street address is never adequate. L.O. 5.1

35. **d** The answer is lead-based paint disclosure. This disclosure is only required for properties that were built before 1978. However, many brokers automatically include the printed disclosure form in all contracts. L.O. 5.2

36. **b** The answer is one year after the date of transfer of title or the buyer's taking possession. An implied warranty against structural defects on new construction continues for one year after the date of transfer of title or the buyer's taking possession. L.O. 5.3

37. **c** The answer is the power of sale clause in the deed of trust gives the right to sell to the lender. If the borrower defaults, the lender can declare the entire debt due and payable. The power of sale clause gives the trustee the right to sell the property for the benefit of the lender without going to court. This is a nonjudicial foreclosure. L.O. 6.1

38. **a** The answer is purchase the property if it does not sell. To avoid any conflict of interest, the trustee can only purchase the property with the written permission from the trustor. L.O. 6.3

39. **c** The answer is provide housing financing for low- and moderate-income residents of Virginia. VHDA either provides or insures financing for low- and moderate-income first-time homeowners. L.O. 6.3

40. **c** The answer is the servicer must declare a moratorium on payments if borrower is having difficulty making payment. The CFPB rule requires the lender to work with the borrower to avoid foreclosure, but no moratorium on payments is required under the new rules. L.O. 6.2

41. **c** The answer is both the GFE and the initial Truth in Lending statement. The Loan Estimate must be given to the borrower within three days of application. L.O. 6.2

42. **d** The answer is bonds sold through the private sector. VHDA obtains funds by selling bonds in the private sector. No federal or state dollars are used. L.O. 6.3

43. **a** The answer is the signature of the grantee. The grantee must be legally competent and the grantee's full name should be used on the deed but only the grantor must sign the deed in order for it to be valid. L.O. 7.1

44. **d** The answer is hostile and continuous use of the property. Establishing adverse possession requires unauthorized, hostile, and continuous use over a period of 15 years. L.O. 7.2

45. **a** The answer is after the will has gone through probate court. Until probate, the will is only the legal declaration of a person's intended disposition and could be revoked at any time after execution, L.O. 7.2

46. **b** The answer is the buyer. RESA is the recodification of CRESPA (Consumer Real Estate Protection Act) and requires specific language regarding the choice of settlement agent by the purchaser or borrower be included in the contract. L.O. 7.3

47. **d** The answer is property was sold to a relative for $1 with a recorded deed. This sale would not cause a gap in the chain of title because there would be a recorded deed with the relative's name. L.O. 7.4

48. **c** The answer is appointed by the governor. The Real Estate Board (REB) is one of 19 boards that is part of the DPOR. It is composed of nine members—seven real estate practitioners and two citizens. Appointments are made for a term of four years. L.O. 8.1

49. **d** The answer is July 14, 2017. An applicant has to apply for a license within one year of passing the Virginia licensing exam before being required to retake the exam. L.O. 8.2

50. **a** The answer is impose a prison sentence of no more than one year. The REB has no authority to impose a prison sentence. In some cases, the REB refers the matter to the Commonwealth attorney for further court action. L.O. 8.4

51. **b** The answer is establish requirements for licensure and renewal. The REB issues and renews real estate licenses, takes disciplinary action for violation of the law, approves schools for teaching real estate courses, and determines license fees. L.O. 8.1

52. **d** The answer is no, because she has failed to take the mandatory two hours of Fair Housing, and has not completed a total of 16 hours of continuing education. L.O. 8.2

53. **b** The answer is reinstatement. After 30 days, the licensee must apply for reinstatement, not just renewal. Applicants for reinstatement of an active license must have completed all continuing education requirements. L.O. 8.2

54. **b** The answer is submit to fingerprinting. The applicant shall also disclose all misdemeanor convictions involving moral turpitude, sexual offense, drug distribution, or physical injury within five years of the date of application, plus any felony convictions during applicant's lifetime. L.O. 8.2

55. **c** The answer is fill out the application for the change, obtain the new broker's signature, and send with appropriate fee to the REB. The application for change of brokerage firm can also be done online today. L.O. 8.2

56. **a** The answer is yes, because disclosure is required regardless of an inactive license status. Disclosure of license status, including inactive, is always required. L.O. 8.3

57. **d** The answer is immediately give it to his broker. The broker is responsible to place the check in an escrow account within five business days. L.O. 8.3

58. **a** The answer is 30 hours post-license training. These 30 hours of training include the following: 2 hours fair housing; 3 hours ethics; and 1 hour each of agency, contracts, and legal updates (including flood zone information). These 8 hours count toward the 16 hours required for salesperson license renewal. As of 2016, additional continuing education credits completed in the six months prior to license renewal shall carry-over into the next renewal period. L.O. 8.2

59. **d** The answer is design and mail brochures for the agent. Allowable activities for both licensees and unlicensed assistants are specifically listed in 18 VAC 135-20-165. L.O. 8.2

60. **c** The answer is maintain regular office hours in the brokerage office. The emphasis on the responsibility of supervising brokers has shifted from regular office hours to an availability for reviewing documents and training affiliated licensees. The requirement to ensure that all agents have an active, current license is as of 2016. L.O. 8.3

61. **a** The answer is must be held in a federally insured Virginia bank. The requirement for being in a Virginia bank has been dropped: it must be a federally insured depository, but it needn't be located in Virginia. L.O. 8.3

62. **b** The answer is a court orders disbursement. Otherwise, all parties would have to agree to the disposition, and a broker can only act in accordance with the terms of the contract. If all principals to the transaction have agreed in writing, the funds shall be returned within 20 days of the agreement (new in 2016). L.O. 8.3

63. **a** The answer is electronic media advertising that can be experienced on a web page (not email) must contain disclosure viewable on the main page or no more than a click away. The regulation includes email as well as web pages. L.O. 8.3

64. **a** The answer is continue their lease under current terms. The tenant retains the same rights and privileges when the property is sold unless it is specifically stated otherwise in the lease. L.O. 9.1

65. **a**   The answer is provided the tenant is given adequate written termination notice. The termination notice can specify a 24-hour period, or any longer period of time for the tenant to remove the property. L.O. 9.2

66. **d**   The answer is name and phone number of the owner. The name and address of the owner or authorized property manager must be in writing and provided prior to the beginning of tenancy, but not a phone number. L.O. 9.2

67. **b**   The answer is more than two rental properties. The trigger number for VRLTA was formerly four rental properties in urban areas and a total of 10 statewide. In 2016, legislation clarified that, in order to determine whether an owner of single-family residences is subject to the VRLTA, the owner only needs to count the number of properties owned in Virginia. One residence + two rental properties = VRLTA. L.O. 9.1

68. **c**   The answer is $1,990 (2 × $995). A landlord cannot charge more than two month's rent as a security deposit, even if insurance premiums are to be charged. The combination of insurance premiums and security deposit cannot exceed two months' rent. L.O. 9.3

69. **b**   The answer is a handicapped person requiring major modifications at the landlord's expense. Reasonable modifications must be allowed but at the tenant's expense and may be required to be restored to present condition at termination of the lease. L.O. 10.2

70. **d**   The answer is the applicants do not have adequate income. Refusing a rental applicant on the basis of inadequate income is allowed. L.O. 10.2

71. **d**   The answer is one year. An injured party has one year to file a complaint with the REB if an alleged fair housing discriminatory act has taken place. L.O. 10.4

72. **d**   The answer is $100,000. The maximum amount would be $100,000 for two violations at $50,000 each; both familial status and the elderly are protected. L.O. 10.3

73. **a**   The answer is the nine-member REB. All complaints filed against licensees are heard by the REB. L.O. 10.1

74. **c**   The answer is the second floor residence in a building without an elevator. ADA standards are only required for the first floor in buildings without an elevator. L.O. 10.2

75. **d**   The answer is none of these. A service animal is not considered to be a pet; no pet deposit may be charged. L.O. 10.3.

GLOSSARY

active license   Any broker or salesperson under the supervision of a principal or supervising broker performing real estate brokerage activities.

actively engaged   A broker or salesperson having active licensure with a licensed real estate firm or sole proprietorship and active for an average of at least 40 hours per week. The REB may waive the 40-hour-per-week requirement at its discretion.

adverse possession   The actual, open, notorious, hostile, and continuous possession of another's land under a claim of title. Possession for a statutory period may be a means of acquiring title.

agency   The relationship between a principal and an agent wherein the agent is authorized to represent the principal in certain transactions.

agent   One who acts or has the power to act for another. A fiduciary relationship is created under the law of agency when a property owner, as the principal, executes a listing agreement or management contract authorizing a licensed real estate broker to be his or her agent.

alienation clause   The clause in a mortgage or deed of trust stating that the balance of the secured debt becomes immediately due and payable at the lender's option if the property is sold by the borrower. In effect, this clause prevents the borrower from assigning the debt without the lender's approval.

as-built survey   A house location survey with all other physical features of the subject property shown, including water courses, utility lines, fence lines, outbuildings, and similar features.

attorney-in-fact   An unbiased third party appointed by another person to act in that person's place.

automated survivorship   Intended to place joint tenants in the same situation as tenants in common as far as augmented estates were concerned. Has been abolished in Virginia.

beneficiary   (1) The person for whom a trust operates or in whose behalf the income from a trust estate is drawn. (2) A lender in a deed of trust loan transaction.

boundary survey   Shows the boundary or perimeter of the parcel as taken from and applied to the ground. Corner stakes or other physical landmarks appear.

broker   In Virginia, any person or business entity, including, but not limited to, a partnership, association, corporation, or limited liability corporation, who, for compensation or valuable consideration (i) sells or offers for sale, buys or offers to buy, or negotiates the purchase or sale or exchange of real estate, including units or interest in condominiums, cooperative interest... or time-shares in a time-share program... or (ii) leases or offers to lease, or rents or offers for rent, any real estate or the improvements thereon for others. (§ 54.1-2100)

brokerage relationship   Describes both client and customer relationships with the broker.

broker's lien   A lien on the rent paid by the tenant in the amount of the compensation (commission) agreed on by the owner and the broker.

caveat emptor   "Let the buyer beware." Requires the buyer to examine the property before purchase and to take responsibility for its condition.

chain of title   The succession of conveyances, from some accepted starting point, whereby the present holder of real property derives title.

civil action   A lawsuit in which someone claims to have incurred a loss resulting from another person.

client   A person who has entered into a brokerage relationship with a broker licensee.

Closing Disclosure (CD)   A five-page statement of final loan terms and closing costs. This document should be compared with the Loan Estimate.

cloud on the title   Any document, claim, unreleased lien, or encumbrance that may impair the title to real property or make the title doubtful; usually revealed by a title search and removed by either a quitclaim deed or suit to quiet title.

complainant   The person or entity who files an administrative complaint accusing someone of violating Maryland fair housing law.

conciliation   A form of alternative dispute resolution in which a conciliator meets with each of the parties separately to help them settle their differences voluntarily, without the formality of a hearing or trial.

concurrent license   Brokers who are active in more than one legal entity, that is, who work for more than one brokerage firm.

condemnation   A judicial or administrative proceeding to exercise the power of eminent domain, through which a government agency takes private property for public use and compensates the owner.

condominium   The absolute ownership of a unit in a multiunit building based on a legal description of the airspace the unit actually occupies, or a separate dwelling unit in a multiunit development, plus an undivided interest in the ownership of the common elements in the building or development, which are owned jointly with the other condominium unit owners.

conflict of interest   Acting for more than one party in a transaction without written consent.

consent order   Resolution of a matter by accepting, making a counteroffer, asking for exhibits, or requesting an IFFC (if one has not been held).

continuing education   An approved course of study that meets the requirements for maintenance of a real estate license.

cooperative   A residential multiunit building whose title is held by a trust or corporation that is owned by and operated for the benefit of people living within the building who are the beneficial owners of the trust or shareholders of the corporation, each possessing a proprietary lease to a property unit.

customer   The third party or nonrepresented consumer for whom some level of service is provided.

deed of trust   An instrument used to create a mortgage lien by which the borrower conveys title to a trustee, who holds it as security for the benefit of the note holder (the lender); also called a trust deed.

defective drywall   Imported drywall, commonly referred to as Chinese drywall. Some consumers who live in these homes have reported problems, including a strong sulfur smell, like rotten eggs; health issues, like irritated and itchy eyes and skin, difficulty breathing, a persistent cough and headaches; and premature corrosion or deterioration of certain metal components in their homes, like air-conditioner coils and wiring behind electrical outlets and inside electrical panel boxes.

deferred purchase money   Sellers with no immediate need for cash from the proceeds of a sale may choose to defer the income of the sale and obtain an installment tax treatment by creating an annuity in this form of deed of trust, held by the seller.

designated agent   One or more of a broker's licensee affiliates assigned by the broker to represent one client to the exclusion of all other clients in the same transaction, as well as to the exclusion of all other licensees affiliated with the broker.

distress warrant   The order to seize tenant property.

dual agent   A broker who simultaneously has a client relationship with both seller and buyer or both landlord and tenant in the same transaction.

due-on-sale clause   A provision in the mortgage stating that the entire balance of the note is immediately due and payable if the mortgagor transfers (sells) the property.

dwelling   Any building or part of a building designed for occupancy as a residence by one or more families.

easement by necessity   An easement allowed by law as necessary for the full enjoyment of a parcel of real estate (e.g., a right of ingress and egress over a grantor's land).

easement by prescription   An easement acquired by open, notorious, continuous, hostile and adverse use of the property for the period of time prescribed by state law.

elderliness   For purposes of the fair housing law, elderly persons are those individuals who have attained their 55th birthday.

elective share   The amount of a decedent's estate that a surviving spouse is entitled to claim by law. This prevents a person from disinheriting a spouse, unless the spouse agrees to receive less than the elective share.

eminent domain   The right of a government or municipal quasi-public body to acquire property for public use through a court action called *condemnation*, in which the court decides that the use is a public use and determines the compensation to be paid to the owner.

equitable title   Property ownership rights held by the purchaser in conjunction with transferring legal title to the lender by a security deed. Owner retains a right of redemption to reacquire the legal title from the lender when the loan is paid off.

estate   That which is owned by a person including insurance policies, retirement benefits (exclusive of Social Security), annuities, pension plans, deferred compensation arrangements, and employee benefit plans.

eviction   A legal process to oust a person from possession of real estate.

familial status   One or more individuals under age 18 living with a parent or guardian; also includes a woman who is pregnant and anyone who is in the process of assuming custody of a child under age 18.

firm   Any real estate business entity, including but not limited to a corporation, partnership, limited liability company, and sole proprietorship.

four-corner doctrine   All agreements must be present within the "four corners" of the contract in order to be valid. An oral agreement between builder and buyer is not valid.

government-sponsored enterprises (GSEs)   Organizations created by the federal government (Fannie Mae, Freddie Mac, Farmer Mac, Ginnie Mae) to help increase loan opportunities for homebuyers.

grace period   A provision for a late charge if a monthly payment is not made within a certain period after the due date.

grantor   The owner transferring title to or an interest in real property to a grantee.

grantor tax   Tax the seller pays on the transfer of property.

handicap   A person who suffers from a physical or mental impairment that substantially limits one or more major life activities.

hoarding   A newly classified mental disability pertaining to the difficulty of discarding or parting with possessions feeling the need to keep them.

holographic will   A will that is written, dated, and signed in the testator's handwriting.

home equity line of credit (HELOC)   Permits the note holder to make advances from time to time, secured by the real estate described in the deed.

homestead exemption   A householder is entitled to hold a certain amount of real or personal property exempt from unsecured debts.

house location survey   A boundary survey with the location of the house shown.

inactive license   Any broker or salesperson who is not under the supervision of a principal broker or supervising broker, who is not affiliated with a firm or sole proprietorship, or who is not performing any real estate activities.

independent contractor   The broker-licensee relationship where at least 75% of the compensation is based on commissions earned and the broker does not withhold payroll taxes.

informal fact-finding conference (IFFC)   A hearing conducted at the offices of DPOR; presided over by an REB member and supported by DPOR staff.

intestate   The condition of a property owner who dies without leaving a valid will. Title to the property will pass to the decedent's heirs, as provided in the state law of descent.

joint tenancy   Ownership of real estate between two or more parties who have been named in one conveyance as joint tenants. Upon the death of a joint tenant, the decedent's interest passes to the surviving joint tenant or tenants by the right of survivorship.

judgment   The formal decision of a court upon the respective rights and claims of the parties to an action or suit. After a judgment has been entered and recorded with the county recorder, it usually becomes a general lien on the property of the defendant.

judicial foreclosure   Some states require the use of a mortgage instead of a deed of trust, which requires court action to foreclose.

just compensation   The fair market value of the property at the time of the taking.

land surveyor   A licensed architect or engineer when surveying is incidental to a particular project.

land trust   A trust in which property is conveyed, and in which real estate is the only asset.

landlord's lien   A lien on a tenant's property for the satisfaction of unpaid rent or property damage.

law of descent and distribution   Establishes the rights of ownership to property by a surviving spouse and others.

limited service agent   A licensee acting only on the duties in a written brokerage agreement. The status as a limited services agent must be in writing noting a list of the services that will be provided, along with a list of the duties required of a standard agent.

lis pendens   A recorded legal document giving constructive notice that an action affecting a particular property has been filed in either a state or a federal court.

Loan Estimate (LE)   A three-page form you receive after applying for a mortgage which includes important details about the requested loan.

loan origination fee   A fee charged to the borrower by the lender for making a mortgage loan. The fee is usually computed as a percentage of the loan amount.

lot-and-block (recorded plat) method   A method of describing real property that identifies a parcel of land by reference to lot and block numbers within a subdivision, as specified on a recorded subdivision plat.

mechanic's lien   A statutory lien created in favor of contractors, laborers, material suppliers, and others who have performed work or furnished materials in the erection or repair of a building.

Megan's Law   Federal legislation that promotes the establishment of state registration systems to maintain residential information on every person who kidnaps children, commits sexual crimes against children, or commits sexually violent crimes.

metes and bounds   Legally sufficient real property description that surveys a property's boundaries by courses and distances with an identifiable starting point.

ministerial acts   Routine acts that a licensee can perform for a person that do not involve discretion or the exercise of the licensee's own judgment.

mixed-use developments   Properties that accommodate more than one use, such as commercial, residential, retail, office, or parking.

money judgement   The formal decision of a court upon the respective rights and claims of the parties to an action or suit. After a judgment has been entered and recorded with the county recorder, it usually becomes a general lien on the property of the defendant.

net listing   A listing based on the net price the seller will receive if the property is sold. Under a net listing, the real estate professional can offer the property for sale at the highest price obtainable to increase the commission. This type of listing is illegal in many states.

nuncupative will   An oral will declared by the testator in his final illness, made before witnesses and afterward reduced to writing; not permitted by all states.

nonjudicial foreclosure   Gives the trustee the right to sell the property (foreclose) without going to court.

parol evidence   Evidence of facts and circumstances not included in the deed or contract.

pay or quit notice   The landlord may issue a written notice giving the tenant five days to pay the rent or vacate the property.

place of business   Where the business of real estate brokerage is normally transacted and where business calls can be directed and received.

post-licensing education   Proscribed by the Real Estate Board as that education required to obtain the first renewal of a real estate salesperson license.

power of attorney   Legal document that gives individuals the right to sign legal documents for another. In Virginia, a specific power of attorney specifying the transaction and the parties involved is generally preferred for real estate transactions, rather than a general power of attorney. The power of attorney must be notarized and recorded with the deed.

power of sale clause   A clause in the deed of trust which gives the trustee the right to sell the property (foreclose) without going to court.

prepaid rent   Rent paid more than one month in advance of the rent due date.

principal broker   In a brokerage, the broker who is responsible for all the activities of both the firm and all its licensees.

principle of uniformity   All property shall be levied at fair market value and shall be uniform upon the same class of subjects within the territorial limits of the authority levying the tax (i.e., residential, commercial).

promissory note   A financing instrument that states the terms of the underlying obligation, is signed by its maker, and is negotiable (transferable to a third party).

property management agreement   A written agreement between a property manager and the owner of real estate for the management of the real estate.

public offering statement   Written document providing a full property disclosure to purchasers. The sale of a cooperative, a condominium, or a time-share requires the POS to fully and accurately disclose the characteristics of the project. Additionally, the Virginia Property Owners Association Act may require the use of the POS.

purchase-money financing   A note secured by a mortgage or deed of trust given by a buyer, as borrower, to a seller, as lender, as part of the purchase price of the real estate.

qualified residential mortgage (QRM)   Loan terms and practices that regulatory agencies have determined are less likely to end up in default; meets standards set by Consumer Financial Protection Bureau.

reasonable accommodation   Changes to existing rules and procedures that may be needed in order for the tenant to enjoy full use of the dwelling place.

reasonable modification   Adjustments made to a property that affect the physical features.

recordation tax   Tax the purchaser pays on the transfer of property.

referral agent   A real estate licensee who does not engage in real estate activities such as listing and selling property.

resale certificate   In the event of an intended resale, the seller must obtain certain documents from the unit owners' association.

respondent   The person or entity who is being accused in a complaint filed alleging violation of Virginia fair housing law.

retaliation   Conduct by landlord such as rent increases, a decrease in service, or termination of the lease.

"run with the land"   The owner is responsible for paying real estate taxes for the current tax year from the date of purchase until the end of the year. In Virginia, the buyer is said to own the property on the date of closing or settlement.

salesperson   Any person, other than an associate broker, who acts on behalf of a real estate broker in performing any act authorized to be performed by the broker in this unit.

security deposits   The sum held by a landlord as a guarantee that the rental property will be returned in satisfactory condition.

service animal   Trained animals that perform tasks to assist people with disabilities.

settlement agent   Either an attorney or a title company; must be registered with the Virginia State Bar, carry errors and omissions or malpractice insurance at a minimum of $250,000, and maintain a surety bond of not less than $100,000.

short sale   When a lender agrees to accept less than the amount due on the mortgage note.

sole proprietorship   Business ownership by an individual in which all profits and losses are reported through personal tax returns.

special assessment   A tax or levy customarily imposed against only those specific parcels of real estate that will benefit from a proposed public improvement like a street or sewer.

specific power of attorney   Certain limits are imposed upon the person appointed.

standard agent   A licensee who acts for or represents a client in an agency relationship.

statute of frauds   That part of a state law that requires certain instruments, such as deeds, real estate sales contracts, and certain leases, to be in writing to be legally enforceable.

stigmatized property   A property that has acquired an undesirable reputation due to an event that occurred on or near it, such as violent crime, gang-related activity, illness, or personal tragedy. Some states restrict the disclosure of information about stigmatized properties.

structural defect   A flaw that reduces stability or safety of the structure below accepted standards or that restricts the normal use of the structure.

subdivision plat   A map of a subdivision indicating the location and boundaries of individual properties.

subrogate   Permitting action against the licensee to recover the amount of claims paid due to the licensee's misconduct.

tacking   Concept providing that successive periods of continuous occupation by different parties may be combined to reach the required total number of years needed to establish a claim for a prescriptive easement.

tenancy by the entirety   The joint ownership, recognized in some states, of property acquired by spouses during marriage. Upon the death of one spouse, the survivor becomes the owner of the property.

tenancy in common   A form of co-ownership by which each owner holds an undivided interest in real property as if each were sole owner. Each individual owner has the right to partition. Unlike joint tenants, tenants in common have right of inheritance.

tenancy in partnership   A partner is co-owner with the other partners of real property.

testate   Having made and left a valid will.

testator   A person who has made a valid will. A woman might be referred to as a *testatrix*, although *testator* can be used for either a man or a woman.

time-share   A form of ownership interest that may include an estate interest in property and that allows use of the property for a fixed or variable time period.

title examination   Review information specific to the title condition of the property, such as any unrealized deeds, existing title insurance policies, and any known unrecorded deed, lien, or encumbrance information.

title insurance   A policy insuring a property owner or mortgagee against loss by reason of defects in the title to a parcel of real estate, other than encumbrances, defects, and matters specifically excluded by the policy.

title theory   Some states interpret a mortgage to mean that the lender is the owner of mortgaged land. Upon full payment of the mortgage debt, the borrower becomes the landowner.

trustee   One to whom something is entrusted and who holds legal title to property and administers the property for the benefit of a beneficiary. Can also be a member of a board entrusted with the administration of an institution or organization, such as a cooperative.

unlawful detainer warrant   The landlord may begin eviction proceedings immediately after issuing this warrant. The tenant remains obligated to pay the rent.

unsecured debts   Not secured by real property, for instance, credit card debt.

usury   Charging interest at a higher rate than the maximum rate established by state law.

vendor's lien   A lien that belongs to a vendor for the unpaid purchase price of land, where the vendor has not taken any other lien or security beyond the personal obligation of the purchaser.

walk-through inspection   Purchaser makes final inspection of premises before settlement.

will   A written document, properly witnessed, providing for the transfer of title to property owned by the deceased, called the *testator*.

writ of execution   A court order issued to enforce a judgment of possession.

writ of possession   A court ordered judgment where a debtor's real property may be conveyed to a sheriff.

INDEX

W

Notes